HEALTH AND HEALING
THE NATURAL WAY

THE STRESS
FACTOR

HEALTH AND HEALING
THE NATURAL WAY

THE STRESS FACTOR

PUBLISHED BY

THE READER'S DIGEST ASSOCIATION LIMITED

LONDON NEW YORK SYDNEY MONTREAL

THE STRESS FACTOR
was created and produced by
Carroll & Brown Limited
20 Lonsdale Road, London NW6 6RD
for The Reader's Digest Association Limited, London

CARROLL & BROWN

Publishing Director Denis Kennedy
Art Director Chrissie Lloyd

Series Editor Arlene Sobel
Series Art Editor Johnny Pau

Project Editor Caroline Turner
Assistant Editor Madeleine Jennings

Art Editor Michelle Tiley

Photographers David Murray, Jules Selmes

Production Lorraine Baird, Wendy Rogers,
Amanda Mackie

Computer Management John Clifford

First English Edition Copyright © 1995
The Reader's Digest Association Limited,
11 Westferry Circus, Canary Wharf,
London E14 4HE

www.readersdigest.co.uk

Copyright © 1995
The Reader's Digest Association Far East Limited
Philippines Copyright © 1995
The Reader's Digest Association Far East Limited

Reprinted 2001

ISBN 0 276 42263 5

Reproduced by Colourscan, Singapore
Printing and binding: Printer Industria Gráfica S.A., Barcelona

SENIOR CONSULTANTS

Prof Cary Cooper, BSc, MBA, PhD,
MSc, CPsychol, FBPsS, FRSA
*Manchester School of Management
University of Manchester
Institute of Science and Technology*

Dr Adam Ward, MSc, MB, BS, MRCGP,
M F Hom, Dip Orth Med
The Royal London Homoeopathic Hospital NHS Trust

MEDICAL ILLUSTRATIONS CONSULTANT

Dr Frances Williams, MB, BChir, MRCP, DTM&H

Dr Lesley Hickin, MB, BS, BSc, DRCOG, MRCGP

CONTRIBUTORS

Susanna Dowie, LicAc, MTAcS, RWTA
Nancy Duin
Richard Emerson
Sue George
Clare Hill
Siobhan McGee
Ursula Markham
Vera Peiffer, BA (Psych), CAHyp
Kate Swainson
Stephen Ulph

FOR READER'S DIGEST

Series Editor Christine Noble
Editorial Assistant Caroline Boucher

READER'S DIGEST GENERAL BOOKS

Editorial Director Cortina Butler
Art Director Nick Clark

The information in this book is for reference only;
it is not intended as a substitute for a doctor's diagnosis and care.
The editors urge anyone with continuing medical problems
or symptoms to consult a doctor.

THE STRESS FACTOR

More and more people today are choosing to take greater responsibility for their own health rather than relying on the doctor to step in with a cure when something goes wrong. We now recognise that we can influence our health by making an improvement in lifestyle – a better diet, more exercise and reduced stress. People are also becoming increasingly aware that there are other healing methods – some new, others very ancient – that can help to prevent illness or be used as a complement to orthodox medicine.
The series *Health and Healing the Natural Way* will help you to make your own health choices by giving you clear, comprehensive, straightforward and encouraging information and advice about methods of improving your health. The series explains the different natural therapies now available – aromatherapy, herbalism, acupressure and many others – and the circumstances in which they may be of benefit when used in conjunction with conventional medicine.

The aim of *The Stress Factor* is to examine the causes of stress and its effects and to give solutions to the problems it raises. Stress has many causes: demanding children, traffic jams, financial worries, heavy deadlines at work – the list is endless. These stressors can take a huge toll on your health, especially if they're repeated. Research shows that stress leaves us vulnerable to infections, high blood pressure, back pain, allergies and a host of other ills.
In *The Stress Factor* you'll learn how to recognise the warning signs before stress gets out of hand. We help to equip you with an armoury of stress-handling skills, showing in true-life cases how others have successfully overcome stress-related difficulties. And you'll find easy-to-follow instructions for many natural therapies that will help you and your family to keep stress at bay and ensure a healthier and happier way of living.

CONTENTS

5 STRESS AND THE FAMILY

6 A STRESS-FREE HOME

7 STRESS AT WORK

8 STRESS AND THE ENVIRONMENT

STRESS – A FACT OF MODERN LIFE

Stress lurks in every corner of our daily lives. The pressures of life themselves are not the problem; rather it is how we react to them that counts.

HARRY S TRUMAN
Former US President Harry S Truman was known for his daily 5 mile walk. It was his way of working off the pressures of the job. Walking is an ideal stress buster, and it can be done anywhere and at any time.

LAZY DAYS OF SUMMER
You don't have to wait for your holiday to unwind from stress, there are many easy techniques to help keep you free from stress every day.

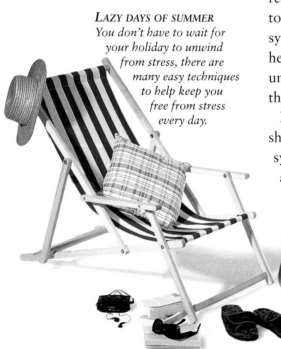

The traffic is moving at a snail's pace, and you are worried that you will be late for work. At home, the washing machine has broken down and needs to be mended and you haven't had time to start your Christmas shopping. Your neighbour's dog keeps barking at night, keeping you awake, but you do not want to risk a confrontation that might cause bad feelings. All of these situations, and thousands of others which are encountered in daily life, have the potential to generate stress. However, it is not the pressures of life themselves that create stress: it is how we react to them and deal with them that matters.

Stress is difficult to define. For example, the stress of a crying baby will give some of us a tension headache, whereas others will simply shrug their shoulders with a resigned smile. Our individual reactions to stress can be just as varied as what each of us perceives as being stressful. Some of the more common psychological reactions to stress are resentment, anxiety, low self-esteem, inability to cope, lack of concentration, and feelings of isolation. Physical symptoms include the loss of appetite (or overeating), indigestion, heartburn, sweaty palms, muscle cramps, and fainting spells. As uncomfortable as these symptoms are, they usually disappear once the stressful situation has passed.

However, this is not so if the stress is chronic. New research shows that continued exposure to stress can depress your immune system, lowering your resistance to illness and, in extreme cases, be a major factor in the development or aggravation of problems as wide ranging as depression, impotence, eczema, migraine, asthma, high blood pressure (hypertension), peptic ulcers, coronary heart disease, and cancer. An awareness of the ways in which stress can affect our health is vital because taking too long to recognise the signs of stress may result in serious mental or physical harm.

WHAT IS STRESS?

Stress, as one writer put it, is 'an associate of Strain and a consultant to Nag, having been referred by Job'. Although stress is an innate part of the human condition, it wasn't defined until the 1930s when an endocrinologist named Hans Selye observed that his laboratory rats would develop peptic ulcers in response to various toxic substances. He borrowed the word *stress* from physics, where it means 'external pressure exerted on a malleable object to produce distortion or strain'. When people under pressure describe their feelings, the aptness of this definition is obvious – they feel pushed and pulled in all directions, crushed, wrung out, overloaded, at breaking point, about to snap. Their symptoms, however, often sound vague: 'I'm not sleeping well'; 'I can't concentrate'; 'I feel run down'; 'I can't cope with all my family's demands'.

Stress is not a condition on its own, but rather a *reaction* to something, or what stress pioneer Selye called 'an adaptive response to a noxious event'. Selye invented the word *stressor* to describe such events. Typically, the most worrisome stressors are unpredictable and uncontrollable events. But what is so fascinating and confusing about stress is that these uncontrollable events can be real (for example, a speeding car) or perceived (such as rumours of redundancies at work). Either way our bodies do not recognise the difference between a real threat and a perceived one, and the stress reaction is the same.

GONE FISHING
Although fishing is a means of survival for some people, others find that it is a great stress-relieving activity, perhaps because it offers the opportunity to simply let your thoughts drift away, in natural, peaceful surroundings.

WHY DO WE EXPERIENCE STRESS?

Stress may seem a disease of modern times caused by fast-moving, ever-changing lifestyles, but it has been with us since time immemorial. Our ability to cope with stress has been critical to our continued survival. In fact, our bodies have retained the same primitive responses that protected it from the kinds of physical dangers encountered during the prehistoric age. Often termed the fight-or-flight response, this reaction enabled our forebears to deal effectively with threatening situations, such as a charging animal or a forest fire, by preparing the body to either confront the threat (fight) or to run from it (flight). To provide extra strength in a fight

LAURENCE OLIVIER
Performing or speaking in public is usually high on everyone's stress list. The actor Sir Laurence Olivier suffered from such intense stage fright that for a time he considered abandoning his acting career.

SOOTHING MUSIC
Playing a musical instrument uses the creative part of your brain, diverting you from negative and stressful thoughts. It can also bring physical benefits, such as lowering blood pressure.

or the ability to run speedily away, various physiological changes occurred – a faster heartbeat, higher blood pressure, increased muscle tension, and quickened breathing.

Once we perceive the threat to have passed, our body relaxes – the muscles lose their tension, breathing slows down, and blood pressure drops to normal. Walter Hess, a Swiss physiologist who studied the action of relaxation on the body, considered the relaxation response 'a protective mechanism against overstress'. Indeed, that is exactly what relaxing is designed to do – help the body return to its normal state after the strain of either fighting or fleeing. After a stressful ordeal has passed, the physical response of relaxation is automatically guaranteed. In earlier times, the act of running from a charging animal would allow a hunter to expend the pent-up physical energy that a threatening situation evoked.

Men and women today face threatening situations that are usually of a very different nature from those experienced by our ancestors; however, our bodies have not updated our response mechanisms. We react to causes of mental stress – such as losing a job, the break-up of a relationship, or the unpredictability of public transport – as if they were physical dangers. Our hearts race, our muscles tense, our blood pressure rises, to name just a few of the typical reactions to stress. In today's world, however, it is unacceptable to run away from a difficult meeting or vent your anger by slamming your fist into the wall. The result is an accumulation of stress that cannot be off-loaded by the physical activity of fight or flight.

GOOD STRESS VERSUS BAD STRESS

Stress is not necessarily all bad. It can occur in response to certain welcome events. Preparing for a holiday, going on a first date, and getting a promotion are only some of the many happy occasions with a large stress component. Stress can also be the vital spur that motivates us to learn, improve, and mature. We need a certain amount of stress to remain interested in life and to face challenges. Stress can even bring out the best in people, galvanising an actor's stage performance or helping a student or worker to maintain a keen level of concentration. Road planners, for instance, take active steps to include stress-inducing elements in their designs of road markings at dangerous junctions to keep drivers alert. Without the spur of stress, people often succumb to boredom and listlessness.

While some kinds of stress are good, in that they improve concentration and motivation, others are harmful, inducing fear and anxiety that can be emotionally paralysing. But what is the difference between good and bad stress? For one thing, good stress is accompanied by a feeling of being in control; bad stress arises from a sense of being overwhelmed by difficulties that you feel powerless to overcome. In short, stress is interpreted as good or bad depending on whether we feel we can control what is causing it and, if not, then at least respond to it with confidence.

REACTIONS TO STRESS

Thanks to recent scientific research, we now know much more than we previously did about how stress occurs and why different people experience different levels of stress from the same causes. For example, those who experience a number of stress-inducing events – such as a death or divorce in the family, moving, and job loss or relocation during any one period – are much more likely to fall victim to illnesses than those whose lives over the same period have been relatively incident-free. Fortunately for most people, the stress accompanying such major life events, whether they are happy or sad ones, tends to be finite.

This is not the case with the less dramatic but constant, niggling irritations and worries that assail us, day in and day out. In fact, the cumulative stress of everyday concerns, what researchers refer to as chronic stress, can have as much of an impact on our health as stress produced by major life changes. Chronic stress can be caused by a number of things: worries about putting on weight, the cost of living, having too much to do, misplacing, breaking, or losing things, irritating noise, and constant interruptions. Luckily, while we may be powerless to avoid a major life-event, such as the death of a spouse or the loss of a job, we can try to modify or eliminate many of the little things that create chronic stress.

HANDLING STRESS

How stress affects you depends more on your temperament and your personality than on how many major life changes or minor irritations you are exposed to. Psychologist Suzanne Kobasa used the term hardiness to describe the capacity to respond positively to stress. There are three key elements to hardiness: *commitment*, or the strength of your belief in the value of who you are and the work

JACK NICKLAUS
Sportsmen, such as golfer Jack Nicklaus, use visualisation techniques to help perfect their game and offset the stress of the crowds.

you do; *control*, or the conviction that you can influence the course of events affecting your life; and *receptivity to challenge*, or the belief that change presents opportunities for personal growth, rather than a threat to security. Her research showed that people with a high degree of hardiness were more resistant to illness than those who were less hardy.

In the early 1960s, two American cardiologists, Drs Meyer Friedman and Ray Rosenman, discovered that personality played a huge role in stress management. They distinguished two broad categories of personality – Types A and B. Under this classification, people with a Type A personality are driven, competitive, impatient, aggressive, with a free-floating sense of hostility and a tendency to get angry easily. They also suffer from 'hurry sickness' – a constant sense of urgency and a compulsion to achieve too much in too little time. Type B people lack these Type A traits; thus, they are more relaxed, more patient, less driven, they pace themselves and their work more sensibly, and feel less angry and hostile. While most of us are a mixture of Type A and Type B, those who are primarily Type A appear to run a much higher risk of succumbing to coronary heart disease than Type B. Recent research, however, reveals that it's not the competitiveness or the hurried lifestyle of Type A people that is harmful, but rather their free-floating hostility. One study conducted by Dr John Barefoot of Duke University, in the USA, showed that doctors who scored high in hostility on personality tests were four to five times more likely to develop heart disease than low scorers.

Another important factor in determining how well an individual handles stress is whether there is adequate 'social support' – that is, whether a person has close and fulfilling relationships with a spouse, relatives, and friends. Researchers at three different hospitals in New York found that heart attack patients were at twice the risk of suffering another attack in a six-month period if they lived alone than if they lived with a spouse or carer. Unfortunately, the patterns of modern Western life often mean moving away from friends and family and a familiar community, and people who move away from their roots often find it difficult to meet new people and make new friends. Researchers have found that a lack of social contact and support can be stressful in itself as well as intensifying and provoking other stressors – things or events that cause stress.

MASSAGING TENSION AWAY
Stress often manifests itself in muscle tension, and massage is a highly effective way to ease this tension away. Aromatherapy oils can be used for a range of complaints.

TREATING STRESS

Scientists and doctors agree that stress contributes to illness and that taking measures to reduce it will promote health. The problem for the sufferer from stress is how to choose from the extensive range of countermeasures. The number and variety of the physical and mental manifestations of stress seem to be matched by the number and variety of ways in which people seek to treat it.

Modern Western medicine has little to offer when it comes to stress management. It is geared toward relief of symptoms. Often a doctor will prescribe tranquillisers or sleeping pills to patients under acute stress. Although they may help during a crisis or in the period immediately after a major stressful event, they do nothing to combat the problems of long-term stress. When the course of pills is stopped, or when the body builds up a resistance to them, the symptoms will return. Thus, an increasing number of people have turned to 'natural' therapies – ones that address the causes of stress and the responses of the body as a whole, rather than using the stop-gap measure of treating a particular symptom. In some cases people seek therapies because they are wary of the possible side-effects of sedating medications and they do not want to become dependent upon them. Others believe that 'holistic' therapies that emphasise the interrelation between the mind and the body are the most powerful antidotes to stress.

NATURAL THERAPIES

Strategies for beating stress using natural therapies are varied. Some practices are modern and Western in origin, others are very ancient and come from the East. For practitioners of holistic therapies, balance and inner harmony are the key terms in the treatment of stress. These therapies seek to uncover why and how this balance is lost and help to restore it in the patient.

What the natural remedies all have in common is the desire to avoid treating specific symptoms and causes with modern Western pharmacology and medical practice, and instead to use techniques that take into consideration the whole person – mind, body, soul.

There is a multiplicity of stress therapies available. As different stressors affect different people so one type of therapy may help one individual and not another. Some therapies make use of herbal remedies, some manipulate the body to create beneficial effects, and others encourage corrective diets, exercise, and relaxation regimes.

BARBARA BUSH
Former First Lady Barbara Bush is shown here with her beloved spaniels. Animals have a wonderful ability to help humans cope with stress. Studies show that the simple act of stroking a pet lowers blood pressure several points.

TONY BENNETT
One form of art may be used to replace another as a way of alleviating stress. Here Tony Bennett exchanges the stage for the easel, which is his way of relaxing from performing.

WINSTON CHURCHILL
Hobbies that engage both the mind and body are a wonderful way to offset stress. During and after the Second World War, Churchill devised an unusual way to relax from the pressures of public office. He took up bricklaying and built a long wall around the kitchen garden at his country home in Kent.

Our reaction to stress is complex, involving highly individual elements of personality, physiology, and psychology. The many ways in which stress shows itself justifies a very broad approach to its understanding, and a particular openness to the methods of its treatment. That the various treatments for stress pay far greater attention to the complete physical, biochemical, social, and emotional profile of the sufferer makes them at the very least a useful support for conventional medicine.

IN THIS BOOK

Inside *The Stress Factor* you will find a wealth of information on the subject of stress. You will discover how stress affects your body and how it can affect (both positively and negatively) your health, your marriage or relationship, your children, even your job. And you will learn about a number of stress-relieving natural therapies that can help you to offset the effect of stress in your life.

Learning to recognise the signs is not as easy as you might think. In Chapter 1, you will learn about the physical and emotional signs of stress and you can take a stress quiz to help you determine just how stressed you really are. Chapter 2 focuses on stress management and how diet and exercise as well as several alternative therapies, such as tai chi and meditation, can help you to deal with stress. Chapter 3 explores the link between stress and illness and looks at a range of natural therapies that can reduce stress. Chapter 4 considers the role of stress at each stage of life and teaches you how to take control over difficult situations.

Chapters 5 to 8 provide a detailed analysis of stress in four key areas of our lives: family, home, work, and the environment. Chapter 5 explains how certain stressors can upset the family unit. Chapter 6 shows you how to turn your home into a stress-free haven. Chapter 7 explores the leading adult health problem: work stress. And Chapter 8 describes how you can guard against the stresses caused by environmental factors.

The Stress Factor contains a number of special features, such as case studies of how people have coped under various stressful situations. There are also descriptions of therapies, conventional and alternative, such as massage, homeopathy, yoga, and much more. The goal of this book is simple – to provide you with useful tools to help you to combat the stress in your life.

CHAPTER 1

RECOGNISING STRESS

*Some stress is a necessary part of life,
but too much can result in a wide range of
ailments and disorders. Fortunately, there are early
warning signs that can tell you when something is
wrong. This chapter will show you how to recognise
the physical, mental, and emotional symptoms of
too much stress, so that you can take action
before it leads to a serious illness.*

THE STRESS RESPONSE

The interplay between the senses, the brain, and the central nervous system allows us to respond instantly to danger, and once the threat to our safety has passed, to relax.

Stress is subjective, that is, different people feel differently about a stressful experience. How you feel depends on several factors: personality, hormones, or even the type of day that you are having. Sometimes the same situation may cause feelings of stress one day but not the next. For example, you may have a plane to catch. If your schedule is tight you may be fuming as you wait in traffic, worrying that you will be late. If your schedule is open and you can get a later plane, you are likely to feel much more relaxed.

Although the events that cause stress are subjective, what happens inside your body when you are under stress follows a set pattern, which can be objectively measured. Dubbed the fight-or-flight response, this reaction was first studied in the early 1900s by the American physiologist, Walter B. Cannon at Harvard Medical School. Cannon discovered that when we are threatened, our bodies secrete catecholamines or 'stress hormones'. Produced by the adrenal glands, a pair of triangular organs located on top of each kidney, these hormones are known as adrenaline and noradrenaline. Their job is to orchestrate the body's reaction to stress.

FIGHT OR FLIGHT

When the brain registers a threat, catecholamines are released that instruct certain body systems to shut down temporarily so that more of the body's efforts can deal with the threatening situation, either by staying and fighting or by running away. Also known as the automatic primary stress response, this instinctive physiological reaction gives the body extra power, speed, and energy in times of danger.

You are probably familiar with some of these responses to danger. For instance, if you step off the kerb without looking and then see a car bearing down on you, your heart will pound and you will breathe faster. As your heart rate and breathing rate increase, your blood pressure rises. Extra blood is channelled to the brain and muscles and away from the stomach and intestines – there is little point in wasting energy digesting a sandwich when staring death in the face. This shutdown of the digestive tract is experienced as a dry mouth because saliva production is decreased. To supply the extra energy you need, your liver releases energy-giving sugars. Blood sugar and cholesterol levels go up. Your vision improves. To cope with the possibility of injury, more clotting factors are produced in the bloodstream so that bleeding will be minimised.

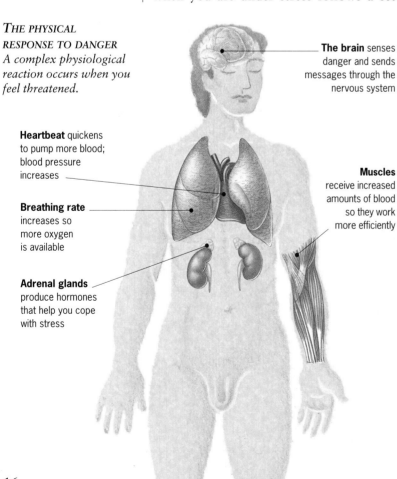

THE PHYSICAL RESPONSE TO DANGER
A complex physiological reaction occurs when you feel threatened.

The brain senses danger and sends messages through the nervous system

Heartbeat quickens to pump more blood; blood pressure increases

Breathing rate increases so more oxygen is available

Adrenal glands produce hormones that help you cope with stress

Muscles receive increased amounts of blood so they work more efficiently

As a way of surviving physical danger – or helping others survive – the fight-or-flight response is extremely effective. It can help participants at major accidents find the incredible strength they may need to lift heavy loads as they search for survivors, or to perform other 'miracles' of effort.

GAINS AND LOSSES

The most efficacious aspect of the stress response, however, is also its main draw-back – it is not under conscious control. The response is immediately set in motion whenever your brain perceives you are threatened. In an instant, this lifesaving reflex ensures that stress hormones are produced that put your body on red alert.

As an effective response to immediate danger, the fight-or-flight response cannot be beaten. But while the short-term benefits can be lifesaving, over a prolonged period this reaction can cause health problems.

In the 1930s, the Austrian-born endocrinologist, Hans Selye, was intrigued to find that his laboratory animals developed ulcers and weakened immune systems when they were subjected to noxious substances. He called what his lab animals were suffering from 'stress', which he defined as a 'nonspecific response of an organism to any demand for change'.

But what if the demand for change was continuous? How would an organism cope? To answer that question, Selye began investigating the physiological reactions to such continuous noxious events as loud noises, bright lights, or extreme heat or cold. From his research he developed what he termed the General Adaptation Syndrome. According to Selye, there are three stages of reaction to continued stress. The first is the alarm response which is marked by the stimulation of the sympathetic nervous system – heart rate speeds up and blood pressure rises. If the stress continues then the organism goes into the second stage, termed resistance, where the adaptive defences are maintained, but immunity is compromised. The final stage is exhaustion.

After analysing the physiology of stress, Selye discovered another remarkable feature of stress. The body is unable to distinguish between physical danger and psychological distress. The worries, fears, and anxieties that are a part of everyday life can trigger the same physiological response as a brush with danger. If you miss the only train that will get you to an important meeting on time, your body will respond just as if the train nearly ran you over. In both cases, you will experience such physical symptoms as a racing heart, shaking hands, and dry mouth.

TRAINED FOR DANGER
Studies have shown that life-threatening jobs, such as firefighting, can in some circumstances cause less stress than more mundane jobs, for which you not have been properly trained or have little control over.

THE BIOCHEMISTRY OF STRESS

When your body registers that you are stressed, the frontal lobes of your brain alert the hypothalamus, a tiny section of the brain that is responsible for many bodily functions, such as temperature, sleep, and appetite. During stress, the hypothalamus engages in a feedback loop with the pituitary gland. The hypothalamus secretes a hormone called corticotrophin-releasing factor or CRF which travels to the nearby pituitary gland and signals it to produce adrenocorticotropic hormone or ACTH. Once ACTH is produced, the pituitary gland releases it into the bloodstream, where it then triggers the release of the hormones adrenaline and noradrenaline (see page 16). These hormones are synthesised in the adrenal medulla – the inner core of the adrenal glands which sit on top of the kidneys.

This incredible relay system of hormones is responsible for setting off the body's numerous reactions to stress, such as rapid heart and breathing rate, dilation of the pupils, increased perspiration, and reduction of inflammation.

THE BODY'S RESPONSE TO STRESS
When stress occurs, the hypothalamus triggers a chain reaction of chemical and nervous system activities.

Hypothalamus

Hypothalamus

Pituitary gland

The best medicine

Two of the greatest natural ways to relieve tension, laughing and crying, may also work to keep the side-effects of the fight-or-flight response from causing you harm. Laughter helps soothe the body's nervous system and enhance circulation. It may also trigger the release of endorphins (natural compounds that mimic the action of morphine) which improve mood and reduce pain. Studies have shown that people who cry after major traumas, such as a bereavement, are more likely to remain healthy than those who refuse to exhibit any emotion.

LAUGH AND THE WORLD LAUGHS WITH YOU
The relief that comes from laughter helps the nervous and circulatory systems recover from stress.

If you were to escape by running from the train, your body's stress reaction would have been put to good use. And when the crisis was over, your body would return to normal. But when you miss a train and anxiety sets in because you will now be late for an important meeting, the body experiences no physical release, nor does the brain signal the all-clear. If this happens too often, over a long time, these stress reactions can cause physical damage and mental strain.

THE PHYSICAL DAMAGE OF STRESS

Researchers have found that the immune system does not adapt well to chronic stress. To function under the strain of chronic stress it simply works at a lower level, making people more prone to infectious diseases. In one landmark study, the carers of loved ones with Alzheimer's disease were tested over a five-

---

THE EFFECTS OF STRESS ON PERFORMANCE

When people live with a constant sense of pressure, they feel on edge and stretched, and eventually become ill. It is well known, however, that some stress is necessary for optimum performance, and human beings need a balance where they feel energetic by day and tired at night. Although the right relationship between stress and performance varies with each person, the general pattern follows the curve shown below.

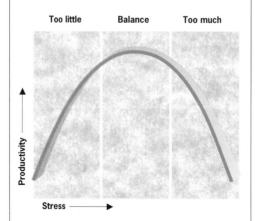

HUMAN EFFICIENCY CURVE
The right level of pressure will spur you on to work efficiently and productively. But pushed too far, you will make mistakes and your efforts will be counterproductive.

---

year period to see how this long-term stress affected their immunity. Compared to non-carers of the same age and gender, the Alzheimer carers came down with more colds and respiratory tract infections.

Because the fight-or-flight response unleashes adrenaline and other stress hormones into the bloodstream where they surge through the body like a tidal wave, a number of organs are affected, none more so than the heart. Sudden, acute stress, for instance, can trigger such a precipitous rise in adrenaline that it can induce a dangerous and lethal disturbance in the heart's rhythm. The chronic activation of stress hormones can also lead to elevated blood pressure. Moreover, it is thought that a chronic oversupply of stress hormones can accelerate the build-up of fatty plaque in blood vessels, including the coronary arteries, leading to heart attacks.

COPING WITH TENSE SITUATIONS

There are some individuals who seem better able to handle the physical challenge of stress than others. Athletes and people who are physically fit, for example, have lower pulse rates when they are under stress than unfit people. In one study, the pulse rates of a group of university students taking a major exam were measured. Although the rates of all of the students went up, the pulse rates of the fitter pupils were slower than the others and returned to normal more quickly. It has also been found that people who exercise regularly run less risk of a heart attack, and it is thought that part of the reason for their lowered risk may be because such people are offsetting any damage caused by the fight-or-flight response by virtue of their fitness.

STRESS: THE SIGNS AND SYMPTOMS

Knowing the danger signs of too much stress can help you defuse its effects before your physical and emotional health are adversely affected.

Since the early 1930s when Hans Selye first developed the concept of stress, researchers have been trying to quantify and qualify the elusive nature of everyday stress. The first problem they faced was determining whether the stress was due to an external event, such as a missed bus connection, or because of some internal disposition, for example, a shy person having to go to a party alone. Stress resulting from external events was somewhat easier to quantify. Researchers called these 'life events'. Two researchers, Dr Thomas Holmes and Dr Richard Rahe, devised a scale to illustrate the impact that life events can have on our health. Called the Social Readjustment Rating Scale, it ranked a number of stressful events. The death of a spouse, for instance, was rated 100; a major illness 53. Note that these events are seen as simply happening to people and are not the consequences of their personality or behaviour. (For more information on measuring your reaction to life events, see pages 64–65.)

During such life changes most of us are more than aware that we are under stress and try to make a special effort to take care of ourselves by eating properly and getting enough rest. But what about ordinary, everyday events? Why do some people get stressed by little things, such as traffic jams, and others do not? Here researchers look at stress in tandem with a person's personality and psychological traits. Needless to say, this type of stress is harder to study because it is relative to each individual. For instance, an impatient person is going to be more upset about standing in line at the supermarket checkout than a patient person. This type of stress can only be rated individually on our own personal distress scale. Because

everyday stress is so pervasive, finding out what irritates you can be difficult. To recognise the first signs of stress, look for nervous habits and mannerisms. Fiddling with one's hair or clothes, biting fingernails, foot tapping, and restlessness are all signs of stress.

COPING STRATEGIES

Stress can also be the culprit behind a variety of physical complaints. Notice that the symptom list (see the column on the right) applies to both acute and chronic stress. It all depends on one's temperament and personality. For this reason, researchers realised that they had to look at how people perceived the stress in their lives and how well they coped with it. What researchers learned was that stressors (stressful events) which required active coping, for example, confronting one's boss or asking for help, were more likely to adversely affect a person's health than stressors that could be coped with passively, such as ignoring the noise from rush hour traffic.

Stress that calls for passive coping is not innocuous, however. Although we may not be aware we are under stress, our body is. One clue that we are passively coping with

---

DID YOU KNOW?

Up to 75 symptoms of stress have been recognised by Arthur Rowshan, author of *Stress: An Owner's Manual*. The symptoms fall into five different categories – physical, emotional, mental, spiritual, and social – and are often elaborately interlinked. For example, arguing with someone can bring on a headache. This may affect your sleep, which in turn makes you irritable.

THE PHYSICAL SIGNS OF STRESS

A variety of problems may become manifest – all with their roots in the fight-or-flight response. Many different areas of the body are affected.

► *Headaches*
► *Teeth grinding, aching jaw*
► *Muscle spasms*
► *Aching shoulders, neck, and back*
► *Indigestion*
► *Nausea*
► *Ulcers*
► *Diarrhoea or constipation*
► *Shortness of breath*
► *Heart palpitations*
► *Cold hands and feet*
► *Skin problems (acne, eczema, psoriasis)*
► *Dry mouth*
► *Gum disease*

EFFECT OF STRESS ON BEHAVIOUR

When people are under pressure, they may exhibit or suffer from the following habits:

▶ *Pacing and fidgeting*

▶ *Nervous tics such as wringing hands*

▶ *Talking too fast and rushing everywhere*

▶ *Hyperventilation*

▶ *Inability to relax*

▶ *Crying*

▶ *Constant fatigue*

▶ *Indecisiveness*

▶ *Sleeping problems*

▶ *Impotence*

▶ *Increased eating and weight gain*

▶ *Decreased eating and weight loss*

▶ *Loss of effectiveness at work*

▶ *Recklessness*

▶ *Overspending*

▶ *Increased smoking and drinking*

stress is a flare-up of a particular body system or target organ that habitually breaks down when we are under too much stress. For example, some people always get cold sores when they are under stress, others develop headaches. Often a person's vulnerable stress spot is determined by heredity, for instance, psoriasis or nettle rash. Lifestyle also plays an important role – old sport injuries often flare up during physical stress, such as a competitive game of tennis.

Try to become aware of how your body feels under such stress. Do you feel tension in your lower back? Are you having problems sleeping? Is your stomach in knots? Are vulnerable areas acting up? For those who are under chronic stress, focusing on the physical symptoms is often the best way to recognise those events that are stressful.

INAPPROPRIATE RESPONSES TO STRESS

Another way to gauge how much stress you are under is to look at any inappropriate, self-defeating reactions you may have to it.

Comfort eating is one popular solution. Many people pamper themselves with tasty sugary snacks when life is getting them down. While chocolate bars will raise your blood sugar level quickly and give you a burst of energy and a feeling of satisfaction, this is quickly followed by an energy low, which can make you feel tired and irritable.

Smoking cigarettes is a common method of relieving stress as it can make you feel more alert and less anxious. But while the habit of smoking may be very reassuring to those who indulge in it, it is so harmful that it cannot be recommended as a form of stress reduction.

Many people look forward to a drink at the end of the day. When used in moderation alcohol can make you feel less tense. A glass or two of beer or wine relaxes you and makes you feel more cheerful. Heavy drinking, however, often leads to anxiety and depression. Additionally, heavy drinkers report that they are often unable to sleep or do not sleep well. With alcohol, therefore, it seems that less is more effective.

MONITORING STRESS

Because prevention is the best cure, it's best to be aware of personal stress levels before they become too high. The Monthly Stress Test on page 24 can help assess the previous month's status. Keeping a daily diary of stressful times may help you to pinpoint those situations that you find most troubling. Once you have recognised them, you can take steps to eliminate them from your life, perhaps by changing your situation or simply organising your time better. Or you may at least defuse them by learning to relax or using the techniques outlined in the following pages.

In your diary you should write down how well you are eating and sleeping, and if you are drinking more than usual. You can also use it to keep track of the emotional problems associated with stress such as tearfulness or loss of interest in sex. This kind of diary will enable you to monitor how stressed you feel. Since stress is so subjective – something that you find easy might cause a colleague great anxiety – you know best how you feel.

COPING WITH ALCOHOLISM

Work stress is known to be a main cause of excessive drinking in men, whereas women are more likely to drink when stress comes from problems in relationships. Because excessive drinking can lead to alcoholism, it is vital to learn how to cope with stress. One of the best ways is to talk about your problems with a sympathetic listener. In fact, Alcoholics Anonymous believes that only by sharing your experiences at meetings can you overcome your drinking problems and learn to live with stress.

SELF-HELP MEETINGS
Founded in 1935 by Bill Wilson, an alcoholic Wall Street employee, Alcoholics Anonymous (AA) is a well-known organisation that helps its two million members worldwide to achieve and maintain sobriety.

The Perfect Mother

Women who try to 'have it all' are under particular stress. This may cause a variety of physical symptoms, such as headaches and nausea, which can be confused with a serious physical illness. As with all suspected illnesses, you should consult your doctor. Worrying about your health will only create more stress.

Penny has three bright children, a loving husband, and a job she enjoys. When her youngest child started school, she was given promotion at work. Although her workload and responsibilities increased, she continued to help out with her children's activities at school, did all the housework, and cooked all the meals. In a few months, she began feeling tired and run-down, and then she developed headaches, neck pains, and nausea. She worried that she was seriously ill and confessed her fears to her husband, Bill. He insisted she visit the family doctor. After a thorough examination, her doctor could find no signs of any illness and said her symptoms were due to stress.

WHAT SHOULD PENNY DO?

Her doctor explained that her headaches and neck pains came from her habit of keeping her jaw tightly clenched all the time, which is a very obvious sign of stress. He advised her to cut back on some of her activities and to take some time out for herself – and not feel guilty about it. He said it was vital to her health and well-being that she find other ways of meeting her responsibilities at home and at work without taking all the strain on herself. He suggested she look for ways of learning to relax, such as taking up yoga or meditation; he also urged her to ask her family for more help with the household chores so that the burden was spread more evenly.

Action Plan

WORK
Stop trying to pack every moment with activity. Learn to realistically schedule the day's activities – don't be afraid to let less urgent things wait until tomorrow.

EMOTIONAL HEALTH
Join a hobby or support group, such as a Bible study group, a women's group, an assertiveness group, or a parenting group.

HEALTH
Learn some form of relaxation, perhaps tai chi, meditation, or yoga. Take time off when stress is too great.

HEALTH
Our body is often the first to point out to us that we are taking too much on or we are neglecting ourselves.

WORK
As responsibilities increase in certain spheres, the impact will be felt in other areas. Something has to give before you do.

EMOTIONAL HEALTH
Setting too high standards can make enjoying life almost impossible. It also isolates you from other people.

HOW THINGS TURNED OUT FOR PENNY

Penny took a course in time management and learned how to prioritise her work and to delegate tasks to others. She analysed her workload and asked her boss for an assistant, who has helped reduce her workload so that she no longer has to work overtime. At home, Penny assigned specific household tasks to her children. Weekends became a time to relax. She started taking a weekly yoga class. After a few weeks, Penny's headaches and neck pain were gone.

The Acupuncturist

People often visit an acupuncturist because of the stress caused by chronic pain. Using ancient Chinese diagnostic methods, the acupuncturist identifies the cause of the malaise and begins a course of treatment that can relieve painful symptoms.

PAINLESS NEEDLES
Many people worry that acupuncture will be painful, but because the needles are very fine and sharp, insertion is virtually painless.

MERIDIAN LINES
Two energy channels run down the centre of the body, with the remainder duplicated on either side.

Red: Heart, small intestine, pericardium

Black: Lungs, large intestine

Blue: Kidneys, bladder

Grey: Sexual organs

Green: Liver, gallbladder

Yellow: Spleen, stomach

Acupuncture has been used in China for over 2000 years, but was almost unknown in the West until the 1970s, when Westerners first saw photographs and films of people undergoing major surgery while they were still conscious. Acupuncture was the only pain relief the patients received, and yet they seemed to feel no pain. The secret lay in the use of very sharp, ultra-thin needles inserted at particular points in the body to redirect energy away from those areas of the body that were being operated on.

Intrigued by acupuncture's effectiveness as a form of pain relief, Western scientists tried to find out how it worked. They learned that according to the theory of Chinese medicine upon which acupuncture is based, energy moves through the body in set pathways, called meridians. During an illness, this energy, known by its Chinese name as *chi*, is not distributed properly. There might be a deficiency or a build up of energy, or the energy might be flowing too fast or too slowly. This theory made little sense to scientists at first, but as they investigated acupuncture, they found electromagnetic energy within the body that seemed to run along the pathways used by acupuncturists.

By inserting the needles into particular points along these pathways, the acupuncturist rebalances the flow of energy. Once the chi is flowing properly again, health is restored.

Origins

Acupuncture is said to have been discovered by a Chinese warrior who noticed a connection between the sharp arrow wounds he received during battle and the complete relief of pain due to several chronic ailments. Brought to the West by Chinese immigrants in the mid 1800s, it achieved little publicity outside Chinese communities until 1970, when an American journalist, James Reston, on a trip to China, experienced acupuncture-induced pain relief after emergency surgery. When he wrote about the experience in the US press, Americans took note. Since then acupuncture has

TREATMENT BY ACUPUNCTURE
Although it is Chinese in origin, acupuncture is also well known in Japan as shown by this picture.

been widely recognised, and even the World Health Organisation has acknowledged its value.

Scientists still do not understand how, or even if, this rebalancing of energy works, and yet acupuncture is known to be effective in relieving chronic muscular pain. It may also help lower blood pressure and can be used in the treatment of certain minor infectious diseases.

How does an acupuncturist diagnose stress?

Before treatment, the acupuncturist will conduct a physical examination during which you will be asked questions about your health and habits. He or she will also take your pulse at 12 different positions on your wrist, and look at your tongue. This examination will reveal your overall state of health and well-being.

How does acupuncture relieve stress?

Practitioners believe that a balanced flow of energy, or chi, within the body is the key to good health. When you are ill, they believe the body's energy is out of balance, and that by redirecting the energy they can return you to health.

What stress-related complaints can acupuncture treat?

Acupuncture is particularly effective for stress-related illnesses such as sleep disturbances, headaches, and joint pain. It may also be used to aid relaxation.

What is acupuncture like?

Most people say that they feel little pain when the needles are inserted. The sensation is most like tingling. Sometimes, patients feel energy shooting from one end of their body to another during insertion.

What will happen at an acupuncture appointment?

Once a diagnosis has been made, the acupuncturist will ask you to lie on a couch and to remove clothing covering the areas he or she intends to work on. During a typical session, an acupuncturist will insert one to 15 sterile needles. They will remain in place for between 10 and 30 minutes.

THERAPIST WITH PATIENT
An acupuncturist places needles along energy pathways, known as meridians, to balance the flow of chi through the body.

Needle insertion
causes a slight tingling

While one session may do the trick, typically six weekly sessions are required before you see results. As part of your treatment, the acupuncturist may discuss how you can improve your diet or lifestyle.

How long does it take to work?

The initial treatment often brings some relief, but a course of treatments is usually necessary to completely cure the condition. The time it takes depends on how severe the condition is, how old the person is, and how long he or she has been ill.

Are all acupuncturists registered?

You do not have to be registered to practise acupuncture in the UK. To find an acupuncturist who is also a qualified medical practitioner, write to the British Medical Acupuncture Society, Newton House, Whitley, Warrington, WA4 4JA.

WHAT YOU CAN DO AT HOME

Instead of needles, you can apply pressure to key meridian points to release blocked energy flow. Use your fingertips to press on the appropriate pressure point.

PRESSURE POINT FOR HEADACHES
Relieve headaches by applying pressure to point B10 on either side of your spine, two finger-widths below the base of your skull.

Press firmly but gently

MONTHLY STRESS TEST

Listed below are some of the ways that people react to stress in their lives. Think back over the past month, and on a photocopy of this page score each symptom according to your personal experience – 3 if it occurred regularly; 2 sometimes; 1 rarely. Add up your total and check your stress level below.

SYMPTOMS	REGULARLY	SOMETIMES	RARELY
Lying awake at night worrying about work or waking with disturbing dreams			
Overreacting to minor problems with anger, anxiety, hurt feelings and/or frequent crying			
Overeating or a decline in appetite			
Increased use of alcohol or tobacco			
Long periods of boredom			
Unable to let go of tension easily; difficulty in relaxing, even in quiet moments, or finding that there is no time to relax			
Experiencing a change in sexual behaviour			
Exhibiting a drop in performance at work			
Having difficulty setting priorities or making decisions			
An increase in the occurrence of any of the following: headaches, digestive problems, aching neck or back, breathing problems, heart palpitations, teeth grinding, muscle spasms, or a worsening of skin conditions such as acne, eczema, or psoriasis			
A greater susceptibility to colds or flu			
An unreasonably anxious need to improve performance at work, or unreasonable worry over seeking higher pay or promotion			
A frequent desire to consult outside professional help, be it from your doctor, your vicar, priest or minister, or from counselling agencies			
Needing a great deal of personal support from friends and family, often more than they are willing or able to give			
Feeling rushed or that there is not enough time to get everything finished			
TOTAL			

RESULTS

15–25: UNSTRESSED

Suggests that there is not much stress in your life, or, which is more likely, that you deal with it very effectively when it does occur. You should probably keep on doing what you're doing as it works for you.

26–35: MILDLY STRESSED

Points to your experiencing high levels of stress at certain times, but that the feelings subside after a while. If you score 30 or over you would probably benefit from embarking on a programme of stress relief and relaxation.

36 OR MORE: HIGHLY STRESSED

Indicates that your life has more than its fair share of stress, and that you are not coping with it very well. You should immediately reflect on your lifestyle and take action to make it more manageable and less stressful.

CHAPTER 2

STRESS MANAGEMENT

In today's world, most people have to cope with the noise, pollution, traffic, and other hallmarks of progress. Luckily, minimising the effects of these stressors on the body is not as difficult as you might think. This chapter reveals how an improved diet, an increase in fitness, and enhanced home surroundings can do wonders to minimise the damaging effects of too much stress. Better still, learning new and improved ways to relax will help to keep stress to a minimum.

PROTECTING YOUR BODY FROM STRESS

You can strengthen your physical defences against whatever life throws at you by eating and sleeping well, giving your body the attention it needs, and maintaining a tranquil mental outlook.

A body that is fit is best able to cope with stress. Proper nutrition arms the body with the resources it needs to fend off the increased demands that stress places on it. An inadequate diet, on the other hand, will deplete your nutritional reserves, leaving you vulnerable to disease. This in turn will cause greater stress because you won't feel that you have adequate resources to cope successfully.

Stress is frequently the culprit behind poor eating habits. In an effort to save time or energy many people just grab whatever is available, such as sweets, crisps, cakes, and biscuits. Typically, these snack foods are high in salt and sugar, and when eaten in excess lead to obesity. Unfortunately, stress can also make sticking to a slimming diet difficult. Knowing this, most reputable weight-loss programmes include behaviour modification as part of their diet plan.

When under stress the best solution is to choose foods that provide the most nutrition. Current dietary thinking lays considerable emphasis on eating plenty of whole grains, pasta, rice, and potatoes – foods that contain complex carbohydrates – as well as lots of fibre-rich fresh fruits and vegetables. Meat, fish, and poultry should be eaten in moderation, as should dairy products. Fats such as butter and oil should be eaten only sparingly, except in the case of children.

Such a diet supplies most people with all the vitamins and minerals they need, as well as enough energy to deal with life's challenges. Instead of getting a quick surge of glucose, followed by a drop as you do when you eat chocolate bars, doughnuts, and other refined foods, complex carbohydrates are broken down in your body into glucose and gradually released into your bloodstream, providing you with steady, sustained energy throughout the day.

STRESS-INDUCING FOODS
Some foods have been especially implicated as stress inducers, making you more at risk of certain illnesses. Although sugar is a great energy source, it also contributes enormously to the development of obesity, which is a leading risk factor in high blood pressure, heart disease, osteoarthritis, and diabetes. Eating foods high in sugar affects your mood: once ingested it leads to a surge

THE FOOD PYRAMID
An effective way of illustrating what foods we should eat and in what proportions is by a pyramid. It separates the food groups and represents what a balanced diet should consist of each day.

Fats and oils should be kept to a minimum (saturated fats such as butter and lard should be used sparingly, if at all)

Dairy products (2–3 servings)

Proteins – lean meat, poultry, fish, and beans (2–3 servings)

Fruits and vegetables, preferably fresh (3–5 servings)

Carbohydrates – bread, pasta, rice, and potatoes (6–11 servings)

DID YOU KNOW?

Under prolonged stress, carbohydrates, fat, and protein are depleted, in addition to the B and C vitamins. When resources run out, the body becomes more susceptible to illness. However, if you maintain a balanced diet throughout the period of stress, you can replace the reserves. Don't be tempted by a quick fix of sweets, biscuits or cake; these foods are high in refined sugar and usually have little nutritional value.

in blood sugar levels followed by an almost equally rapid drop, which can produce symptoms of hunger, weakness, and depression. Try to avoid excess sugar; replace sweet snacks with fresh fruits or pieces of raw vegetables, and reduce the amount of sugar in drinks and cooking.

Coffee, tea, and some colas often contain a significant amount of caffeine. While a little can act as a mood lifter and a physical booster, too much may cause palpitations and raise blood pressure (especially if you smoke), give you jittery nerves and insomnia, and trigger anxiety attacks. Try to kick the caffeine habit; switch to decaffeinated beverages, fruit juice, or water.

The body needs fats for growth and for repair, but a diet that is high in saturated fat, the kind found in butter and animal fat, will contribute to high blood cholesterol and heart disease. To reduce your intake of saturated fats, slash the amount of red meats you eat, cut away visible fat, cook with unsaturated fats (olive oil or sunflower oil), and eat low-fat cheeses.

In times of stress, it is more sensible to eat comforting foods rather than indulge in comfort eating. For instance, homemade soups on a cold day may remind you of being cared for in childhood. A steaming bowl of porridge, scented with cinnamon and sweetened with raisins, can sustain you through the toughest day.

A GOOD NIGHT'S SLEEP

Sleep deprivation is one of the leading causes of stress; and conversely stress is one of the leading causes of insomnia. Extended periods of sleeplessness result in a lack of efficiency and make you tired, irritable, and short-tempered – symptoms that are only too readily compounded with stress. Effects

of sleep deprivation were highlighted by a study of the sleep patterns of young doctors based at a New York hospital. Research showed that towards the end of the standard 36-hour work shift, these young doctors suffered from short-term memory lapses, an inability to react to complex problems, and an increasing lack of concern about their patients. Research has also revealed that people who suffer from insomnia experience the same rapid brain wave patterns as people who are under stress (see page 43). This may explain why falling asleep after a stressful day is difficult.

Getting to sleep

A regular routine will help you if you have trouble getting to sleep. Rising early in the morning, of course, will often make it easier to fall asleep at a decent hour at night. Part of getting a good night's sleep involves paying attention to eating habits, such as avoiding large meals late in the evening, as well as getting enough exercise. The more regular exercise you do, the more likely it is that you will sleep better at night. Start your exercise programme slowly and build up the amount and intensity gradually. Always consult your doctor before you begin.

A BED FIT TO SLEEP IN

Buying a good bed could be the best investment in your health you ever make. The place you rest your head must be conducive to sleep, not something that adds to your day's worries.

Buy the best mattress you can afford. A sagging, lumpy bed will be uncomfortable and may also lead to backache by not supporting your spine properly. Although the amount of give in a mattress is a matter of taste, doctors recommend the firmer the better.

Choose natural fibres – such as cotton or linen – for your nightwear and sheets. They allow your skin to breathe and will keep you cool in summer and warm in winter.

Use several layers of covers, such as a sheet and one or two thin blankets. Then you can roll back a blanket if you are too warm, and also have one at hand should you wake up feeling cold.

STRESS-BUSTING FOODS

You may be able to reduce stress by changing your diet. Foods and beverages you can try are:

▶ *Herbal teas, such as camomile and peppermint, which have a calming effect.*

▶ *Foods high in vitamin B_6 – yeast extracts, liver, whole grains, nuts, bananas – which have been claimed to be stress preventers.*

▶ *Citrus fruits, red, green and yellow peppers, and baked potatoes are rich in vitamin C, which helps your body to maintain resistance to infection when under stress.*

GOOD NIGHT'S SLEEP
To aid sleep, try sleeping on a pillow filled with hops (Humulus lupulus) or other soporific herbs obtained from health food stores.

As bedtime approaches, do something that takes your mind off your problems but does not mentally or physically stimulate you – listening to music, reading, or taking a warm bath. To ease insomnia, the old standby of a glass of milk and biscuits at bedtime works. The reason is that a combination of carbohydrates (biscuits, cereal, or bread) and milk increases the amount of tryptophan in the body. Tryptophan is an essential amino acid that synthesizes serotonin, the neurotransmitter associated with feelings of calm. A tryptophan-rich snack at bedtime can help to induce sleep.

Other substances, however, will keep you awake. The nicotine in cigarettes, which increases the secretion of adrenaline, is likely to make you too alert to sleep. The caffeine in tea and coffee will keep you awake; moreover, it can have a diuretic effect causing an urge to urinate, which will awaken you from sleep.

Although many people believe that an alcoholic drink will help them to sleep, this should also be avoided because alcohol disturbs sleep patterns. Like other sedating drugs that affect the central nervous system, alcohol slows brain activity and depresses rapid eye movement (REM) sleep, thus inhibiting dreaming.

Remedies for insomnia

When sleep is slow in coming, try pushing your worries to one side and visualising a pleasant, nonstimulating scene, perhaps by doing one of the visualisation exercises explained on pages 41 and 147. If noise from traffic or aircraft – or even from your partner's snoring – keeps you awake, try blocking it out with earplugs or consider buying an inexpensive 'white noise' or 'wave' machine that emits soothing sounds which mask unsettling noises.

To calm yourself down before bed, you can try a herbal preparation, ideally a tea. Herbalists often recommend a particular mixture, tailored to each individual's needs, that can help you to get to sleep. However, ready-made herbal teas are available from most health food shops. Camomile tea is one well-known sleep inducer, so is tea made from the root of the valerian plant.

If you still can't get off to sleep, or if your mind is overcrowded with worries or depressing thoughts, see your family doctor, who may prescribe a sleeping drug or sedative. Such medications, however, will often produce an unsatisfactory, artificial sleep and can be addictive, which is why doctors usually recommend them as a short-term remedy only.

RELAXING FOOT MASSAGE

Built-up tension and a poor diet will sometimes cause cramp in your feet and legs, which can interfere with sleep. If you massage your feet, you will ease the cramp that is causing the pain. In addition, if you gently stimulate the nerve endings on your skin, your circulation will improve.

CAUTION
Do not massage your feet if you have a fever or any circulatory problems.

1 STROKING THE FEET
Place one hand on top of your foot and hold it firmly. With the other hand, massage the sole of your foot, stroking with even pressure. Use smooth movements and cover the whole foot, from your toes to your ankle and then back again.

2 THUMB PRESSURE
Put one thumb on top of the other and draw them in a line down the centre of your sole, pressing firmly. Then make similar lines on either side of the foot. With one thumb, press in a circular motion all over the ball and arch of your foot.

3 KNEADING WITH KNUCKLES
Make one hand into a loose fist; support your foot with the other hand. Ripple your fingers in small circular movements to make knuckling pressures all over the sole of your foot.

FINDING YOUR BALANCE

Getting enough sleep will not be sufficient to counteract stress if at the same time your body is full of the tension, aches, and pains arising from bad posture. Unfortunately, the human body is not designed to cope with an upright stance, and so can easily be damaged if held or moved in the wrong way, especially when standing. This is one reason why back pain is the most common complaint that is seen by doctors.

Other parts of your body are also vulnerable. If you continually round your shoulders and back, you will squeeze your internal organs, making it harder for you to breathe properly and to digest your food. In addition, your hips, knees, ankles, and feet will have to take the strain of the weight imbalance to which they are subjected, and this can lead to osteoarthritis in later life. Exercising your back muscles will help you to maintain your flexibility and ease the wear and tear on your joints.

Standing tall, looking good

An important aspect of good posture is balance. The slightest shift in your body weight produces reactions all over your body as it adjusts your centre of gravity to keep you upright. Posture that puts you out

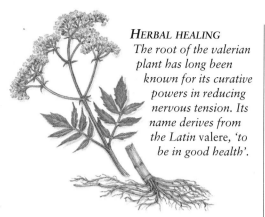

HERBAL HEALING
The root of the valerian plant has long been known for its curative powers in reducing nervous tension. Its name derives from the Latin valere, *'to be in good health'.*

of balance can result in a painful lower back, aching feet, and a sore neck from holding your head at an awkward angle. All this is tiring and places a great strain on your body. Improving your posture will relieve this, and it will also make you feel more confident and alive. Good posture not only benefits your physical well-being, it can also do a lot for you psychologically. Standing and sitting straight and tall will make you feel more alert and active. This positive body language will communicate itself to other people.

Most human beings are born with good posture: just look at the way young children hold themselves when they sit on the floor. Nor is it something that people naturally lose as they age. Men of the Masai people in

Fashion victims

High heels tilt the legs forwards and the body has to angle backwards to compensate. When switching to flat shoes or walking barefoot after wearing high heels regularly, a woman may develop sharp pains in her back and legs. This is because her muscles and ligaments have adjusted to the high heels and will not readjust readily to the lower heel height. You can compromise by wearing shoes with a 2.5 cm (1 in) heel, rather than shoes that are completely flat.

A BODY ALIGNED

When people think of good posture, they often imagine the rigid stance of soldiers. In fact, this chest-out-belly-in position may cause back pain by exaggerating the hollow in the small of the back, and putting too much strain on the muscles there. Correct standing places no extra strain on your back.

To stand correctly, imagine that there is a string running through your body and coming out of the top of your head. Then think of someone pulling the string up and feel your body fall into line. Your hips should be held straight – they should not tilt backwards. If you find that when you stand your weight is thrown forwards, simply raise your toes off the ground. This will shift the weight back to centre you.

To get your body into alignment, perform the following four steps.

1 Stand up straight with your feet slightly apart. Sway gently forwards until you feel your weight on your toes. Return to the starting position and sway slightly back so that the weight lies, correctly, in front of your ankles.

2 With your hands on your hips, gently move your pelvis forwards. You should feel that this puts your body out of alignment. Now realign your pelvis, imagining your body weight passing through your knees.

3 Make sure your knees are not locked. If you can wiggle your kneecaps with your hands, your knees are relaxed.

4 Finish by stretching the neck gently upwards, eyes facing forwards, chin and jaw making a right angle to your neck, your arms hanging loosely by your sides.

Chin held high

Back should be erect but not ramrod stiff

Arms relaxed

Pelvis centred above your knees

Knees relaxed

Feet slightly apart

SITTING CORRECTLY

Slouching in your chair can be just as damaging as failing to stand correctly. You should sit with your back as straight as possible, remembering the following rules:

▶ *Keep your shoulders in line with your hips.*

▶ *Keep both feet flat on the floor and balance your head comfortably on top of your spine.*

▶ *When reading, tilt any reading matter towards you so that you can sit straight.*

▶ *Position your chair and typewriter or computer so that you can sit straight, feet flat on the floor, with your forearms at right angles to your body.*

East Africa, for instance, can balance for long periods on just one leg, and women in developing countries walk gracefully while carrying large burdens on their heads.

In the West, life is a lot easier physically, and so bad postural habits are more likely to develop as people spend more of their time sitting, in cars, at desks, or in front of television sets.

Standing, sitting, and moving correctly are all essential parts of good posture. Therefore, it is an excellent idea to examine how you use your body from time to time. Think of how you sit when you answer the telephone, drive a car, read a book, or even just sit and relax. Do you hold your head on one side, pressing the telephone against your shoulder? Is your back rounded? When you sit at the dinner table, are you bent over? Do you twist your legs around each other? All these simple activities can strain your muscles, tendons, and bones.

Pay close attention to how you use your body at work. Incidences of repetitive strain injury (RSI) have soared because of the growing use of computers (see page 131). Most repetitive strain injuries of the hand

are due to carpal tunnel syndrome. Here, constant typing with the wrist in a cocked position causes numbness and weakness in the hands and fingers. This type of soft-tissue injury is usually treated with anti-inflammatory drugs and rest. It is important to get prompt medical treatment for stress injuries, especially to your hands and wrists; waiting too long will hinder recovery.

THE BENEFITS OF EXERCISE

Of all the natural stress beaters, regular exercise is one of the best. It helps to dissipate tension, makes you sleep better, and can aid concentration. Moderate exercise also has a beneficial effect on the heart and circulation, helping to ward off illness.

When stressful situations arise, you'll be better able to relax and take them in your stride if you are fit. If you quickly become exhausted in everyday situations, you will almost certainly benefit from doing some regular exercise. Then, when you have to face fresh challenges, such as moving to a new home or starting your own business, you will have the energy to handle it better.

continued on page 34

LIFTING AND CARRYING

The bones and muscles of the legs are strong and can be used to protect the back. Therefore, when you lift a heavy object, take the weight with your legs instead of bending over – and never carry more than you can manage.

LIFTING
With your feet shoulder-width apart, bend your knees and squat behind whatever you are lifting. Keeping your back upright (but not rigid), slowly straighten your legs as you rise.

Wrong

Spine bent

Right

Head held in line with spine

Spine held straight

CARRYING A BAG
When holding a heavy shoulder bag, keep your weight evenly balanced on both feet. This puts the least strain on your back.

Wrong

Right

Shoulders should be relaxed

Back and shoulders unbalanced

Knees should be kept loose

Hips should be kept straight

A Strong Back

*Stress makes you mentally and physically tense.
This can quickly lead to back pain and thus more stress.
Appropriate exercises can relieve your aching back and
break the vicious circle.*

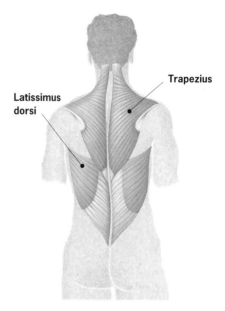

When people are stressed, they frequently feel as if the weight of the whole world is on their shoulders. In physical terms, this often means that people unconsciously hold the large muscles of their backs in a state of tension, and adopt a habitually slumped posture. Eventually they suffer from a painful neck and an aching back.

But back pain can usually be avoided by exercising to make your back stronger and more supple. A strong and properly aligned back will also improve your posture.

By becoming more aware of how you hold and move your back and then strengthening it and making it more flexible, you will ease any strain and free yourself from an added source of stress – back pain.

The exercises below are specially designed to help you to keep your back functioning properly and prevent pain. Be sure to consult your doctor before attempting them.

THE SPINE'S SUPPORT
Thick bands of muscle hold the spine in position, giving your body the flexibility it needs to twist and turn, as well as the strength to lift and carry.

SPINE-STRENGTHENING EXERCISES

Start your day with ten repetitions of the following exercises or include them in your regular exercise routine. Make sure all your movements are smooth and gentle to protect your spine from jarring.

SIDE STRETCH
Raise one arm: bend to the side. Hold. Repeat with the other arm.

The opposite arm should hang down by your side

Legs should be comfortably apart, and knees slightly bent

SPINAL CURL
Lie on your back. Bend your knees, then bring them and your head towards each other, tucking your chin into your chest.

Knees to forehead

SPINAL STRETCH
1 *Lie face down, with your arms at your sides. Raise shoulders and head off the floor. Hold for a count of five.*

2 *Cross your hands under your chin. Raise your head, shoulders, and legs, and hold for a count of five. You can also do this exercise with your arms stretched out in front of you.*

> **W A R N I N G**
> *Stop immediately if these exercises cause back pain. If the pain continues, see a doctor. If you have chronic back pain, you should exercise only after obtaining medical advice.*

Head and neck should be kept in a straight line

Arms should be by your sides, with palms up

Feet should be slightly higher than your head

Alexander Technique

Bad posture can become an ingrained habit and may lead to back pain. The Alexander technique helps you to avoid physical stress by teaching you how to use your body effectively, so that you can sit, stand, and move about in an easy, relaxed manner.

BACK TO INFANCY
The Alexander technique will help adults to recapture the free posture and graceful movements of childhood.

Babies have beautifully straight backs, but as people grow older, gravity and incorrect posture take their toll. Remaining in a static position for long periods – such as when sitting at a desk typing – makes back problems almost inevitable.

Over time, these poor body habits come to feel normal, but they place the body under considerable stress. Since the bad habits work against the way the body would move naturally, they are also very tiring.

The Alexander technique aims to re-educate the body. In keeping with this idea of education, Alexander technique practitioners are called 'teachers' and their clients 'pupils' or 'students'.

Origins

A professional orator, Frederick Matthias Alexander (1869–1955), found his career was in jeopardy when he started to lose his voice whenever he went on stage, only to regain it after the performance.

To find out why, he set up three mirrors, watched himself as he spoke his lines, and saw that when he did so he stiffened his neck, retracted his head, raised his chest, and hollowed his back. He found he could restore his voice by relaxing his neck, allowing his head to go forwards and up and his back to lengthen and widen.

Over a period of ten years, he gradually formalised his technique

THE TEACHER OF MOVEMENT
F.M. Alexander travelled the world teaching his technique until his death at the age of 86.

of movement and posture, and taught it in Australia, the US, and the UK, attracting such pupils as the writer George Bernard Shaw.

What do Alexander teachers do?
During the lessons, which are conducted on a one-to-one basis, teachers use their hands to align and direct their pupils' bodies, primarily concentrating on the relationship between the head, neck, and back. The pupil is taught the correct way to get in and out of a chair, to sit, to stand, and to move.

For instance, once you are standing as straight as you can, your teacher will correct your stance by altering the position of your head, neck, and back, or even changing the angle at which you may be leaning. At first, you might feel uncomfortable, but with practice, you should become accustomed to a new set of postures.

As your teacher realigns your body, he or she will repeat key phrases called directions, such as: 'Neck free, to allow the head forwards, back to lengthen and widen'. As you slowly relearn the correct positioning of your body, you will come to connect this with the directions, so that in daily life you can correct your own bad habits.

How many lessons will I need?
To see lasting results, a minimum of 20 to 30 lessons, each 30 to 45 minutes long, is recommended. Most teachers suggest three lessons a week for the first few weeks – after that, weekly lessons are sufficient. Some pupils continue to visit their Alexander technique teachers for years to be sure of maintaining correct posture.

Can I teach myself the Alexander technique?

No. You need the guidance of a trained teacher who can observe your posture and movements, assess any individual problems and show you how to overcome them.

Is the Alexander technique difficult to learn?

No, it just takes time to rediscover exactly how your body is meant to work. Some pupils find it difficult to avoid making unconscious muscular movements when their teachers guide their bodies into position.

How can the Alexander technique relieve or prevent stress?

It reduces muscular tension and improves your breathing, thus helping you to relax. If you can recognise when your body is not being used properly and when your muscles are tense, you can take steps to correct these faults. Teachers believe that virtually every movement you make can be influenced by using their technique, which help you to move correctly and stay comfortable while sitting, standing, or lying still.

LEARNING TO STAND UP CORRECTLY
Rising to a standing position from a chair is a common movement, but there are few people who do it correctly. Your teacher will show you how to stand and sit with the least strain on your body.

Head, arms, and back are guided into the correct position throughout the movement

The body is guided to achieve the correct fully aligned standing position

Arms should be relaxed as you take your weight on your thighs and raise your body, always leading with your head and maintaining the length of your neck

Do not push up with your hands

Knees take less weight, with your head and back in alignment

WHAT YOU CAN DO AT HOME

To learn the Alexander technique properly it is necessary to take lessons from a trained teacher, but certain positions can be tried out at home. Before you begin, make sure that you will have an uninterrupted half hour in a warm, draught-free room. Wear loose, comfortable clothes, and as you use your body, try to concentrate on the way your muscles and joints feel.

The semisupine position is a particularly relaxing and refreshing pose. When you lie in this position, your rib cage is relaxed and open, easing the pressure on your lungs, freeing your breathing, and giving your internal organs room to relax. When aligned in the semisupine position, your spine is well supported by the muscles in your back. This frees your whole body from the tension and muscular strain that are so often caused by poor posture.

THE SEMISUPINE POSITION
Once you have learned how to assume this position, you can use it to align your spine correctly.

The head will need supporting with some books, but make sure that your breathing is not restricted

Feet should be flat on the floor, and your knees bent

Helping yourself

Exercise is one very important way to reduce the effects of stress. Among its other benefits, physical activity will burn up excess fatty acids and glucose released by the fight-or-flight response. Moreover, it will relieve muscle tension – for many, the hallmark of stress.

Relaxation techniques (see pages 38–43) are another effective weapon in counteracting the symptoms of stress.

CYCLING TO HEALTH
A daily bicycle ride is a great way to stay fit as it provides the benefits of aerobic exercise.

If you can stretch and bend your body easily, you will be much more resilient to the normal stresses and strains of daily life. To check how supple you are, try to touch your toes with your legs straight. If you can touch the floor in front of your toes, you are supple; if you can only touch your toes, you could benefit from some stretching exercises; if you can only reach your ankles, you may want to start working on becoming more flexible.

Almost everyone can exercise, with very few exceptions. If you are suffering from a medical condition, are taking any form of medicine, or are recovering from an illness, always check with your doctor before taking up exercise or a new sport. If you have been ill, when you first start, choose a gentle exercise such as swimming, and don't push yourself.

Assessing your fitness

You can get a good indication of your general fitness by measuring your resting pulse rate – your pulse rate when you first wake up in the morning.

To take your pulse, place the tips of your forefinger and index finger on the inside of your wrist. Press gently until you can feel your pulse. Count the beats over 15 seconds, then multiply by four to get your pulse rate per minute. If your resting pulse rate is under 70, you are physically fit – the average rate is about 80. If your resting pulse is between 80 and 100, chances are you are out of shape. You should see your doctor if it is more than 100, as you may have a medical problem. As your fitness improves through regular exercise, your resting pulse rate will fall.

You can also monitor your fitness by timing how long it takes your pulse to return to its resting rate after exercise. The average is about 4–5 minutes, and the fitter you get, the shorter that time will become.

EXERCISE ROUTINES

According to the Health Education Authority, vigorous exercise is not the only way to keep healthy. Research shows that just 30 minutes every day of physical activity, such as walking or climbing the stairs, will maintain your health. A study carried out in 1993 showed that walkers had fewer cold symptoms than nonwalkers. Although an increase in strength is important, improving

endurance will probably help you the most in coping with stress. Brisk walking and cycling, for instance, are excellent ways to improve stamina, so instead of going by car, plan to make your shopping trips and other journeys on foot or by bike. If you have far to go, park the car or leave the train or bus some distance from your destination and walk the rest of the way.

You can also increase your fitness as you carry out tasks around the house and in the garden. Gardening, especially heavy digging, will strengthen your arms and legs, while vacuuming and making beds contribute to flexibility and strength, but take care not to strain your back. Take good care of your back by practising bending, lifting, and carrying correctly (see page 30).

Many sports and hobbies, such as swimming, dancing, and rambling, have physical benefits as well as being relaxing and stress reducing in themselves. Make exercise part of your social life – a weekly swim with a friend, for example.

Exercising regularly

For people who need the discipline of a formal exercise programme or simply like the idea of exercising with others, most towns have leisure centres where classes are held. Or you can carry out a simple but effective exercise programme in your own home.

It would be counterproductive, however, to take up any form of exercise that you do not enjoy. A boring routine will soon be dropped. To avoid boredom, try to combine activities, such as exercising in a class and

THE IDEAL EXERCISE ENVIRONMENT
Whether you swim or perform exercises in the shallow end of a pool, water offers resistance, thereby increasing the amount of energy you use up. It also reduces the gravitational pull on your body, taking the strain off muscles and joints.

swimming one or two evenings a week, or taking a brisk walk at lunchtime and cycling at the weekend.

When you exercise is a matter of individual preference. Some people like to do it first thing in the morning, while others find evenings preferable, particularly if the day has been emotionally stressful. Working the frustration out at night can be a great release.

The golden rule of all exercise is never to attempt too much too quickly. Studies show that heart attacks occur more frequently during, or after, strenuous physical activity in a person who had been sedentary. This holds for the couch potato who suddenly decides to work out and overdoes it or the

weekend athlete who has returned to sports after missing a few weeks. The reason that exercise can trigger a heart attack in the physically unfit is not clear; researchers think that the sudden rise in heart rate and blood pressure disrupts plaque in the heart's arteries, causing a blockage.

When you begin to exercise, start slowly, especially if you have not exercised in a while. Begin by finding a level of exercise that is comfortable for you and stay at that level for at least a week. Then slowly increase the difficulty or length of time. Also, be sure to start off any activity with a gentle warm-up and allow 5 minutes of cooling-down exercises at the end.

EXERCISING SUCCESSFULLY

To get the most out of exercise, bear these points in mind.

▶ *Exercise should not hurt. If it does, stop.*

▶ *Fresh air is healthy, so exercise outdoors as much as possible.*

▶ *Replace liquid lost from your body during exercise by drinking plenty of water.*

A GENTLE EXERCISE ROUTINE

Aerobic exercise is any sustained exercise that makes your heart beat faster, and increases stamina by conditioning the heart, lungs, and muscles. It improves circulation so that more oxygen reaches the brain cells, and it may stimulate the production of endorphins, which are the body's own 'feel good' chemicals.

Do the following gentle exercise routine for no more than 15 minutes, with a

minute's march between each stage. You can use them to get off to a good start in the morning or to banish workday stress in the evening. Be sure to wear sports shoes and comfortable clothes.

These exercises can be adapted easily to your own level of fitness, but if you are over 40 and do not usually exercise, check with your doctor before starting any exercise programme.

Make a large circle with your arms

Keep elbows high and bent

Arch back

Keep your weight over each knee

1 *With your feet apart and your knees bent, swing your arms up over your head, breathing in deeply. As you breathe out, bring your arms down slowly and cross them in front of you. Repeat exercise three times.*

2 *Stand with your feet apart and your knees bent. Bend your elbows up and push off to either side, moving your weight over alternate feet, coming back to the centre each time. Meanwhile, move your elbows back and forwards to stretch your chest muscles. Repeat exercise 20 times.*

3 *With your feet apart and your knees slightly bent, drop your torso forwards. Interlock your fingers, then stretch your arms and body up, palms to the ceiling. Hold briefly, then drop your torso forwards and swing gently. Now slowly stand, straightening your spine. Repeat exercise three times.*

Tai Chi Chuan

Also known as tai ji quan, tai chi chuan *is a combination of exercise, Chinese medicine, and Oriental philosophy. Called tai chi (or tai ji) for short, its slow, harmonious movements can help people to relax and alleviate stress.*

YIN AND YANG
According to the Chinese philosophy, Taoism, all things under the sun consist of a mixture of two principles: yin (the earth, passive, dark, and feminine) and yang (the heavens, active, bright, and masculine).

Watching a group of people slowly and gracefully going through the precise movements that comprise tai chi, you can hardly believe that this is one of the martial arts – but, when performed at lightning speed by an expert, it can inflict a great deal of damage. Today, however, tai chi is primarily practised to reduce stress, increase overall tone and flexibility, and achieve inner harmony.

What does tai chi consist of?
There are a number of styles of tai chi. The most common one in the West has two forms: a short one of about 40 movements, which, when learned thoroughly, takes about 10 minutes to perform; and a long one with over 100 movements, which takes about 25 minutes. The movements are precise, and there are many rules on how to hold the body. You need to carry out each exercise very slowly – in fact the slower the better, as long as balance can be maintained. This will give you time to examine all parts of your body to ensure you are doing a particular movement correctly. Your teacher will instruct you in how to blend each movement into the next in a continuous flow.

How does tai chi reduce stress?
Tai chi is a form of meditation in motion. It calms the mind and helps to disperse negative thoughts. The deep, slow breathing that is practised helps to induce a state of relaxation. As you concentrate on the feel of the balances and imbalances of your body while you go from one movement to another, you lose track of the outside world and its worries. In addition, tai chi demands natural movement, and muscle tension is released as you step forwards and back, turn, swing around, and bend with coordinated arm movements.

Does tai chi improve fitness?
Adherents believe that the movements improve the flow of the body's natural energy, *chi*, along various meridians (see page 22). The movements exercise all the joints of the body, increasing flexibility. Because

Origins

Tai chi has its philosophical roots in Taoism, which can be traced back to China in the sixth century BC. Taoism emphasises patience, simplicity, and harmony with nature, and states that all things are composed of different combinations of the two complementary forces, yin and yang. Yin represents yielding and evasion; yang denotes firmness and resistance.

According to tradition, the Taoist philosopher Chang Sen-feng dreamt of a snake being stabbed at by a crane. As the snake alternately evaded and resisted the crane's bill, Chang saw these animals as the embodiment of yin and yang, and from this he devised the first series of movements that

TAI CHI IN SHANGHAI
The relaxed and graceful tai chi exercises are often performed by groups outdoors in a park.

was to become tai chi. In 1956, the Chinese government, under Chairman Mao, standardised tai chi into 24 movements.

it is performed in slow motion, tai chi calls for deep breathing, which increases the amount of oxygen going to the heart, and improves the lungs' capacity.

Can anyone learn tai chi?
Tai chi is suitable for virtually everyone. Because it helps to improve blood and lymph circulation, it is ideal for those in poor health. If you are not certain about your fitness, check with your doctor.

Can I teach myself tai chi?
No. Tai chi teachers emphasise that the only way to learn properly is by watching a physical demonstration of the movements. Personal guidance is essential for learning correct body

alignment and maintaining mental and physical concentration. But after lessons with an experienced teacher you can, and should, practise tai chi on your own.

Does it take long to learn tai chi?
If you take a weekly 1 hour lesson, it will take 12 to 18 months to learn and remember all the 100 or so movements of the long form of tai chi. Attending more often will speed up this process, but it can take decades to become an expert.

What are the classes like?
Initially, you will be in a class of beginners, all learning the movements for the first time. Later, you may attend classes with students of

different abilities. The teacher may have you carry out a sequence you have learned, then teach you the next few movements to work on for the rest of the class, or he or she will take the entire class back to an early sequence to perfect their style. If you want to get individual attention, it is best to join a class with fewer than a dozen people.

WHAT YOU CAN DO AT HOME

These exercises are the beginning of a series of movements called 'Heaven and earth'. Wear loose clothing; wear socks or slippers or go barefoot.

SQUATTING SINGLE WHIP
This position is the beginning of a sequence of movements known as 'Snake creeps down to the water'. Reflecting Taoist philosophy of harmony between human-kind and the Universe, many movements have names incorporating nature.

Left hand is open with the fingers pointing up

Right hand should shape into a 'bird's beak'; fingers and thumb should touch and face the ground

Energy flows from the centre of the body to the hands and feet, and the face and head

Body weight should rest on left leg

Feet are kept apart, with weight evenly distributed

HORSE STANCE
With feet apart at shoulder width and knees bent, put your arms by your sides. There should be space between your arms and your body – about the width of a fist. Hold for 5 to 10 seconds.

Back should be straight, with knees slightly bent

Arms are held away from the body

HEAVEN STANCE
From the horse stance, raise your arms out in front of you, as though holding a ball. Hold for 2 to 5 minutes, breathing calmly and evenly. Experts hold this pose for up to 20 minutes.

LEARN TO RELAX

If you are anxious, your body will become tense. Relaxation can help you to feel calmer and more controlled. At least once a day, try to turn off the pressure and relax.

Is television relaxing?
Many people list watching television as their favourite method of relaxation. But whether it is really relaxing depends very much on what you watch. Viewing a romantic film or a comedy can be both enjoyable and stress reducing. Studies have shown, however, that watching violent programmes does little or nothing to lessen anxiety and stress; in fact, it can have the opposite effect. In addition, compared with people who use different forms of relaxation, television addicts are more likely to mistrust others and see the world as a hostile place.

RELAXING AT HOME
A family may often feel that the only time they get to relax together is when they are watching television.

No matter what makes you feel stressed out – your boss in a bad mood, your children misbehaving, having to admit to making a mistake, or trying to deal with bumper-to-bumper traffic – you need to find a way of relieving the pressure.

One of the most effective ways of curbing stress is to learn to relax. But relaxing is more than putting your feet up and watching television. Instead, relaxation is a way to consciously turn off everyday worries. This is highly therapeutic and beneficial for both mind and body.

DIFFERENT WAYS OF RELAXING

Relaxation is as subjective an experience as stress. Just as there are many stressors that evoke different reactions, there are many ways to relax which, depending on your personal make-up, provide varying degrees of relaxation. Going for a walk, gardening, taking a bath, or enjoying a quiet evening at home with friends are well-known relaxing activities. You can add to the list reading, going out for dinner, writing to a friend, and watching a video of an old movie. At the very least, these reassuring activities will take your mind off your problems.

Although it does not really matter where you relax, safety, peace, and quiet are essential. You could, for example, watch the world go by in the local park during your lunch break or meditate in the evening at home. A change of scenery can be relaxing in itself. If you work indoors all day, go outside for a walk. If the walk is brisk, you will have an added aerobic benefit. This will help to improve sleep patterns (see page 27) and increase your resistance to stress. If you work away from home, getting home and sitting down in your favourite chair with a book or newspaper can be relaxing. Gentle stretching exercises can also ease tension.

BIOFEEDBACK

For many people, the simple act of relaxation needs to be relearned. One excellent way is to use biofeedback to teach you how your body feels when it is stressed and how it feels when it is relaxed.

In this procedure, electrodes are placed on various parts of your body, for example, your scalp to measure muscle tension, or your finger to measure body temperature; the electrodes are then connected to a piece of equipment (typically no bigger than a small radio) which is called the biofeedback monitor. The monitor registers changes in body functions, such as slight changes in heart rate, blood pressure, skin temperature, or minute amounts of perspiration on the

THE BODY RELAXING
Changes take place as your body relaxes, which help to increase your physical and mental resistance to everyday pressure.

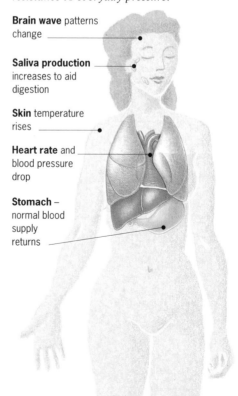

Brain wave patterns change

Saliva production increases to aid digestion

Skin temperature rises

Heart rate and blood pressure drop

Stomach – normal blood supply returns

Muscle Relaxation

Learn to ease the tensions of daily life through deep breathing and progressive muscle relaxation. Easy to master and beneficial for all ages, this routine can help to relieve your tensions and enhance your life.

Complete physical and mental relaxation can rarely be achieved simply by putting your feet up. When stress has been prolonged, or if there is a related condition such as high blood pressure, you may need to take positive steps towards reducing tension.

You can combine deep breathing with simple muscle-relaxing exercises to get the maximum benefit in the shortest possible time. It is best to practise this routine as frequently as possible. Regular relaxation has a cumulative effect, and the more you do it, the more quickly you will be able to enter a state of deep

relaxation, and the longer its effects will last. All that is needed is the discipline and dedication to integrate it into your life.

Ideally, you should perform progressive muscle relaxation exercises twice a day. Choose a time when you are feeling alert; do not do the exercises when you are tired, as you might become so relaxed that you fall asleep.

You should soon find that, after practising these relaxation exercises, you feel a great deal more at ease and better able to deal with daily stresses and tensions.

DEEP BREATHING

When you're tense, your breathing becomes shallow. Therefore, a simple and effective method of reducing tension is to breathe deeply and evenly.

One method of deep breathing is called *pranayama*, which is a branch of yoga. People who practise pranayama believe that by taking full, deep breaths, you absorb more life energy or *prana* from the atmosphere.

To practise deep breathing, place your hands flat on the area just above your navel. Inhale so that your belly rises and your hands are pushed out. Exhale – your belly will deflate beneath your hands. Repeat.

PROGRESSIVE MUSCLE RELAXATION

Your body will feel as if it is melting into the floor

Feet and legs will fall sideways when you are fully relaxed

Hands and arms should fall slightly away from the body

Lie down in a warm room and close your eyes to help your concentration. Breathe in and out deeply for 2 or 3 minutes to establish a regular pattern of respiration. Follow the sequence (right), tensing each part of your body in turn without involving any other muscles.

1 *Tense your feet and toes hard. Hold for a moment, then relax. Now tense your calf muscles; hold for a moment, then slowly relax.*

2 *Continue in the same way in the following order: thighs, abdomen, chest, hands, arms, shoulders, neck, jaw, and face.*

3 *Clench your teeth and shut your eyes tightly so that the muscles of your face are tense. Then relax them, and feel your face soften.*

WINNING THOUGHTS
Many top sports people use positive visualisation (see opposite) to excel in their chosen fields. Imagining performing a routine perfectly may help to ensure success.

skin. These changes are not normally consciously felt, but when they are monitored by biofeedback machines, they can provide many meaningful clues to how your body registers stress.

Listening to your body

During a biofeedback session, meter read-outs or tones will tell you whether the tension in your scalp muscles or your body temperature is increasing or decreasing. However, by visualising a pleasant scene, concentrating on a piece of lyrical music, or repeating a mantra or affirmation, for example, or by using some other relaxation technique, you can reduce your stress level and muscle tension. This mental effort will reduce the number on the meter read-out or lower the sound. Biofeedback only makes your stress visible or audible; it is the power of your mind that actually effects the changes that reduce the tension in your body. Eventually, when you have practised your visualisation technique sufficiently, you will be able to reduce muscle tension without being attached to the machine.

THE RELAXATION RESPONSE

Just as stress produces a variety of specific changes in the body, so, too, does deep relaxation. Dr Herbert Benson of Harvard Medical School has called these physical changes 'the relaxation response'. They include slower breathing and heart rate, a lower blood pressure, and an improvement in digestion and circulation.

But what brings about this relaxation response? Dr Benson believes that it is due to the brain's increased production of the large, slow alpha waves (see page 43), which occur after meditation. These replace the shorter, faster beta waves that are produced by the 'active' brain. Alpha waves allow the brain to quieten down and possibly become more receptive to communications between its left and right hemispheres, which some theoreticians believe is essential for creative thinking.

Connected with these physical changes, which return the body to its natural balance, are changes in the mind and emotions. Apart from feeling calmer and more composed, your concentration and memory improve,

TRANQUILLITY THROUGH SENSORY DEPRIVATION

One way to escape from the unrelenting pace of the modern world is through sensory deprivation. Flotation tanks and rooms are designed for this purpose. The tank is a large box that, when shut,

FLOTATION TANK
Spending half an hour in a flotation tank would relieve your cares. Isolated from all intrusions, you could relax in utter peace.

excludes all light. In the bottom there is enough water to fill three baths. The water is highly salted so that you float easily. The absence of all types of stimuli and the gentle sensation of floating effortlessly in the water combine to make this a relaxing experience.

For those who feel nervous about entering such a dark and confined space, flotation rooms are a useful alternative. These consist of a sauna-sized room filled with 25 cm (10 in) of saline solution in which you have room to stand, move around or float undisturbed. The temperature of the solution is kept at just below that of the body so you do not feel the water. You are also in control of the door and interior light.

Sensory deprivation is a good treatment for stress-related conditions including:

▶ *High blood pressure*

▶ *Headaches/migraines*

▶ *Persistent anxiety*

▶ *Muscle tension and fatigue*

you feel more resilient mentally, your mood lifts, and you are better able to put your difficulties into perspective. Because you are able to think more clearly, you will be able to assess situations better and find solutions to problems more easily.

VISUALISATION

The brain is a very powerful organ. Just by thinking you can either increase feelings of stress or reduce them. This is because the subconscious mind cannot tell the difference between a real experience and an imagined one. For example, having a near accident in your car will bring on such symptoms of stress as a racing pulse or churning stomach. These reactions will also occur if you vividly imagine a car crash. Lying in the sun on a peaceful balcony overlooking a deep blue sea will relax most people, but so will visualising it.

In addition, visualisation can help you to meet difficult situations. This use of visualisation is based on the principle that it is easier to do things when you have done them before. Thus, by vividly imagining the procedures that you are going to follow when you begin a new task, when you do finally tackle it you will proceed with much more confidence.

Visualisation is especially effective in sporting endeavours. It has been shown that people, having learned the basics of a sport such as golf, perform better at the game if they have spent time visualising the necessary movements or strokes than players who do not. Professional sports people who spend time visualising perfect performances as part of their training are finding that their performances do indeed improve.

Mental preparation

A great many potentially stressful situations can be eased by visualisation. For example, if the thought of attending a party at the weekend makes you feel very nervous or anxious, then begin the week by imagining that you are watching some other guest at the gathering. Imagine that person chatting away happily to the other guests and moving about confidently. Think about this image as often as you can over the next couple of days.

Now imagine yourself as the person you visualised, but still remain on the outside looking in – watch yourself having a good time. Let this image run through your mind as frequently as possible over the next few days prior to the gathering. Then put yourself fully into your imagined scenario. Be that person who is conversing and socialising happily and confidently, and keep this thought uppermost in your mind right up to the time of the party. Once you get there, you may be surprised at how easy it is to mingle with the guests and enjoy yourself – but then you've done it all before!

Can I do it?

People often think that they will be unable to produce any mental pictures, claiming that they have no imagination whatsoever. These self-doubts are quite frequently caused by a misconception of what a mental image is supposed to be. Individuals think they should expect to 'see', with their eyes closed, a picture that exactly mirrors the images that they see with their eyes open. Although some people can indeed produce very powerful mental images, it is not essential to be able to do this for visualisation to work for you.

Everyone is capable of visualising. For example, if you have to describe your bedroom to an acquaintance, you will bring it to mind, perhaps internally focusing on particular features – the covers on your bed, your bedside table, or your wallpaper or curtains. You may even narrow your eyes while staring at a spot on the opposite wall – trying to 'see' a pattern clearly, or you may use your hands to indicate a particular size or shape, or texture to help you to visualise more effectively.

Accessing pictures from your memory is very common in everyday life. In fact, you probably haven't realised that you have used the act of visualisation hundreds of times in the past.

Music and soothing sounds can be great aids to visualisation. Certain sounds on their own – the gentle noises of the rain forest, or the ocean lapping at the shore, or the wind in the trees – are often sufficient to ease tensions and evoke peaceful visual images, which can calm you completely. Today, listening to 'new age' music, which is noted for its soothing melodies and instrumentals, has become an extremely popular form of relaxation, as are affirmation or subliminal tapes in which positive words and phrases are repeated.

Soothing sounds
Effective relaxation can be aided by appropriate background music. This is especially suitable where visualisation is being used to unwind from a hectic and stressful day. You can choose from a range of commercially available audio tapes that provide a wide assortment of background effects.

DEEP RELAXATION
Some people find that listening to the beautiful and haunting sounds of a whale song mentally transports them to the stress-free shores of the ocean.

Meditation

The simple act of concentrating the mind on a single word or object has been found to slow down body processes and increase serenity. People who meditate regularly find that their stress levels are greatly reduced.

BUDDHIST MONK MEDITATING
Proponents of Buddhism incorporate meditation into their worship.

MEDITATION TEACHER WITH PUPIL
Your teacher will help you choose a mantra, and answer your questions.

For thousands of years, meditation has been a major part of many religions, including Buddhism and Hinduism. The best known and most researched method in the West, transcendental meditation (TM), was revived from its ancient form by the Indian teacher Maharishi Mahesh Yogi. Introduced to the West in 1959, TM was developed and made more accessible to modern, industrialised populations and by the mid 1990s over 180 000 people had learned the technique in Great Britain and there were about 4 million followers around the world.

How do you meditate?

Although there are many variations, the three basic strategies are: contemplation, concentration and TM. During contemplation your mind freely associates around a subject; concentration involves focusing your attention on a single thought, word or object; while TM requires that you sit comfortably and use a *mantra* (a Sanskrit term for a specific sound without meaning) in a natural way. The aim of all three strategies is to achieve a particular state of awareness called 'restful alertness'.

What do you meditate on?

In contemplative meditation, as the name suggests, you are encouraged to contemplate spiritual concerns, whereas during concentration meditation you focus on an object, such as a candle flame or a crystal, to help purge your mind of all distractions. With TM, a mantra that is suited to you is given in confidence by your instructor and you must repeat this over and over again to clear your mind of unnecessary thoughts.

How does meditation relieve stress?

Meditation produces a state of very deep relaxation. Your heart rate slows down, your level of oxygen consumption decreases, and after

Controlled breathing helps to calm the mind

Candles can be used as an object of meditation

Sitting cross-legged may not be comfortable for everyone. Find your own position, such as sitting on a chair habitual practice your blood pressure will lower. Through meditation, your mind will become calmer, which will enable you to cope more effectively with the tensions of everyday life.

Can I learn meditation by myself?

Yes, there are a number of books available on the subject; ideally, however, the entire TM process and the correct posture and breathing techniques for other forms of meditation should be learned from a qualified teacher.

Who can teach me meditation?

Meditation is taught by people who have usually studied meditation techniques for many years. Teachers of

Origins

Meditation is an ancient Eastern practice that may have originated with shamans and witch doctors in order to achieve a trance. In this way these early Asian tribesmen thought they could communicate with the spiritual worl... Later, mantras and yoga poses were introduced as aids to meditation.

WHIRLING DERVISH
Muslim ascetics achieve, through rhythmic dance, a state of higher consciousness that is quite similar to meditation.

TM complete a year-long training course; they are then registered with their country's national office.

What happens in a session?

In concentration and contemplative meditation, your teacher will show you how to adopt a posture for meditating: sitting with legs crossed and back straight, for example. Next, you will be told to concentrate on breathing slowly and rhythmically. With TM you repeat your chosen mantra in a natural manner, whereas with other techniques you might be asked to chant, close your eyes, or focus on an object or thought.

While repeating your mantra you will begin to empty your mind of all nagging concerns and tensions and let the word or object fill your consciousness. Do not fight distracting thoughts or noises, just be passively aware of them and gently bring your mind back to the object of your meditation. Initially, you will be asked to try to meditate for about 10 minutes. Experienced individuals may practise for periods extending to days, but most beginners are amazed at how much their minds wander during 10 minutes.

How long does it take to learn how to meditate?

Learning the basics of TM typically should only take four sessions with each session lasting about 2 hours, although the number will vary from teacher to teacher. Follow-up sessions may be given to see whether your meditation technique can be improved upon in any way. Some people can learn other techniques after even one session, but it is a process of constant refinement.

How does meditation differ from self-hypnosis?

Self-hypnosis usually has a specific goal in mind and is a very good tool for reducing levels of stress or giving up smoking. Meditation is much more open-ended, because it helps people to achieve long-term, physical and mental well-being.

BRAIN WAVES

In different states of awareness the brain displays characteristic types of electrical activity. This electrical output can be recorded in wave patterns. Meditation has been shown to slow down the fast beta waves that characterise a busy working day, and to help to maintain more alpha waves, which are associated with feelings of calm and relaxation.

Alpha waves (8–13 Hz)
Normal, calm state of mind

Beta waves (14–30 Hz)
Active, busy state of mind

Theta waves (4–7 Hz)
Drowsiness

DEDUCING YOUR STATE OF MIND
Your mental state can be determined from your brain wave patterns.

WHAT YOU CAN DO AT HOME

You don't need special training to meditate, but it is important to have an idea of the basic technique. You can begin now by choosing a word or a short sentence or statement, such as 'I will succeed', or 'I have unlimited potential'. Take time each day (first thing in the morning is best) to repeat your phrase wordlessly over and over for at least 10 minutes. Make sure you are sitting or reclining comfortably; close your eyes. While focusing on your word or phrase, breathe deeply and slowly; when distracting thoughts come, return to your word or phrase.

POSITIVE THINKING

You may not be able to change the weather or your job, but by changing the way you think, you can turn a negative experience into a positive one.

The philosophy of positivism

The French pharmacist Emile Coué (1857–1926) became famous for his belief that it's possible to teach our subconscious minds to be more positive. To do this we have to clear our minds of negative thoughts through repeating the positive phrase: 'Every day in every way, I am getting better and better.'

Coué's philosophy was expanded by Dr Norman Vincent Peale (1898–1955), a Protestant minister in New York, who advised that anything is achievable if you have faith in yourself and refuse to accept the possibility of failure. His book, *The Power of Positive Thinking* (1952), is still in print and has sold over 20 million copies worldwide.

HOW FULL?
Positive thinkers would see this glass as half full, pessimists as half empty.

Positive thinking, also known as auto-suggestion, can help you reduce stress by enabling you to look at potentially stress-filled situations in a new light. For example, in the past a teacher may have often told you that you were stupid. This entered your subconscious, together with hurt and helpless feelings. Now, at work, your boss might draw your attention to a mistake you have made. This awakens childhood memories of being told you were inadequate, and you think that you really must be incompetent. But the more you dwell on it – perhaps imagining your boss laughing at your discomfort – the angrier you become, and your frustration, depression and anger add up to increased stress.

You could, however, break out of the straitjacket of the past by deciding to find a new way of seeing things. If you can accept your boss's comments as constructive criticism intended to help rather than hurt, you will begin to feel that you and your boss are on the same side, and in turn this will help you feel more comfortable about asking when you are unsure of something, thereby avoiding further mistakes. At first, it may be hard to believe such positive thoughts, but with practice you will find yourself approaching life and its problems with more optimism and less stress.

A NEW LOOK AT LIFE

Another way to develop a positive attitude (and so decrease stress) is to make a point of noticing the good things that happen to you, then take them into your subconscious by sending yourself positive messages – for instance, 'I did that job very well', 'I am perfectly capable of tackling that task', or 'This person likes me'. Once you begin talking to yourself in more positive terms, you will notice an improvement in your self-esteem and your performance.

Just avoiding negative thoughts and vocabulary when thinking about yourself can raise your self-esteem. For example, rather than believing that you are ignorant about a subject, tell yourself that you are capable of finding information about it if you need to. Try substituting words such as challenging for impossible, opportunity for risk, fallible for incompetent. Keep reversals of fortune in perspective, and try to see some of them as minor setbacks rather than disasters. If you feel buried under an impossible workload, view it as a challenge you can learn from – and resolve to avoid in future. If you feel positive you will be more in control, and your actions and words will be noticed.

HYPNOTHERAPY

Hypnotherapy is widely acknowledged today as an effective treatment for many stress-related conditions, including anxiety, insomnia and irritable bowel syndrome. The therapist first induces a light trance in the patient, then makes suggestions aimed at reducing the symptoms of the problem. Although no one really knows how it works, there is a growing body of documented evidence to show that it does. In some cases, patients can be taught techniques of self-hypnosis to enable them to control a condition themselves.

Anyone seeking to try hypnotherapy for a stress problem should take care in choosing a therapist. A hypnotherapist who has also trained in medicine or psychotherapy may be better able to reach the root of a problem, helping you to change negative attitudes and feelings of guilt or anger. Perhaps the most important factor, however, is to choose a therapist whom you trust and feel comfortable with.

CHAPTER 3

STRESS-RELATED DISEASES

*New research shows that too much stress
is a key factor in a wide variety of illnesses. In
fact, more than half of the ailments that are treated
in doctors' surgeries have some connection to stress.
Alternative therapies have long recognised the link
between our emotional state and our physical well-
being. The ones offered in this chapter provide
a wide range of healing remedies to ease stress
and return you to health.*

STRESS AND HEALTH

Medical evidence shows that stress influences the immune system. Be aware of the role of stress in various ailments and you may be able to guard your health more effectively.

For centuries the theory that too much or prolonged stress can cause disease and aggravate existing conditions has been just that – a theory. While doctors had a great deal of anecdotal evidence to support a cause-and-effect connection between stress and illness, there was little actual scientific proof. But circumstances changed dramatically in the early 1970s when neuroscientists unravelled the way the brain transmits messages. What they saw revolutionised how we think about the brain. They knew that the brain had an intricate system of communications that relied on natural chemicals (known today as neurotransmitters) to act as a kind of chemical bridge, sending and receiving information from one brain cell to another. What they didn't know was how these neurotransmitters worked. Thanks to steady research, they discovered that certain neurotransmitters were connected to specific sites in the brain using a lock and key system. This explained why the painkilling drug morphine, for instance, was effective against pain – it bonded to particular receptor sites in the brain that relieve pain.

Further study soon revealed that under special circumstances, such as prolonged physical stress caused by long-distance running or childbirth, the brain would manufacture its own morphine-like substance (known today as endorphins) that bonded to the same pain-relieving receptors.

If the brain had the ability to relieve pain, could it also affect the emotions? This question was answered by the discovery of the function of other neurotransmitters, such as serotonin and dopamine. Low levels of serotonin, for instance, were found in people with severe depression; diminished amounts of serotonin and dopamine were found in those suffering from anxiety. The impact of these neurotransmitters on the emotions has spawned new drugs to treat depression that affect the level of serotonin in the brain; one such drug is Prozac (fluoxetine).

New research, however, now shows that the receptors for these neurotransmitters are found not just in the brain but also in the digestive tract and the immune system, including the lymph nodes, thymus gland, bone marrow, the spleen, and the specialised lymphocytes.

To a number of researchers, this startling discovery suggests that the immune system must be connected to the nervous system,

STRESS HITS WHERE IT HURTS

From migraine to irritable bowel syndrome, stress causes a wide range of ailments. The suppression of the immune system when you are under pressure can also make you more vulnerable to infectious diseases such as colds and flu.

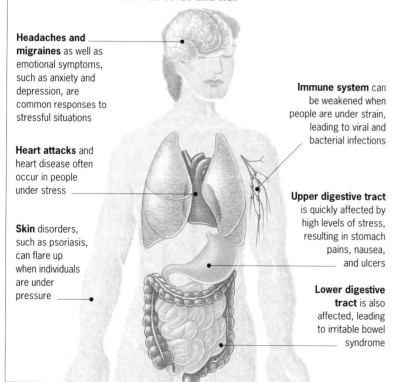

Headaches and migraines as well as emotional symptoms, such as anxiety and depression, are common responses to stressful situations

Heart attacks and heart disease often occur in people under stress

Skin disorders, such as psoriasis, can flare up when individuals are under pressure

Immune system can be weakened when people are under strain, leading to viral and bacterial infections

Upper digestive tract is quickly affected by high levels of stress, resulting in stomach pains, nausea, and ulcers

Lower digestive tract is also affected, leading to irritable bowel syndrome and that fear and anxiety, two common emotions associated with stress, have a direct impact on the immune system. Others, however, feel that stress and the associated emotions are too varied and complex to make a direct connection between emotions and illness. Nevertheless, scientific proof is just around the corner and therefore most health care practitioners urge people to start using stress management techniques to prevent illness and promote health.

Alternative therapies have long recognised the mind-body link. Thus their approach is to treat a person's mental and emotional state as well as the physical condition. They do this by relieving the stress along with its physical manifestations. Their success has encouraged orthodox doctors to take a new look at the role of stress in disease and in many cases has helped to transform the way they treat their patients.

STRESS REACTIONS

Numerous studies have tried to pin down the role of stress in disease. Researchers know that when a person is under stress, the entire body is affected. The heart beats faster and more forcibly, blood pressure rises, stores of fatty acids and glucose are released into the bloodstream, and the bronchioles (breathing tubes) in the lungs expand to let in more air. Certain blood vessels dilate and others constrict to divert blood to where it is most needed. The blood also becomes stickier to encourage clots to form so that bleeding will be reduced if any injury occurs. There are other changes as well, such as an increase in stomach acids, reduction in the production of saliva, and an increase in the urge to urinate.

The stress response also calls for the immediate suppression of the immune system. The stress hormones (adrenaline and noradrenaline) act to inhibit the way white blood cells (which are part of the immune system) respond to bacteria, viruses, and cancer cells. Usually the suppression of the immune system is not harmful, and once the stress has subsided, all the body systems return to normal.

Long-term stress, however, can result in many health problems: heart disease, high blood pressure (hypertension), hormonal disorders, backache, and migraine. It also aggravates disorders connected with the immune system, such as allergies.

Heart and circulatory problems

A specialist in heart disease at London's Charing Cross Hospital, Dr Peter Nixon, has described what he calls the human function curve (see below). This shows what happens when stress makes people attempt increasingly demanding tasks at increasing risk to their mental and physical health, and in particular their heart.

Here is how it works: as the body copes with physical exertion and minor stress, it is normal to have peaks of raised blood pressure. The chemicals secreted by the body in these circumstances cause the arteries to constrict, so that their diameter is reduced. This means that pressure must be increased to keep the blood going through the circulatory system.

High blood pressure (hypertension) refers to a consistent measurement that is greater than 160/95. If blood pressure levels are very high – or have been elevated for a long time – the arterial walls become more rigid and prone to damage, and there is an increased risk of kidney disease and stroke.

In addition, hormones released during stress break down the body's fat stores in order to provide more fuel for energy requirements. As a result, levels of fatty acids and other lipids in the blood increase, contributing to the fatty deposits inside the arterial walls that gradually block the blood flow. This can lead to coronary heart disease in susceptible individuals, especially those with high saturated dietary fat intake, who may already have increased coronary artery clogging.

Heart disease: the international view

The incidence of heart disease varies across the world. It is high in the UK and in Eastern Europe, while in Mediterranean countries it is strikingly low. In the UK, a high saturated fat diet has been implicated, and so have the levels of stress among the general population. This is partly due to a faster and more pressured pace of life. In the Mediterranean countries, the lifestyle is more relaxed. Moreover, the diet includes olive oil, a monounsaturated fat, and moderate levels of red wine – both of which protect against heart attacks.

THE HUMAN FUNCTION CURVE
The first part of the blue curve shows how a person's performance improves while under stress. The second part of the blue curve represents what the person still believes he or she is capable of achieving while the stress continues. The red curve, which drops sharply, actually reflects a person's diminished capability and decreased health.

Stress ⟶

Performance

Intended performance

Fatigue

Ill heath

Healthy tension

Breakdown

Getting away from it all

Going to a retreat for a few days, or even a week, is an option for stressed-out souls who seek calm, spiritual contemplation, or just rest and recuperation. In the UK there are hundreds of retreats and recent years have seen a steady increase of interest in them.

Retreats have been organised by Buddhist centres, convents, monasteries, yoga healing centres, and New Age groups. Each offers an individual approach to help people to refresh their lives, from days of silence or prayer, to one-to-one counselling, to chanting, dancing, and walking. Most retreats are inexpensive and make a novel holiday from the stresses of everyday life.

Digestive disorders

Some of the most common symptoms of stress are pains in the stomach, indigestion, heartburn, and nausea. Irritable bowel syndrome (a chronic malfunction of the intestines that causes abdominal pain, diarrhoea or constipation, and heartburn) can also be caused by high anxiety levels, and it worsens when sufferers are under pressure.

While stress may be the culprit behind many ailments, you should not rule out other factors. Ulcers are a case in point. Doctors once believed they were caused solely by stress. New research reveals that most peptic ulcers are the result of a common bacterial infection. Once the bacteria in question, *helicobacter pylori*, is treated with antibiotics and antacids, peptic ulcers clear up. However, an interesting question remains. Since most adults harbour *helicobacter pylori*, why are so few afflicted with ulcers? The answer to date is that stress contributes to peptic ulcers by lowering the immune system's defences against the bacteria.

Reproductive problems

While anxiety depresses sex drive in both men and women, it can also have a direct effect on fertility. Studies of male fertility show that emotional stress, such as the kind caused by the death of a close relative, can reduce sperm count by 12 per cent.

Stress can also play havoc with a woman's menstrual cycle. Menstrual irregularity, which can have a number of causes, is often related to increased stress. Moreover, stress can precipitate 'spontaneous' abortions (miscarriages) and premature labour.

Allergies, asthma, and skin disorders

An allergy is the severe reaction of the body's immune system to various substances, such as pollen or dust, that are usually harmless. Responses can vary widely, but sneezing and watery eyes are common.

Asthma – another disease that often has an allergic component – is thought to be affected by stress, but the attacks cause anxiety in themselves, and the reaction is hard to separate from the trigger. In one investigation, however, the asthma of 70 per cent of the sufferers being studied had a significant emotional component.

Many skin problems are exacerbated when the sufferer is under pressure. Such complaints include nettle rash (urticaria), which can flare up in direct response to stress. Psoriasis, which occurs irregularly, can erupt when stress levels are high, as can acne, neurodermatitis, and alopecia (excessive and sudden hair loss). People who suffer from allergic eczema often find the condition worsens when they are stressed.

Treatment for stress-related illness

Unlike modern Western medicine, which targets a specific problem, alternative remedies are holistic in nature. That is, they aim to treat the whole person, physically, mentally, and, in some cases, spiritually, in order to restore the body to a state of balance so it is able to withstand disease successfully.

Alternative medicine presents a unique approach to the problem of stress because it attempts to address the cause of the stress as well as the physical manifestation of disease and illness. Thus, alternative practitioners usually ask a great many more questions concerning their patients' quality of life than Western doctors would. This is so that they can accurately identify the underlying causes of the symptoms. In that way these therapists are looking to provide 'whole health' to sufferers.

Alternative therapies consist of a variety of different approaches to treating disorders and ailments of the body. A number of these therapies, such as acupuncture, acupressure, and homeopathy, work on the principle that disease is due to various imbalances in the body; if balances are restored, the body's ability to combat disease is strengthened, and its capacity to heal itself renewed. If excessive stress is the culprit behind a health problem, alternative therapies can help to bring about healing simply by teaching the person how to relax.

Other techniques, such as the Alexander technique, osteopathy, chiropractic, and massage, concentrate on reducing tension and relieving pain that was caused by stress, either through physical manipulation or by the correction of poor posture.

Eastern practices, including yoga, tai chi, and meditation, emphasise the power of the mind in overcoming the sources of stress and teach their followers ways of harnessing their mental energy to maintain health.

Finally, therapies like aromatherapy, which uses oils to aid relaxation, are especially suited to self-care.

Working Up to An Illness

Persistent anxiety can lead to various physical discomforts or to real illness. Minor ailments, like indigestion, may not be life-threatening, but can cause misery, whereas major stress disorders, like hypertension, can be dangerous. For these reasons we must recognise signs, such as irritability and sleeplessness, that tell us we are under pressure, and take steps to prevent serious consequences.

Philip, a 45-year-old social worker, works long hours. Staff shortages have forced more cases onto his workload, and he is finding it hard to complete all his duties. His long hours at the office leave little time to be with his wife, Judy, and when they do meet he is irritable and tired. He has heart palpitations frequently and suffers extreme fatigue. Philip feels overwhelmed by his work, and yet he feels powerless to do anything about it.

One morning, Judy is shocked to find Philip sitting in his car having a panic attack before an important meeting at work. He tells her he is terrified he might die during these attacks, and is afraid he could have a serious heart problem.

WHAT SHOULD PHILIP DO?

Rather than pushing himself beyond the limit of endurance, Philip needs to share his concerns with others. First, he should go to his doctor for a thorough checkup and find out whether his health is as bad as he fears. If tests prove he has a heart problem, he will have to take steps to protect himself from a possible heart attack. However, if his concerns are groundless, he will need to think about the causes of his symptoms, and look for ways of alleviating them.

Philip also needs to consider his marriage. His irritability is driving Judy away. If he wants her continued support, he must become aware of how his work is affecting his relationship with her.

Action Plan

HEALTH
Visit a doctor for a checkup. Try to restore a healthy sleep pattern. Find out which therapies may help to keep heart disease at bay.

PARTNERS
Reopen lines of communication with Judy to air problems. Suggest taking a holiday together to get away from work pressures.

WORK
Discuss ways of alleviating work pressures with colleagues. Arrange a meeting with the boss and ask if some of his duties can be delegated, at least in the short term.

HEALTH
Stress at work can manifest itself in a range of physical and emotional symptoms.

PARTNERS
Workaholics often have little time to give to their personal relationships. This can lead to marriage breakdown.

WORK
Overwork causes many unpleasant symptoms and can make people resentful of their employer.

HOW THINGS TURNED OUT FOR PHILIP

Philip's electrocardiogram and other tests are normal, but he does have high blood pressure (hypertension). The doctor explains that it is due to stress, and suggests he exercises and learns relaxation techniques. Philip begins to run every day and signs up for a class on meditation. He tells his boss that his excessive workload is affecting his health, and his boss agrees to lessen his case load. His blood pressure soon returns to normal, and the panic attacks disappear.

The Homeopath

Homeopathy is a system of medicine that uses highly diluted substances to boost the body's natural ability to cure itself. Practitioners view illness as a sign of inner imbalance, and consider all aspects of patients' lives when treating complaints.

DEADLY NIGHTSHADE (BELLADONNA)
Tiny doses of both the flowers and berries of this poisonous plant are used by homeopaths to treat stress-related headaches, particularly those that produce throbbing pain.

Homeopaths define illness differently from conventional physicians. They believe that the symptoms of an illness are signs of how the body is attempting to cure itself, and their efforts are directed towards enhancing those efforts. To do this, they prescribe substances that induce similar symptoms when given to healthy people in large amounts. This is called treating 'like with like' (from the Greek *homoios*, 'like'). Practitioners use a holistic approach, considering the psychological as well as the physical needs of their patients, and tailor remedies to the individual.

Origins

Homeopathic medicine was founded as a discipline in the 18th century by the German physician Samuel Hahnemann (1755–1843).

Hahnemann experimented on himself with a malaria remedy called cinchona bark. He took the medicine and experienced malaria-like symptoms, even though he was healthy. He wondered if other medicines also produced the symptoms of an illness in a healthy person but relieved them in someone who was sick, and he began to investigate this possibility.

In 1811, the *Homoeopathic Materia Medica* was published, in which Hahnemann described his theories, as well as giving a list of remedies. His ideas gained approval, and homeopathy spread to France,

HAHNEMANN'S REMEDIES
Hahnemann's own medical kit, containing around 200 bottles of homeopathic medicines, can be seen in the National Museum of American History, Washington, DC.

then to Great Britain and the United States. Homeopathy was supplanted by other medical therapies in the early part of the 20th century, but it is regaining popularity as a helpful adjunct to conventional medicine.

What are homeopathic remedies made from?

Most are based on extracts from minerals, plants, and animals. A number have long-established histories of medicinal use, including those that are derived from poisons. For instance, doctors and homeopaths use foxglove (*Digitalis purpurea*) as a medicine – digitalis.

How are homeopathic medicines prepared?

First, the beneficial substance is soaked in either alcohol or water to form a tincture. Next, a drop of the tincture is added to a vial of water in a ratio of 1:10 or 1:100 (1 drop of tincture to 9 or 99 drops of water). Finally, the vial is shaken. This procedure is repeated until an effective potency is achieved. The remedies are sold as liquids or as pills.

How dilute are homeopathic medicines?

No trace of the original beneficial substance can actually be found in the remedies. It is thought that, despite this, the medicines have imprinted themselves on the molecular structure of the liquid or solid they were diluted with, and remain effective.

If nothing remains of the original substance, how can it treat illness?

Surprisingly, homeopaths believe that the more dilute a remedy, the more powerful it is. They think that the original 'vital force' of the beneficial substance is imparted to the final remedy by the mixture being shaken vigorously, or 'succussed', after each dilution.

How do homeopaths treat patients?
Homeopaths take a detailed history of the patient, including personal circumstances, general health, and the medical aspects of the complaint. They will also ask a wide range of questions so that they can build up a comprehensive psychological profile. The homeopath will then prescribe a remedy tailored to the particular patient. As a result of this individualised treatment, people with the same illness may be given quite different medicines. Homeopaths may prescribe different remedies, or the same remedy at different potencies,

THERAPIST WITH PATIENT
In the first consultation, the homeopath will ask questions about your medical history, energy level, sleep patterns, and food preferences.

in subsequent consultations. The aim is to cure each 'layer' of disorders until the central, underlying condition is resolved.

How is homeopathy effective in treating stress?
Homeopaths take a two-pronged approach. If stress is the underlying disorder, the homeopath will prescribe remedies to deal with the specific symptoms. Homeopaths will also often suggest changes in their patients' lives that can help them to tackle the underlying causes of their anxiety.

Homeopaths spend a great deal of time talking to patients, who derive much psychological benefit from this. Homeopathy has a good success rate with people whose problems –

Patients find it very therapeutic to discuss their problems.

such as migraine or irritable bowel syndrome – have an emotional or psychological component.

How quickly does homeopathic treatment take effect?
Serious treatment may require several stages with at least four to six weeks between visits. Symptoms may worsen for a time, known as 'a healing crisis'. This is a good sign, so long as the reaction is not too severe, because it shows that the treatment is stimulating the body to heal itself.

How do I find a homeopath?
Many doctors practise homeopathy as well as conventional medicine or will recommend a local practitioner. Alternatively, write to the Society of Homeopaths, 2 Artizan Road, Northampton, NN1 4HU, which has a register of qualified practitioners.

WHAT YOU CAN DO AT HOME

Once you have your homeopathic remedy there are a few simple rules that you should follow. Store all remedies in a cool, dry place. To maintain their potency, remedies must never be handled, allowed to come into contact with any strong scent, or transferred into a container that previously held any other remedy. Don't drink coffee or alcohol during the course of treatment; some homeopaths also ask you not to eat peppermint or use mint-flavoured toothpaste.

TAKING A REMEDY
Tip the remedy onto a clean spoon, and place it in your mouth. Suck it or allow it to dissolve under your tongue; do not swallow it whole.

The Chiropractor

Stress-related tension can cause nerve compression, which in turn may induce head, neck, and back pain. To relieve it, chiropractors apply manual pressure to muscles, bones, and joints, particularly the spine.

7 cervical vertebrae

12 thoracic vertebrae

5 lumbar vertebrae

Sacrum

Coccyx

THE STRAIN ON THE SPINE
Powerful muscles attached to the spine contract as the body moves, sometimes pulling heavily on the spine. Many backaches stem from strain and tension in these muscles, and disappear quickly when the stress is relieved.

The word *chiropractic* (from the Greek words *cheiro* and *prakrikos*) means 'done by hand'. The principle behind chiropractic is that misalignments, often called subluxations, of the vertebrae can impinge on the spinal nerves and cause pain and illness.

If a nerve is pinched, pain can occur at any point along its path. Pain that occurs away from the site of the entrapment is called referred pain. For example, the sciatic nerve extends from the base of the spine to the foot. If it is pinched near the spine, there may be pain in the lower back, the knee, or toes.

Stress is a particularly insidious factor in many ailments because it can cause pain, which in turn can lead to muscle spasm, causing more stress, and so on. Chiropractic treatment can help to relieve muscle spasm and disrupt this cycle.

How does a chiropractor make a diagnosis?

At the consultation, the chiropractor will ask the patient about family history, recent stressful events, and habits and diet. The chiropractor will then make a visual and manual examination of the patient, looking for signs of injury, bad posture,

Origins

Chiropractic was founded in 1895 by Daniel David Palmer (1845–1913), a Canadian healer who practised in Iowa. Before he developed his own system of manipulation, Palmer had learned osteopathy, an earlier practice which had been established in Missouri by Dr Andrew Taylor Still and involved less vigorous manipulation of the spine.

Palmer's first success was with a deaf man who claimed that his affliction was due to a back injury. Physical examination revealed that the man had a misaligned vertebra, which Palmer manipulated back into place, thereby restoring the man's hearing. After this, Palmer formulated a theory that all living

things have an 'innate intelligence' that flows through the central nervous system and regulates all its vital functions. He developed treatments to free this intelligence from interference and allow it to flow freely in the body.

After Palmer died, it took another 50 years before chiropractic gained acceptance (and state licensing) throughout the United States. It is now the third largest primary health care system, with more than 40 000 practitioners worldwide.

As chiropractic grew, divisions began to appear within the practice. Some chiropractors began to use high-tech equipment such as X-ray and ultrasound machines, which others thought was a departure from Palmer's natural approach. The British founder of McTimoney chiropractic, John McTimoney (1914–81), established his

DANIEL DAVID PALMER
Modern chiropractic was founded by Daniel David Palmer. The treatment seeks to cure disorders through spinal manipulation.

own school in Oxfordshire in 1972 to teach 'pure' chiropractic, using no special equipment, no drugs, and usually no X-rays.

muscle spasm, tenderness, excessive or restricted limb movement, or displaced joints. Usually he or she will take X-rays.

Which disorders can be treated by a chiropractor?

Several stress-related ailments – for example, neuralgia, and certain rheumatic and arthritic disorders – can be relieved by chiropractic treatments, as can nonspecific neck and back pain. A chiropractic manipulation, more commonly called an adjustment, can help to ease many of the symptoms of nerve compression such as tingling, numbness, or 'pins and needles'. To ease muscle spasms, some chiropractors apply heat packs to the affected area.

Is chiropractic treatment better for back pain than orthodox treatment?

A 1988 study of 20 000 back injury cases in Florida found that subjects who chose chiropractic therapy returned to work in a third of the time compared with individuals who had chosen orthodox treatment (which included bed rest, physiotherapy, and painkillers). However, in 1994, in a randomised trial of patients with low back pain, the Iowa Spine Research Center found that there was no significant difference in outcome between massage, chiropractic manipulation, and wearing a corset.

Are there any disorders that chiropractic cannot treat?

Pain from fractures, infections, tumours, or arthritis that involves inflammation cannot be treated. Children should not undergo chiropractic manipulation.

Is chiropractic ever dangerous?

It can be dangerous in the hands of an unqualified person. Each of six different government inquiries worldwide, however, concluded that modern chiropractic therapy, when carried out by an adequately trained chiropractor, is quite safe. Be sure, however, to check with your doctor

before visiting the chiropractor to find out if chiropractic treatment is advisable in your case.

How is treatment carried out?

A combination of over 30 different adjustment techniques is used, most commonly a series of short, rapid, shallow thrusts. Chiropractors may also employ heat therapy, ice packs, traction (when a weight is attached

to part of the body to pull it into alignment), or ultrasound (when very high sound waves penetrate the skin and the energy of the vibrations dissipates as heat).

Where can I find a chiropractor?

A list of qualified chiropractors is available from The British Chiropractic Association, 29 Whitley St, Reading, Berkshire, RG2 0EG.

THERAPIST WITH PATIENT
In one adjustment technique, the chiropractor uses both hands to manipulate the joints.

The chiropractor applies the appropriate degree of pressure to the affected area

The patient lies face down on the table, arms hanging loosely over the side

WHAT YOU CAN DO AT HOME

A regular stretch of your shoulders will help to keep your upper spine flexible, and release any tension you are holding there. Do the stretch slowly and smoothly whenever you can.

STRETCH ONE
Clasp your hands behind your back.

STRETCH TWO
Push your chest forwards and up and stretch your arms back. Hold for a few seconds.

ANXIETY AND DEPRESSION

It is estimated that up to 30 per cent of the Western world's population will suffer periods of depression from too much pressure, and many more will suffer stress-related anxiety.

Some degree of anxiety and fear is a natural human response to a challenge. In the right circumstances they will help you to spring into action. However, constantly heightened levels of anxiety and fear can lead to physical as well as emotional problems, especially if they are caused by situations in which you are powerless, such as impossible schedules or deadlines you can't meet. For some people the anxiety may be external, such as living in a high-crime area. In such cases, the fear of crime and your lack of control over it may lead to debilitating panic attacks or depression.

Anxiety and fear can also play a role in numerous physical complaints. Common symptoms include tension headaches, chest and neck pains, and backache. Sometimes, people with acute anxiety develop psychosomatic symptoms that mimic an organic disease, for example, chest pains caused by anxiety that can feel like a heart attack.

Sometimes stress is so acute that it causes a panic attack. This is a brief period of acute anxiety and profuse sweating, light-headedness, palpitations, tightness in the chest, and a sinking feeling in the stomach. These attacks can be so strong that sufferers may believe, unrealistically, that they are going to die. For example, they feel their heart is beating so fast that they are going to have a heart attack. Panic attacks often

---

SEX AND STRESS

Communication problems between partners can cause a great deal of anxiety. This releases stress hormones that counteract the effects of testosterone, the hormone responsible for sexual arousal. If this leads to impotence in a man, or to loss of sexual drive in a woman, tension will increase and sexual failure will then become yet another source of stress.

If you are experiencing a sexual problem you should visit your doctor to discover if anything is physically wrong, or if any medication you are taking is responsible. If there is no physical cause, then ask yourself why you are feeling so anxious, and talk it over with your partner. You could also try changing the times and places you make love. Make plans for a holiday – the change of scene

may reawaken your interest in lovemaking. If the idea of intercourse worries you, simply touch and hug each other; touching in itself will relieve tension and may help to re-establish communication.

VICIOUS CYCLE: EFFECT OF STRESS ON DESIRE

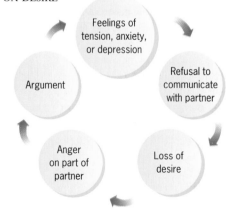

Feelings of tension, anxiety, or depression

Refusal to communicate with partner

Loss of desire

Anger on part of partner

Argument

happen without warning, though they are usually associated with a stressful event, such as a crowded lift. It is also common to hyperventilate, which upsets the balance of oxygen and carbon dioxide in the blood. If you feel that an attack is imminent, breathe in and out of a paper bag to restore oxygen concentrations to normal. Or try holding your breath for as long as possible.

DEPRESSION

Everyone feels down occasionally, but the feeling usually passes. This is not the case with severe or clinical depression. Severe and long-lasting depression produces very specific physical symptoms, such as a loss (or occasionally an increase) of appetite, and sleeping disorders. Other symptoms include constipation, extreme fatigue, and a general feeling of malaise.

It also produces mental and emotional symptoms. People with clinical depression often report a feeling of emptiness, a lack of interest in everything, and a loss of energy. Food is tasteless, meetings with friends and family joyless; in serious cases the sufferer is full of despair, loses hope in everything, and thinks of suicide. It is important that someone suffering from these symptoms seeks prompt medical help. Fortunately there are many treatments available, ranging from counselling to medication.

Causes of depression

Clinical depression falls into two categories. One is the reactive type – the emotional gloom is due to a person's response to a recent stressful event, such as a bereavement, the loss of a job, or divorce. This kind of depression usually abates with time.

The second kind is known as endogenous depression. There are many kinds of this depression, such as manic-depression (also known as bipolar disorder), unipolar depression, and postnatal depression.

There are many theories about the causes of depression. Hormonal imbalance (which is especially the case with new mothers suffering from postnatal depression), genetic factors, and major stressful situations in the past that were never resolved, for instance, the death of a parent when you were a child, have all been implicated. There is evidence that depression is caused by an overwhelming accumulation of stress, which depletes the brain of serotonin (see page 46).

ART THERAPY
For those with stress-related psychological problems, art therapy (left) can release hidden feelings, such as the frustration and anger experienced in the above drawing.

Learned helplessness

One theory about depression has been put forward by the psychologist Martin Seligman. Seligman gave electric shocks to caged animals which, when they tried to escape, found their ways barred. After a while, they began to show the symptoms of lethargy and listlessness typical of depression. Then Seligman gave the animals the same shocks but left the cage doors open. Although now free to leave, the animals stayed in the cages, having learned to be helpless. Seligman extended his theory of 'learned helplessness' to human beings, and proposed that depression comes from people feeling powerless about their lives.

His ideas have been borne out in a study of workers in high-stress jobs, among them assembly-line operators under heavy pressure to perform but with little control over how they worked. The workers took more medicine for depression than their managers did, who had more control over their lives.

continued on page 58

DID YOU KNOW?
Many famous historical figures have suffered from depression. One of the most notable was Sir Winston Churchill, the British statesman and prime minister, who called his attacks of incapacitating depression his 'black dog'.

Reducing Stress with

Yoga

Yoga – the Sanskrit word for 'union' – is an ancient Indian tradition that combines exercise and meditation. It is useful for relieving stress, and the stretching exercises are beneficial for everyone, regardless of age or level of fitness.

A VARIATION OF THE LOTUS POSITION
One of the classic yoga poses, this version is for advanced yoga students.

With its emphasis on gentle stretching and deep, even breathing, yoga postures are good for health in many ways. In particular, the exercises can help to ease muscle tension, lower blood pressure, and calm nerves.

As with any attempt at behaviour modification, yoga works best if practised frequently. Practitioners advocate daily practice, even if it is just for 10 minutes a day and even if each 10 minute session is broken up into 2 or 3 minute periods spread throughout the day.

Yoga's philosophy is noncompetitive and nonstressful. The intention is to make the sessions as pleasant as possible, so that you will be inspired to practise the movements and deep breathing regularly.

GENTLE YOGA EXERCISES

Pick a time when you will not be disturbed, and a space where you can move freely. Breathe naturally while holding a pose. Hold the pose for as long as is comfortable, then slowly come back to the starting position and repeat on the other side.

THE TRIANGLE POSE

Start with legs comfortably apart, feet facing forwards, and arms loosely by your side.

Shoulders should be down and relaxed

Hand and wrist should be relaxed, with stretch coming from the armpit

Exhale slowly as you bend. Inhale slowly and deeply as you straighten up

Hips need to face forward

Stretch from the outside of your leg and up your side

Weight should be kept firmly on your left foot

The hand may not reach this far down, but you will improve with practice

1 *Turn your right foot out and left foot in. Raise arms to shoulder height.*

2 *Stretch out slowly to the right. Do not let your body bend forwards, but be careful to keep it in one plane.*

3 *Bend sideways towards your ankle, until your right hand reaches your leg, with your left arm stretching up.*

THE WARRIOR POSE

Start with feet comfortably apart, facing forwards, with toes slightly in and arms by your side.

The left arm should remain dynamic, as if pulling you to the left

Shoulders should be relaxed and down; don't let them bunch up towards your ears

1 *Turn both feet to the right, while keeping hips aligned to the front. Raise your arms, then turn your head to the right.*

2 *Exhaling slowly, bend the right knee, keeping equal weight on the back leg and the body vertical.*

Weight should remain firmly on your left foot; try to stay evenly balanced

The shin should stay vertical, and not bend forwards over the foot

THE CAT POSE

Place your hands and knees squarely on the floor. Make sure your hips are aligned above your knees and your shoulders above your hands. The exercise is designed to stretch the whole length of the spine.

Shoulders should not be bunched around your ears; keep them loose

THE CHILD POSE

This is a good winding-down, relaxing pose. Kneel down on your heels, back rounded over, forehead on the floor, and arms by your sides.

Aim to stretch the upper part of your back, not just the lumbar region

2 *Exhaling, round your back upwards, letting your head flop down.*

Place a cushion over your heels if you cannot kneel right back on them. It is important to have a firm base from which to stretch forwards

Hands should be flat, and fingers stretched. The exercise will help to strengthen your wrists

1 *Exhaling slowly, lift your head upwards, stretching from your chest. Hold the pose, then relax.*

CAUTION

Before starting any exercise regime, check with your doctor, especially if you are pregnant or suffering from high blood pressure, a back injury, or a heart or breathing disorder.

COPING WITH DEPRESSION

Try one or more of the following 'natural' remedies to ease the symptoms of depression.

▶ *Share your feelings with a trusted friend or relative, and enjoy the support and reassurance he or she can offer.*

▶ *Avoid spending too much time alone. Going out can introduce you to new activities and to people who may help your recovery.*

▶ *Increase your intake of fresh fruits and vegetables, fish, lean meats, whole-grain cereals and low-fat dairy products. A healthy diet will make you feel less lethargic.*

▶ *Eat lightly throughout the day instead of having large meals. This will steady your blood sugar levels and help prevent mood swings.*

SKULLCAP
Found in moist woods and meadows, skullcap is used in a variety of herbal preparations for stress relief.

To improve morale, some companies now give their workers more control over their working procedures, and have mixed routine tasks and duties with new challenges.

TREATING ANXIETY AND DEPRESSION

Although anxiety and depression are common conditions, there is still a considerable stigma attached to them. Many people feel ashamed or embarrassed about admitting to emotional problems, even to their doctors. They worry that they will be regarded as weak or neurotic, and for that reason they struggle on and refuse to seek help as they see it as a 'loss of face'.

And yet, talking about your feelings to a friend or family member can help to ease mild anxiety or depression; indeed, the act of unburdening yourself may not only help you feel better but also enable you to gain perspective on your feelings.

If you are suffering from depression-like symptoms, it might be worthwhile visiting your doctor, who will try to determine if there are any underlying physical causes.

If no physical illness is found and your condition warrants it, your doctor may prescribe tranquillisers for anxiety or antidepressants for depression. Bear in mind, however, that long-term use of such drugs, especially tranquillisers, can lead to depen-

Pathway to health

There are a number of alternative therapies that are very effective in helping to relieve anxiety and depression. Some of these remedies have calming properties; others can invigorate or lift the spirits.

Aromatherapy is one therapy where the soothing scents of the essential oils achieve both of the above results. A regular massage using, for instance, rosemary oil, will ease the rigid, painful muscles in the neck and shoulders that are so often brought on by tension and worry.

Lavender essential oil may help calm those who are suffering from the effects of anxiety, and it will also promote restful sleep. Add a few drops of this oil to your bath, or place 1–2 drops on the edge of your pillow.

dence. While the new antidepressants, such as Prozac (fluoxetine) and Paxil, may cause some unpleasant side-effects in certain people, they have proven effective at treating depression and obsessional disorders.

In cases of severe and intense depression, electroconvulsive (electroshock) therapy has proven effective, especially for those people who are not responding to medication and require additional treatment.

Counselling and therapy

Discussing your problems with a trained therapist – usually on a one-to-one basis – can help a great deal when dealing with either anxiety or depression. You can ask your doctor to recommend one, or look for one on your own; it might take a while to find the right one, but keep looking.

Cognitive therapy is one method offered by therapists. It encourages people to make a conscious decision to change their ways of thinking about themselves and the world. These beliefs often include such convictions that bad experiences in the past are bound to be repeated in the future. Once the anxious or depressed person discovers that this is not necessarily true and breaks the mental habit of thinking in such ways, he or she can take positive steps toward leading a more satisfying life.

There are many other forms of therapy that will help with anxiety and depression, including self-help groups, where individuals discuss their feelings together, with or without a trained therapist. Some people prefer this type of therapeutic setting to one-to-one counselling, or indeed 'graduate' to it after engaging in solo counselling.

If you feel that formal therapy will not suit you, then why not take a creative approach to events that bother you. Writing or painting are good outlets for people who find it hard to reveal deep feelings to others, or who have nobody they can talk to.

Controlling your life is important in helping to combat anxiety. You can do this by learning assertiveness techniques (see page 72), which will give you the confidence to change your circumstances so that they suit your own terms. Exercise is also another good way to relieve anxiety. Researchers at the University of Massachusetts Center for Health and Fitness found that after subjects took a brisk 40-minute walk, they experienced a drop in their level of anxiety.

CHAPTER 4

STRESS
AND THE
INDIVIDUAL

We all react to stress in our own way.
An event that makes one person anxious will be
shrugged off by another, with barely a second thought.
Our response to stress is governed by a number of
different factors – age, health, environment. However,
the most dominant is our personality. By learning
how to assert ourselves, we can offset
the debilitating effects of stress.

THE STAGES OF LIFE

Every age has its special challenges and unique stressors. To live happily and healthily, new strategies for coping with stress need to be learned and previous ones modified at each stage.

Although the human lifespan has increased considerably since Shakespeare's day, the seven ages the Bard described stay much the same. However, the length of time spent in each period and the problems encountered at each stage differ.

CHILDHOOD
Children need extra help in developing skills for coping with problems, and adults are their best teachers. The problems may be minor, like frustration at physical incompetence, or more devastating, like the breakup of the family, but all will provoke a reaction. Any child who becomes aggressive, withdrawn, or 'difficult' is under stress and in need of immediate attention. It is vital, therefore, that parents or teachers be alert to signs of pressure in children.

To ward off potential long-term problems, a responsible adult must react quickly and appropriately. For example, a mother

DEALING WITH COMMON PROBLEMS AT ALL STAGES OF LIFE

LIFE STAGE	GENERAL PROBLEMS	SPECIFIC STRESSES	COMMON REACTIONS	WHAT CAN BE DONE
CHILDHOOD	Physical mastery, competence, and coordination Intellectual mastery Emotional containment and maturity	Frustration: 'I can't do it' Difficulties with communication Jealousy toward brothers or sisters Adjusting to school Rivalries with other school children and friends	Tantrums Playing hooky and bullying Uncooperativeness Moodiness Dependency Bed-wetting Aggression Withdrawal	**By parents:** Be calm and supportive Communicate Be understanding Be realistic about child's capabilities Set clear guidelines for behaviour
ADOLESCENCE	Acquiring independence and self-reliance Establishment of peer group relations Consolidation and development of earlier learning Developing sexual identity Need for application and challenge to achieve competency	Anxieties about having friends; concern over appearance (especially 'being fat' for girls) Loneliness Worries about schoolwork and getting into college Conflicts about forming intimate relationships Exam pressure Pressure to achieve	Eating disorders Rudeness Withdrawn behaviour and secretiveness Refusal to keep 'house rules' Neglect of, or obsession with, schoolwork Sexual adventurousness Drug and alcohol abuse	**By parents:** As far as possible be supportive, positive, encouraging Communicate parental anxieties **By child and parents:** For serious problems, seek family therapy Minimise power struggles by setting 'house rules' together

whose two-year-old child has become aggressive after the birth of a sibling should realise her toddler is fearful of losing parental attention. The mother can allay this fear by paying her toddler extra attention and setting aside special times for just the two of them to do things together. The parents of a schoolchild who seems withdrawn should try to discover what is making their child unhappy. Above all, they need to be supportive of their child. Having frank discussions with teachers will make it clear that they are concerned and would like to enlist their aid.

ADOLESCENCE

Once they reach their teens, young people must balance the need to develop apart from their families with the desire to retain their childhood security. Teens are pressured to conform with their peers, to perform well at school, and to meet the challenges of becoming competent in an adult world.

The adults in teenagers' lives need to be alert for signs of irritability, aggression, or withdrawal, and to make it clear that they are always available for them. A listening and nonjudgmental ear is an excellent antidote to stress, and this may be all your teenager needs to stay stress-free.

At problem times, perhaps when a relationship gets into difficulties, adolescents are best taught to deal with emotional upset by example. If you can express your own feelings and look after yourself when things get tough, your children will learn that the people who take care of themselves are the ones who cope best under pressure.

YOUTH

The major challenge of this period is to take full responsibility for finding one's own direction in the world. If an individual does not know what he or she would like to do, schools often offer guidance counselling, which may help. Counsellors can pinpoint

DEALING WITH COMMON PROBLEMS AT ALL STAGES OF LIFE

GENERAL PROBLEMS	SPECIFIC STRESSES	COMMON REACTIONS	WHAT CAN BE DONE	LIFE STAGE
				YOUTH
Establishing independence at home or leaving to be on one's own	Conflict over leaving home	Using home 'as a hotel'	**By parents:**	
	Achieving financial independence	Refusal to communicate or explain	Making clear limits of parental contribution	
Finding direction for education, training, or work	Choice of college or other degree courses	Being reckless with finances	Suggesting career and financial advisers	
Exploring possible long-term relationships	Worry about getting a job	Sexual experimentation	Listening without judging	
	Concerns over finding 'the right person'	Overdependent relationships	**By youth:**	
			Drawing up budgets	
				ADULTHOOD
Establishment of permanent adult relationship, usually marriage	Finding a suitable spouse	Burying oneself in work to avoid problems at home	Honest acknowledgment of problems	
	Career change	Drinking to relieve stress	Discussions with spouse	
Raising children	Birth of children/infertility	Overindulging in spending or gambling	Membership in support group for specific problems	
	Worries about children	Depression or illness, especially one which has a psychosomatic component – migraine or colitis	Seek counselling for marital, financial, or career problems	
Maintenance of financial viability	Unemployment			
	Moving house			
Development of career	Problems at work	Obesity	Turn to friends for peer-group support	
	Separation and/or divorce			

things that may hold a student back, such as hidden fears or lack of confidence, and help him or her overcome these problems.

On the other hand, things may seem to be going very well, but because the pressure to maintain progress is great, youths may be prone to angry confrontations with friends or superiors; this, too, is a sign of stress. Engaging in physical activity can help release pent-up feelings.

ADULTHOOD

According to Freud, the essence of adult life is love and work, that is finding a loving partner and making the best contribution you can in your working life. These challenges are rarely completed without difficulty. While the average individual may be able to cope with the inevitable marital conflicts and problems with child-rearing, stress at work can compound the whole family's stress. You can alleviate work overload by managing time better and setting priorities.

Nurturing relationships and honing parenting skills can make family life happier and more harmonious. There are many self-help books and adult education courses that will help you improve your interpersonal skills, but if relationships become very troubled, marriage or family counselling may become necessary (see also page 98).

MIDLIFE

This is the prime of your life, a time when you can give to others the benefit of your experience – in other words, potentially it can be a satisfying period. Unfortunately, however, it may also be a time of the so-called midlife crisis, as you realise you may not have achieved all the dreams of your youth and that time is running out to do so.

If the latter is true, then it is important to find new meaning in your life, but some people deny that anything has changed. For this reason, many marriages may become strained or break up. A more positive

DEALING WITH COMMON PROBLEMS AT ALL STAGES OF LIFE

LIFE STAGE	GENERAL PROBLEMS	SPECIFIC STRESSES	COMMON REACTIONS	WHAT CAN BE DONE
MIDLIFE	Recognising limitations of professional or career development

Regret over chances or opportunities missed

Recognition that procreative life and 'youth' are probably over

Departure of children, signalling end of part of one's life

Denial of own mortality and ending of first half of life

Ageing parents making demands on time and money

Older children marrying | Lack of further promotion or possible unemployment

Discontentment with work, boredom, disillusionment

Disagreements with children

Dwindling physical powers and energy

Changes in physical appearance

Forcing self to behave like a younger person

Coping with ageing parents' needs

Changes in libido and sexual abilities

Development of health problems

Divorcing or deserting spouse | Depression

Irritability

Lack of motivation

Bitterness

Criticism of spouse, family, employer

Attempts to preserve youth, often quite inappropriately – for example, dress, choice of partner, behaviour

Wanting to start anew

Resentment and jealousy of friends | Review life and its possibilities

Focus on positive aspects of life

Pay more attention to relationships – perhaps try a marriage-enrichment programme

Development of new interests and hobbies

Make changes to lifestyle

Financial planning to help eliminate future problems

Preretirement planning for next stage

Begin therapy, if necessary

Try relaxation techniques such as meditation

Take care of health – eat better, stop smoking, cut down on drinking, begin regular exercise |

approach is to acknowledge changes and to see this period as a time of opportunity. Now is the time when many women, free of the concerns of child-rearing, go back to work on a full-time basis, while many men find themselves at a crossroads. They can choose between continuing with their careers, changing course completely, or giving work less priority in their lives and devoting a lot more time to their families and interests.

RETIREMENT

The challenge in the years after 60 is to explore new possibilities in oneself while becoming reconciled to changes in your status quo, for example, the loss of work and physical vigour; the death of friends and relatives; a drop in income; the winding down of one's social life and anxiety over financial security. All of these concerns can result in depression, so planning ahead is vital, because if these years are well planned,

retirement can bring many joys. During retirement, there is more time to spend on favourite pastimes, a second or even a third career, travel, or simply time with loved ones. Research has shown that people who have many interests adapt best to retirement. Exercise at this time in life is vital. Yoga is an ideal exercise for older people.

OLD AGE

This is the time to let go of many responsibilities and simply enjoy the freedom to be with friends, children, grandchildren, and great grandchildren without having time constraints. Consider joining a club for the elderly that will provide companions and a range of social activities. Although some chronic ailments are common at this stage, try not to let them restrict your lifestyle. Now more than ever it is important to exercise, if only for a few minutes every day. Also, be sure that you eat balanced meals and drink plenty of fluids.

DEALING WITH COMMON PROBLEMS AT ALL STAGES OF LIFE

GENERAL PROBLEMS	SPECIFIC STRESS	COMMON REACTIONS	WHAT CAN BE DONE	LIFE STAGE
				RETIREMENT
Need to reconcile self to absence of a job and accompanying issues of social status Financial adjustment Prospect of illness or death	Loss of work-related social life Changing structure of the day Sense of loneliness and meaninglessness Anxieties about money, home, illness, aches, and pains	Depression Withdrawal Isolation Rigid routines developing: 'I never go out at night'. or 'I always eat at 6:00 pm'. Inability to discuss problems with spouse or children Closer involvement with religious institution	Find new social context: join clubs or groups or retire to retirement 'village' Greater time spent with family and younger people More involvement in public sector – perhaps doing voluntary work or working in community	
				OLD AGE
Declining mental and physical powers Possible financial anxieties Loss of independence	Forgetfulness Illness Weakness and dependence Loss of home Death of friends and family	Depression Lack of interest in life Personal neglect Bitterness Anger Fear and mistrust Becoming secretive	Choice of best possible physical care – modified house or apartment, sharing home of child, private nurses, or nursing home Continued interest in family circle or other social outlets	

DAY-TO-DAY STRESS

No one is immune from everyday stress. New demands in your life, even pleasant ones, can make stress levels intolerable. Here's a way to check your stress levels before they get out of hand.

The fact that major stressful events can affect a person's physical and mental well-being is well known. But only comparatively recently has it been recognised that the cumulative effect of a number of small stresses can cause just as much damage.

In the early 1970s, Thomas Holmes and Richard Rahe, working at the University of Washington, looked at the effect that a series of expected events can have on a person's life. They found that any change – even a positive one – can cause stress. To measure the degree of stress that a person

PERSONAL STRESSFUL EVENT SCALE

Not everyone is affected by events in the same way, and even if life is stressful some people cope better than others. If you have had what you consider a great deal of stress within a short time, your health could be at risk.

The following chart, developed by Cary L. Cooper, Rachel D. Cooper, and Lynn H. Eaker in their book *Living with Stress,* was designed to measure your stress levels. First

look at the chart and see if any of the events match your experience in the past two years. Then, on a separate piece of paper, jot down the number that best expresses the degree of stress that the event caused you (1 indicates minimal stress and 10 maximum stress). Add up your score. Fifty points is an average stress level. A higher score indicates recurring problems that may prove to be too heavy a burden.

RELATIONSHIPS	1	2	3	4	5	6	7	8	9	10
Engagement										
Marriage										
Arguments with partner										
Marital problems										
Problem relatives										
Problem friends										
Problem neighbours										
End of long-term relationship										
Separation from loved one										
Divorce										
PARENT/CHILD										
Pregnancy										
Childbirth										
Birth of grandchildren										
Disagreements with children										
Disagreements with parents										
Child starts school										
Child leaves home										
Child marries										

had suffered over a period of time, they created an index that listed 43 of the most common stressful events in an average individual's life and rated each event for stressfulness. Death of a spouse had the highest rating, 100, and minor breaches of the law the lowest, 11. The researchers found that subjects with a score of over 150 had a 31 per cent chance of a health problem of some kind within two years; subjects who scored over 300 stood a 79 per cent chance of illness unless effective measures were taken to combat stress. Although Holmes and Rahe's work demonstrated that a relationship existed between stress and illness, it did not take into account individual differences. Stress is relative, so current researchers believe the most important factor in assessing stress is how individuals rate its effects.

Pathway to health

If you're under a great deal of stress, use one of these strategies to help you cope.

Make sure you relax daily. Yoga (see page 56), meditation (see page 42), tai chi (see page 36), progressive relaxation (see page 39), or even an aromatherapy bath (see page 68) can be helpful.

Laughter is good for you, so take home an amusing video to watch, or tune into a favourite comedy show. A change in lifestyle will also be beneficial: cut down on smoking and overeating; avoid drinking alcoholic and caffeinated beverages.

PERSONAL STRESSFUL EVENT SCALE

ILLNESS/BEREAVEMENT	1	2	3	4	5	6	7	8	9	10
Illness of self										
Illness of family member										
Illness of relative										
Having to care for ill person										
Death of partner										
Death of child										
Death of relative										
Death of close friend										
EMPLOYMENT										
Work problems										
Promotion										
Demotion										
Job change										
Threatened loss of work										
Unemployment										
Retirement										
FINANCE/GENERAL										
Home improvements										
House purchase										
Moving house										
Sale of home										
Building work										
Increased borrowings										
Debt problem										
Insurance problem										
Legal problem										
TOTALS										
GRAND TOTAL										

A Woman of a Certain Age

Middle age can be a stressful time for many women. There are anxieties about grown children starting out in the world and worries over aging parents, plus the first signs of the menopause. When additional problems arise – unemployment, debt, or family worries – stress levels can reach the point where a woman's health can be seriously affected.

Sally, a devoted wife and mother, is just about to turn 50. There are a number of disquieting changes going on in her life. Jenny, her 18-year-old daughter, is going away to university in the autumn, and the prospect of her only child leaving home is upsetting. Sally is also worried that she and her husband, Joe, might not be able to help Jenny with her financial needs, especially since they have very little money set aside for their own retirement. Sally

is anxious about looking for work. Before her marriage, 25 years ago, she worked as an infants' school-teacher, but she hasn't worked since.

Adding to her concerns is the failing health of her father. For the past few months, he has become increasingly frail and she is worried that he will have to employ a nurse, move in with her and Joe, or move into a nursing home. On top of all this, Sally has become aware of changes to her mood and body.

She has had a number of hot flushes and unexplained mood swings and she wonders if she is starting the menopause.

Given these pressures, it is hardly surprising that Sally is feeling tense and irritable. She has trouble getting to sleep at night, has lost all interest in sex, and suffers from constant minor aches and pains. She cannot remember the last time she felt so completely besieged by worries and unable to cope with them.

CHILDREN
While their growing independence is gratifying, the idea of children leaving home – creating an empty nest – can be very distressing.

FINANCES
Family purses can be strained by dependent older children, elderly parents, health problems, or the need to put away money for retirement.

HUSBAND
In midlife themselves, husbands may be facing flagging physical capacities and the stresses of early retirement or possible unemployment.

PARENTS
Becoming increasingly infirm, elderly parents are often dependent on their middle-aged children. Some need financial assistance; others need help with everyday tasks.

WORK
The prospect of returning to full-time work after a long absence can cause extreme anxiety because of a lack of self-confidence.

HEALTH
Midlife is the time of the menopause. Changes in hormonal production may cause depression, lack of concentration, and a host of physical symptoms.

WHAT SHOULD SALLY DO?

Stress is greatest when a person feels overwhelmed and powerless. Thus Sally needs to approach each of her problems separately. The first one she should address is her own health. Much of Sally's depression and physical symptoms could be related to menopausal changes; she needs to see her family doctor.

Sally needs to confront her feelings about Jenny leaving home. Rather than anticipating loneliness, she could look upon this time as a new start for herself. Sally might want to consider getting a job, especially since money is a major concern. Returning to work after a long absence can be unsettling; Sally could start gradually by helping out for a day or two at the local preschool playgroup.

Whether Sally's father goes into a nursing home or moves in with her is dependent on a number of factors. She needs to talk to her husband about what they can and cannot afford, as well as how such a move would impact on their marriage and family life. They need to be as realistic as possible, especially if Sally is planning on getting a full-time job.

They might want to see an independent financial adviser who would be able to provide them with a savings plan that would take into consideration their need to put money aside for retirement, the extra costs of having a child in college, as well as caring for an elderly parent.

Action Plan

CHILDREN
Try to accept that Jenny has to begin to live an independent life. Ask Jenny if she would work part time to help defray the cost of being at university and if she has fully investigated all the grant or sponsorship opportunities.

PARENTS
Arrange to speak to a geriatric specialist about her father's health problems and options for care. Discuss these with father. Consult legal adviser and consider getting power of attorney over her father's financial affairs.

FINANCES
Scout around for good financial advice. Discuss with a financial adviser the best way of budgeting their finances. Consider getting a full- or part-time job.

HUSBAND
Stress typically spills over into one's relationship. Be sure to spend some time together alone. Arrange a 'date' for every Friday night – be it dinner out or staying in and watching a movie.

HEALTH
Make an appointment with the doctor. Read up on treatments to relieve menopausal symptoms. Try some self-help relaxation techniques that can be done at home. Start walking half-an-hour a day.

WORK
Contact the education authority to see if supply teachers are needed. Look into courses that would bring her teaching qualifications up-to-date. Visit a job centre to discuss job prospects for those returning to work.

HOW THINGS TURNED OUT FOR SALLY

Sally's doctor confirmed her menopausal status and prescribed hormone replacement therapy (HRT). Within a few weeks her hot flushes ceased and her depression abated. She felt more cheerful and energetic and able to tackle the new challenges in her life.

Unfortunately, her father's health deteriorated rapidly. After talking it over, they moved him into their home as soon as Jenny left, and Sally arranged for a carer to come in part time every day to help him. The sale of her father's home eased Sally's financial worries for the time being, but she thought she should start looking into retirement plans and also find a job. Although she was very nervous about returning to work after 25 years, she found that she was excited about the prospect. After some research, she discovered that there were a number of openings with the local education authority. She got a job working at a nearby day nursery three days a week.

Jenny was doing well in university. In the summer, she found a job working with her mother, and enjoyed it so much she has decided to study early child development.

Aromatherapy

For hundreds of years, people have used the essential oils that give various plants their scent to relax the body and mind. Known as aromatherapy, essential oils are increasingly used to treat disorders and combat work-induced stress.

VERSATILE OILS
Essential oils are contained in some bath and massage oils. You can also add a few drops of essential oil to some water and vaporise them over an incense burner.

Aromatherapy heals by appealing to our sense of smell, the most well developed of the five senses. When inhaled, certain scents can induce calm or invigoration. During an aromatherapy massage, the skin absorbs the oils extremely quickly, speeding the soothing of aching backs and tense shoulders.

Aromatherapists divide the oils into three groups. Uplifting oils (for example, bergamot, basil, or rosemary) invigorate the body and raise the spirits. Calming oils such as cedarwood, jasmine, and neroli have a sedating effect. Toning and regulating oils, such as lemongrass, and myrrh (not to be used during

Camomile from Morocco is a reliable remedy for relieving stress and insomnia

Sandalwood is used for relief of tension and anxiety, and is regenerative and soothing

Neroli – also known as orange blossom – comes from the flowers of the bitter orange, grown in South-east Asia. Used for treatment of anxiety and depression

Ylang-ylang, with its spicy scent, stirs the senses and can be used as an aphrodisiac

Lavender has a wide variety of uses, including treatment for insomnia, depression, and high blood pressure

POWERFUL PLANTS
There are between 60 and 70 essential oils in the aromatherapist's armoury. Some can relieve stress and anxiety and raise the spirits.

Cedarwood, from the aromatic conifer of Lebanon and south-west Turkey, is used to soothe anxiety pregnancy) are said to condition the skin and promote the health of the internal organs. Vaporising such essential oils as jasmine or lavender over a burner can bring a calming atmosphere to your home or office. You may unwind after a hard day at work by giving yourself a shoulder and neck massage using the oils of rose, sandalwood, or camomile.

Oils are also relaxing in baths, in face packs and foot soaks, or as an inhalation (see below). Essential oils can be bought at health food and body-care shops. They should be stored in a cool place (but not in a refrigerator) and kept out of the reach of children.

Most oils are extracted by a method of distillation. Depending on the plant, seeds, flowers, leaves, bark, or resin are placed in a container and steam is passed through them. The oils first evaporate, then condense when the steam cools; after this they can be separated out from the water. Very large quantities are needed – for instance, it can take about 2000 kg (4400 lb) of rose petals to make 1 quart of rose oil. This is the reason why these oils are so expensive.

USING THE OILS

Never apply undiluted oils directly to your skin; they should always be mixed with a suitable medium – warm water or a light, mild base oil. If you have sensitive skin, you should apply only a drop or two of diluted oil at first, and wait to see the results.

Everyone has favourite aromas, so try out a range of oils to discover which you like best, as well as which ones are the most effective to use.

FACE PACK
Mix 1 teaspoon of cold-pressed wheat germ or almond oil with one drop of essential oil (rose suits most skin types, tea tree is good for oily skin). Stir in 3 teaspoons of live, whole milk yogurt, and ½ to 1 teaspoon of fine oatmeal to form a paste. Apply a thin layer of the mixture to your face; leave for 10 to 15 minutes. Rinse off with cool water.

INHALATION
Pour hot water into a bowl and add two to three drops of an essential oil (cedarwood or juniper). Position your face above the rising steam, then cover your head and the bowl with a towel and inhale and exhale deeply until the water cools.

BATHING
Ensure that the bathroom is warm and all windows shut so that the vapours will not escape. Add six to ten drops of oil to hot bath water and swish this around so that an oily film forms on the surface. When you get in, some of the oil will penetrate your skin, and you will inhale more through the steam.

FOOT SOAK
Fill a bowl half full with hot water. Add up to ten drops of an essential oil (peppermint, lavender, or rosemary). Soak your feet for 10 minutes and dry well. Then massage gently.

TACKLING THE STRESS IN YOUR LIFE

Not having control over important facets of your life is very stressful. No matter what your personality, you can use assertiveness to gain back control and cut down on stress.

THE TORTOISE AND THE HARE
Characteristics of people of Types A and B are described in Aesop's well-known fable with the hare being Type A and the tortoise Type B.

No two human beings are alike. Almost from the moment of birth, a baby asserts his or her individual personality and temperament. As life goes on, these characteristics are further shaped by each person's experiences.

Even though everyone is different, it is possible to group people according to various types and classifications. For thousands of years, leading philosophers, theologians, and scientists the world over have devised various systems that classified people by their physique, intelligence, or emotions in an effort to understand how and why people behave the way they do. A number of modern psychologists have created psychological classifications to describe different personality types in order to better treat emotional and personality disorders.

BODY TYPES

In the 1940s, W. H. Sheldon of Harvard University developed Kretchmer's concept of somatotypes. This characterised people according to three distinctive physical shapes, each of which had its own personality.

A mesomorph had an athletic form, with a lot of muscle but not much fat, a large head and broad shoulders. The mesomorph was said to be energetic, aggressive, and competitive.

An endomorph had an overall rounded shape and head with a 'heavy' build and a predisposition for storing fat. An endomorph's personality is relaxed and easy-going like his or her shape.

The ectomorph was sharp and thin in form, with spindly legs and arms, and not much muscle or fat. Matching their physical forms, ectomorphs were said to be tense, taut, sensitive, introverted, and artistic.

While the somatotype theory was largely discredited in later decades, health-care professionals still acknowledge that some body shapes do have health implications.

The 'apple-shaped' individual, with large deposits of fat located on the abdomen, is much more prone to heart disease and breast cancer than are 'pear-shaped' or 'bean-pole shaped' people. Control of weight through diet and exercise can help to reduce this risk for many people.

PERSONALITY TYPES

In the early 1900s, Sigmund Freud, an Austrian neurologist and founder of psychoanalysis, divided personality into three parts: the id (representing our instinctive and unconscious wants and needs), the superego (standing for the often admonishing voice of society), and the ego (our conscious 'I', which tries to reconcile the conflicts between the id and superego).

Freud's groundbreaking work provided a springboard for his famous student, Carl Jung, a Swiss psychologist. Jung classified people into two major groups – introverts and extroverts – according to their social and emotional interaction. Introverts were restrained, retiring individuals, often shy and unforthcoming around others, but who maintained reserves of thoughtfulness, independence, and quiet determination. Their opposites, extroverts, are characterised as energetic and outgoing, at ease in company, and adaptable and flexible team members. Confident and outspoken with others, they require the stimulation other people can give to perform well, and are therefore often less at ease with solitude.

While classifying people by personality type was instrumental in treating their mental health problems, it was not often used to determine physical ailments. That changed in the early 1960s with the pioneering work of two American cardiologists, Meyer Friedman and Ray Rosenman. While treating people with heart disease, they were puzzled by the fact that more than half of their heart attack patients did not have the usual risk factors of high cholesterol, hypertension, obesity, or cigarette smoking. What was causing their heart disease? Careful observation revealed that these patients all had a similar personality. They were all competitive, ambitious, and driven by deadlines. They called this aggressive personality trait Type A. Friedman and Rosenman developed a personality test to determine who had a Type A personality and who did not. The Type A individuals

TABLE OF THE HUMOURS

The ancient Greek physicians Hippocrates and Galen (and those of the Elizabethan era) believed that there were four personality types – sanguine or happy, melancholic or sad, choleric or angry, and phlegmatic or listless. Each personality type was thought to be the result of an excess of a particular humour or body fluid – blood, black bile, yellow bile, or phlegm. The humours were related to the four elements – fire or blood, earth or black bile, air or yellow bile, and water or phlegm.

ELEMENTAL TYPES
Elizabethans believed everyone had a surfeit of one humour.

PERSONALITY AND YOUR HEALTH

There are many different ways of classifying human beings, reflecting factors such as personality types, character traits, and physical features. According to certain philosophies, personality has the potential for affecting the health of the individual. Check the chart to see how you may be at risk.

CATEGORISATION	PERSONALITY AND CHARACTER TRAITS	HEALTH FACTORS
ANCIENT INDIAN PHILOSOPHY		
Hindu philosophers believed that the life energy (*prana*) is manifested in the human body according to the five elements – ether, air, fire, water, and earth in their three basic compound forms – *vata* (air and ether), *pitta* (fire and water) and *kapha* (water and earth).	**Vata:** Small-boned, wiry people, often nervous types, unable to sit still for long. At times highly intelligent, but often abstract rather than practical, and lacking humour.	Susceptible to constipation, arthritis, lower back problems, and lung disorders.
	Pitta: Intense, hardworking people, often with athletic, muscular bodies. Highly energetic with curiosity and a hunger for learning, and prone to impatience and jealousy.	Prone to cancers, strokes, and digestive, blood, and hormone deficiency disorders.
	Kapha: Often stocky and thick-set people with a tendency to put on weight easily. Slow moving, solid, jolly, and emotionally stable, they like the status quo and enjoy the good things in life, and are perhaps a little unimaginative.	A tendency to succumb to illnesses affecting the lungs, lymph glands, and stomach. A sluggish circulation may affect the heart.
TYPES A AND B		
Psychologists use these convenient tags to describe a person's attitudes toward time and tasks, self-image, and self-evaluation.	**Type A:** A self-centred personality, incessantly driven to achieve more and more in less and less time, in competition with other things and other people. Always running 'at full throttle', ambitious and insecure.	Type As are more likely to suffer infections and are 80 percent more prone to hypertension and cardiovascular disease than Bs.
	Type B: People lacking in Type A traits. Unhurried, relaxed, patient, and quietly self-assured, with little need to prove themselves. They pace themselves and their work well, but perhaps they are a little lacking in drive.	Type Bs are not as susceptible to heart disease, but have a higher incidence of depression than Type As.
CHINESE PHILOSOPHY		
In traditional Chinese thought, personality is made up of two opposing attractions – *yin* and *yang*, the female and male forces in nature. Their mutual attraction is the source of all movement and energy – the life force called *chi*.	**Yins:** 'Dark and moist' yins are tranquil, quietly reflective types, mentally alert but also passive personalities who make better followers than leaders.	An excess of yin can lead to sluggishness and deficiencies of some sort, such as underactive organs and pale complexions.
	Yangs: 'Bright, hot, and dry' characters, who are active strivers, are physically more than mentally active, and good leader material, but who are also aggressive, undisciplined, and uncooperative with others.	An excess of yang produces symptoms associated with heat, such as fever, sweating, and flushes.

CALM YOURSELF

Should you become angry, try the following tactics to defuse your emotions.

▶ *Count to 10.*

▶ *Speak slowly and deliberately.*

▶ *Lower your voice.*

▶ *Cross your fingers and breathe deeply and slowly.*

▶ *Go for a short walk.*

were constantly involved in many different activities to which they felt a driving need to compete and win. They had a marked tendency towards aggressive and hostile feelings. They appeared to be unable to relax – hurrying their lives away by eating, walking, and talking too quickly. In short, they were in a constant state of mental and physical hypervigilance. Those who did not share these character traits were called Type Bs. Type Bs were the reverse of Type As in that they were relaxed and easygoing.

Using their personality test, Friedman and Rosenman were amazed to find that Type As had twice the rate of heart attacks and heart disease than Type Bs. For the first time, personality was used to determine physical health. But the question remained: what was causing heart disease in the Type A patients? Friedman and Rosenman concluded that the hard-driving personality and overly demanding behaviour of Type A patients were causing their heart attacks and heart disease. The treatment seemed obvious: help Type As to modify their behaviour so that they could deal with stress more effectively. In short, teach them to become more like Type Bs.

Later research, however, showed that not all Type As had heart attacks and that not all Type Bs were free of heart disease. Researchers reconsidered the relevance of determining the risk of heart disease according to the degree of free-floating anger and hostility people felt. They found a definite correlation between anger and blocked coronary arteries. Subsequent research has shown that anger and hostility literally take a toll on the heart.

MANAGING ANGER

Anger, linked with hostility, puts a person on the alert, and triggers the fight-or-flight response with all its attendant physiological responses. Some people believe that if they vent their anger, they will not experience any ill effects, physically or psychologically. They might express it directly by shouting at the person who caused it, or indirectly, perhaps by hitting a pillow. Neither of these strategies, however, is effective at stopping the effects of anger. Suppressing anger does not work either.

The best way to deal with anger is not to express it or to control it but to try to avoid it. This does not mean giving in all the time, or sidestepping conflict. It means making your feelings known before you reach the boiling point. For example, if your children annoy you by walking mud into the house, simply cleaning up after them will not solve the problem – eventually you will explode in a torrent of angry words. The best solution is to make your feelings about muddy floors known in a calm, straightforward way and to tell your children that you expect them to wipe their feet before entering the house. The technique used for doing this is known as assertion (see page 74), and it is one of the key strategies for reducing your stress level. By solving a problem before it becomes a crisis, you will find that you feel less tense and more at ease.

ASSERTING YOURSELF

The foundation of assertion is that every person has rights. Being assertive means being confident that you have the right to express your feelings. It also means that you remain aware of another person's rights. In this way, you can avoid conflict because you are not attempting to say that your rights and needs are more important than another's. By taking the rights of others seriously, you ensure that the other person takes your rights seriously, too. Also, by

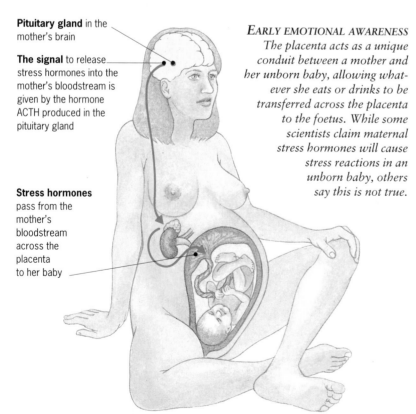

Pituitary gland in the mother's brain

The signal to release stress hormones into the mother's bloodstream is given by the hormone ACTH produced in the pituitary gland

Stress hormones pass from the mother's bloodstream across the placenta to her baby

EARLY EMOTIONAL AWARENESS
The placenta acts as a unique conduit between a mother and her unborn baby, allowing whatever she eats or drinks to be transferred across the placenta to the foetus. While some scientists claim maternal stress hormones will cause stress reactions in an unborn baby, others say this is not true.

becoming more assertive, you will find that you can tell people how you feel. You will be able to say no when you want to, and refuse unreasonable demands.

Why be assertive?

Being assertive sounds easy, but acting assertively can be difficult. Many people prefer to avoid conflict and give in without a fight. They often apologise repeatedly for small infractions and begin far too many sentences with 'I'm sorry'. These old habits can be hard to break.

If you feel you are not assertive enough, take some time to think about the areas in your life where assertion would help. Do you wish you could tell people at work what you want? Or that you could make it known to your spouse that you want help with the housework? Do you feel that your friends never ask you what you want to do when you go out together? Or that you never seem able to ask your doctor to explain things more clearly? Make a list of the situations in which you would like to be more assertive.

Colleges, evening classes, adult education programmes, and the like offer classes in assertiveness training that teach simple techniques. These will enable you to change from a passive person to someone who knows how to make sure your needs are addressed. The secret of true assertiveness is to identify and understand passivity and aggression, and to recognise that passive reactions, such as withdrawal, sulkiness, or reproach, are not only inadequate but also often ineffective.

The language of assertion

The first step in asserting yourself is to be clear about what you want. The next step is to make the other person aware of it by saying it simply, clearly, and directly. Before you speak, take a moment or two to collect your thoughts. For instance if someone has overcharged you, say, 'You've given me the wrong change. I think you'll find that I gave you £10, not £5'. Try to be direct and to the point, avoiding a long explanation. Speak firmly, but be polite. If the person you are talking to is not helpful, you may need to repeat your request, or make a further suggestion: 'If you look in the till, I think you'll find that I gave you a £10 note'. Continue to repeat your request,

ASSERTIVE BEHAVIOUR
Simple, straightforward steps can help to resolve problems.

- Identify the problem
- Approach the person
- Explain the benefits
- Explain the consequences
- Be patient
- Maintain communication
- Problem resolved

remaining calm and polite. If the person refuses to acknowledge your complaint and check the till, then summarise the situation as it stands and state that you will seek out the next level of authority. For example, you could say, 'As you are not prepared to check the till, I would like to speak to the manager of the shop'.

Practising assertion techniques

A good way to learn how to be assertive is to practise. You can do this on your own by mentally rehearsing conversations. For example, you might want to talk to your boss about something that has been troubling you at work. People respond best if you use the word 'I', so that the emphasis is on what you want, rather than on what they have done wrong. Do not say, 'You always make me work through lunch and I am sick of it'. Instead try, 'I value my lunch hour and would appreciate it if we could arrange the work schedule so that I can take a lunch break every day'. This statement lets your employer know how you feel, but avoids apportioning blame. By using the word 'we' and suggesting how to solve the problem, you show that you want to be part of the solution.

When to compromise

Even the best assertion techniques in the world, however, do not always work. Sometimes it is necessary to give in. Some situations are difficult to resolve, either because they have been going on for a long

continued on page 76

ASSERTION CHECKLIST

Since people communicate both verbally and nonverbally, you will have to learn to assert yourself not only by what you say but also how you say it. To get across your point of view, make your feelings known, or ensure that your position is clear, you should:

▶ *Stand up straight.*

▶ *Concentrate on breathing regularly to help keep your voice firm and even.*

▶ *Make eye contact. Averting your eyes makes you look submissive and unsure of yourself, but there's no need to stare.*

▶ *Speak in a firm voice; do not shout or raise your voice.*

▶ *Stick to the point; avoid long explanations.*

▶ *Be polite but do not start a sentence with 'I'm sorry'.*

▶ *Listen to the other person's point of view but be persistent.*

Using Assertion

Some people are happy speaking up whereas others find it very difficult to make their voices (and wishes) heard. By learning a few, easily mastered lessons in assertiveness, you will be able to get more from life.

AN INDIVIDUAL'S RIGHTS

You may feel better about what you want and who you are by thinking about some inalienable rights. These include:

▶ *The right to make mistakes.*

▶ *The right to refuse requests without feeling guilty.*

▶ *The right to express feelings.*

▶ *The right for your own needs to be considered as important as those of other people.*

▶ *The right to object to unfair criticism.*

▶ *The right to be listened to.*

Many of the problems individuals face are linked to their inability to take charge of their relationships at home or in the outside world. Non-assertive people allow their children and spouses free time, while they do all the chores, then sulk or explode in a rage in response to a small demand. At work they find themselves taking on tasks that are not their responsibility, working long hours, not taking holidays, and then becoming ill. Nonassertive people do themselves no good. If they were more emphatic about their needs and feelings everyone would gain. Children would learn self-reliance. Communication between spouses would improve. And companies would be more efficient if their employees were not taking sick leave due to overwork and understaffing.

ASKING FOR A PAY RISE

When you ask for a rise, remember that you are entitled to your worth being recognised in a monetary form, just as your employer is free to grant or refuse your request. If your request is reasonable, then your chances of success are good. But even if your request is well founded, there may be other extenuating circumstances why you are turned down. It is important to discover what these are, as rejection can play havoc with your self-esteem, not to mention your ability to assert yourself in other areas of your life.

Before you make an appointment to see your employer, write down a complete list of the assets you bring to your job. You don't need to recite them all, but they will help you make it clear that you deserve more money, and the list itself will increase your confidence so that you will feel assertive when you do meet your employer.

The employer

The employee

Speak firmly to indicate that you are serious, but vary your intonation to stop you from sounding intimidating

Make eye-to-eye contact occasionally, to engage your boss's attention

To convey ease, sit with your arms loosely placed, not crossed in front of your body

HOW TO BE AN ASSERTIVE PERSON

An assertive person is 'open and flex-ible, genuinely concerned with the rights of others, yet at the same time able to establish very well his or her own rights', according to a definition given by Alberti and Emmons in *Your Perfect Right: A Guide to Assertive Behaviour.*

To achieve this ideal, you first need to identify the areas where you feel least confident. It could be at work, or at social gatherings, where people talk to you but you do not feel you have anything worthwhile to say, or even at home, where other people's needs take precedence over your own. Ask yourself what it is you want. Be specific; it could be as simple as having someone else order the office supplies or telling your partner to remember to buy milk on the way home from work. Next repeat An Individual's Rights (see page 74) until they are ingrained.

MAKING A COMPLAINT IN A SHOP

An important assertiveness technique is to be persistent. We often lose in a conflict because we give up easily. The trick is to keep politely repeating what it is we want.

The salesperson

The shopper

Say positively you would like a refund

Refuse to be diverted if the assistant again tries to put you off. Ask again for a refund

Keep body language open, but do not budge until you receive a satisfactory answer

Don't be intimidated. The assistant may try to put you off, but keep repeating your request

PASSIVE OR AGGRESSIVE?

Changing the way you speak can make you more assertive. Be direct and clear. 'Please do the washing up' is more to the point than 'Am I the only one who cares that the kitchen looks like a pigsty'. When you want to be assertive, you should use assertive words. These include 'I' statements such as 'I think', 'I feel', 'I want'. If you wish to be more co-operative, use 'let's' or 'we could'. Remember, that there are fundamental differences between assertiveness and aggression. When you are nonassertive you are denying your own rights; and when aggressive, you are denying the rights of others.

THE NONASSERTIVE RESPONSE 'That's okay, I don't mind. I will drop what I am doing and do it right now. No, no, I'm not busy'.

THE AGGRESSIVE RESPONSE 'What do you take me for? Why should I jump whenever you call? Find someone else to run around for you, I'm busy'.

time or because the person you are negotiating with is in a stronger position.

For more challenging situations, it may help to practise what you want to say with a friend. Often people who are learning to be assertive are afraid that they are being rude or aggressive. You could try role-playing with your friends taking the part of your adversary. Record or videotape your session, and that way you can find out what you look and sound like. Then you can adjust your voice and manner so that you are less aggressive or more assertive, as you deem necessary.

The bonuses of assertion

Acting assertively will not change your life overnight, but with practice and persistence, you should find that other people will respect you and your wishes more often. Instead of simmering inside with unresolved anger, you will be able to express your feelings and work with others to find a solution that respects the needs and wishes of all, without unnecessary confrontation. Being assertive will help you to be more self-confident and in control of your life, as you take active steps towards achieving what you really want.

ARE YOU ASSERTIVE?

Each one of us likes to have his or her point of view appreciated and considered. But humans are sociable beings, and expressing an opinion in the face of possible opposition is not always something that comes easily.

How good are you at striking a balance between submissiveness and aggression? Add up your 'yes' answers to the questions that are listed below and compare your total with the results.

QUESTIONS	YES	NO
Do you avoid conflict with others at any cost, rather than argue with them, even over issues that are important to you?		
Do you feel that things seem to matter more to others than they do to you, and therefore make allowances for them, for the sake of peace?		
If a salesman, market researcher, or political canvasser calls you, do you find it difficult to tell him or her politely that you are not interested and then hang up?		
If something you purchased was faulty, would you keep it, but resolve to shop elsewhere in the future, rather than take it back for repair or a refund?		
If someone pushes in front of you in the line, do you keep quiet and sulk, hoping the message will be clear rather than voicing your irritation?		
Are others' feelings always more important to you than the 'principle of the matter'?		
When there's a deadline to meet at the office, are you always the one who stays late to finish the work – even when you would rather not?		
Do you prefer your partner to make the shopping decisions?		
Do you drive or walk around for ages before stopping someone to ask for directions?		
Do you find yourself unable to say no to requests for a favour, and worry that you might be asked to do things you would rather not?		
Do you shy away from asking for advice because you are afraid of appearing incompetent?		
If you feel wounded by an unfair remark, do you add it to the stockpile of injuries, rather than firmly but politely correcting whoever said it?		
Do you feel embarrassed or overdemanding in telling your spouse what you want in your relationship?		
If someone makes a mistake, do you prefer to avoid mentioning it, rather than draw attention to it?		

HOW DID YOU SCORE ?

0 to 5 'yes' answers
Your score indicates that you could be a little more sympathetic to others. You seem to express your opinions more aggressively than is necessary or, indeed, warranted.

5 to 10 'yes' answers
You seem to have a reasonable approach to confrontation, and are able to balance your opinions with those of other people so that both of you are satisfied.

Over 10 'yes' answers
You appear to set a very low value on your rights and points of view. You are as important as anyone else, so be more decisive and express what you want.

CHAPTER 5

STRESS AND THE FAMILY

*Because families consist of individuals with
different personalities, desires, and needs that
are changing all the time, conflict and stress are
inevitable. By developing awareness of everyone's
requirements and trying to balance them with plenty
of give and take, stress within the family can be
reduced. This chapter looks at some of the
ways you can make your family life
more relaxed and harmonious.*

THE FAMILY UNIT

Today's families take many forms other than the traditional unit in which the father goes out to work and the mother stays home with the children. Each type has its own joys and stresses.

FAMILY TIES
Years ago, the extended family often spanned four generations. Today, thanks to increases in remarriages, the notion of family extends 'horizontally' to include stepchildren, the birth of new siblings, and stepgrandparents.

In many traditional cultures, people live with their parents until they marry, and afterwards continue to live nearby. Each member of the extended family – parents, grandparents, children, aunts, uncles, and cousins – relies on the others for support, and several generations may live together in the same house. This sort of close family network has much in its favour: it can provide emotional balance, financial stability, a feeling of rootedness, and day-to-day support with child care and housework. It might not, however, allow young people a great deal of individual freedom and can give the older generations unwarranted licence to interfere.

THE CHANGING FAMILY
In the West, the traditional extended family has been eroded by two major factors. The first is that in today's job market people are relocating far more frequently to take up new jobs, and the second is a preference for smaller nuclear families, comprising only parents and a few children. But there are other factors as well. Since the 1960s the number of marital separations and divorces has escalated and the trend has grown for serial marriage – marriage for a second or third time. There has also been a large increase in children born out of wedlock, so that more and more families are now headed by one parent only. The majority of these single parents are women.

While some single parents return to their own parental homes with their children, in a re-creation of the extended family, others bring up their children alone. Sometimes divorced husbands and wives form 'bi-nuclear' families, where children divide their time between two households. Family life can be further complicated when one or both members of the divorced couple remarry and bring a stepfather or step-mother into their children's lives, possibly accompanied by stepbrothers and sisters.

THE STATE OF MARRIAGE

Recent statistics show that for every two marriages one ends in divorce, and that the majority of divorcees remarry. The trend is slightly higher in the US where there are more marriages and, proportionally, more divorces and remarriages.

	UNITED STATES (255 200 000)*	UNITED KINGDOM (57 700 000)*	GERMANY (80 300 000)*
MARRIAGE			
	2 362 000	364 600	405 200
DIVORCE			
	1 215 000	175 100	135 000
REMARRIAGE			
	1 075 000	156 000	85 000

*These figures refer to the overall population of each country. All the remaining figures are for 1992, except US remarriage, which has been estimated from 1988 figures.

The fluid nature of the modern family has made it all too easy to lose touch with members of an extended family. In addition, new people often have to be integrated into the larger family unit. It can be a challenge, with these conditions, to maintain a feeling of closeness with all your relatives. But frequently the desire to renew contact with them gets stronger as you grow older.

PARENTS AND THEIR ADULT CHILDREN

Parents often assume that their children will grow up to have aims and convictions that are similar to their own. They may feel disappointed if their offspring do not decide to follow in their footsteps. Points of conflict can include education, careers, religion, politics, and choices of friends, lovers, and marital partners.

Teenagers and young adults often want to distance themselves from their parents and lead different lives. They can also become angry at their parents, often years later, for the way in which they were brought up. Grievances that have been nursed silently for a long time may suddenly erupt when a child leaves home and discovers a new way of life. In extreme cases, parents and children may disagree about practically everything, leading to anguish for all.

Whether or not parents come to accept their children's choices, or the children become reconciled to the way in which their parents have chosen to live their lives, it is vital to keep the lines of communication open, especially if there are grandchildren involved. The relationship between a grandparent and grandchild is a very special one. It can bring stability and extra attention to the life of a child with busy parents, and great joy and pleasure to the grandparents. It would therefore be an enormous mistake to jeopardise this through anger over past acts or differences of opinion.

As long as parents and children continue to communicate in some way, there is a chance for them to work towards the future. Time does heal to some extent, but it may take some self-examination to see that the anger you are harbouring is hurting you as much as it is an aging parent or adult child. Expressing your feelings in a non-aggressive way (see page 75) can help to take the sting out of old wounds, and clear the way for a more satisfactory relationship.

SIBLINGS

Many brothers and sisters who were close as children remain so in adulthood. Others become closer as they grow up, leading to emotionally rewarding relationships as adults, not just for themselves but also for their families. Some siblings, however, find it hard to forget childhood rivalries. Others cannot come to terms with long-standing disagreements, where the slights and feuds of childhood may have left scars that have not healed. Such simmering feelings can make family gatherings very tense, awkward, and stressful.

Although it may be hard to initiate the conversation, talking through problems that have existed since childhood with your brother or sister can be therapeutic. It might also be revealing, and possibly very funny, to share perspectives on some events that occurred when you were both very young.

If you have difficulty reopening contact with a sibling, start with small gestures, such as sending a birthday card, or making a telephone call about something practical such as asking advice about a repair in the house. Be patient and try to repeat similar gestures regularly, and in time you may reap the benefits of a much closer relationship.

GRANDPARENTS

Senior citizens today do not always conform to the popular image of dear old grandad and grandma, relaxing in rocking chairs. Many modern grandparents have their own interests, careers, and needs, and may not be available to help their offspring as much as their counterparts did in years past – filling in as baby-sitters, for example, or helping out with financial difficulties. Children have to recognise this and, while maintaining as much contact as is practical, they must understand that grandparents have their own lives to lead.

Eventually, however, older members of the family can become frail and require special care. Losing independence because of declining health can be upsetting to people who, finally freed of their work and family responsibilities, have had a relatively short time to enjoy their new status in life. Elderly people can become depressed or morose and difficult to get along with when this happens. Family members can help by keeping in touch and showing that they value the older person's opinions and company.

*ACTIVE SENIOR CITIZENS
Today's grandparents are more youthful and independent and are spending more time away from their family in pursuit of their own interests and hobbies.*

The physical and mental deterioration of a loved one is extremely upsetting, and it may also be a source of guilt, especially if you live far away or work long hours and therefore cannot help as much as you would like. Hard choices may have to be made. Choosing a nursing home for an elderly person is especially difficult, even when it seems like the only option. Alternatively, a son or a daughter may decide to give up work and take care of a parent, which in itself can give rise to unforeseen strains and problems. The views of the elderly people as well as the demands on prospective carers must be taken into consideration before any decision is made.

DISTANT RELATIVES

When family members live far apart, perhaps even reside on different continents, visits may be infrequent. Getting together with relatives you haven't seen in some time can be fulfilling but also stressful, as you may all be virtual strangers to each other and perhaps have very different outlooks and habits. When you don't know what to expect, it might be better to make a limited visit. If you plan to stay longer than a day or two, you should consider staying in a hotel. That way you can call on your relatives for a meal or go on an outing, rather than be with them for the whole time.

Try not to visit only at times of crisis, such as the illness or death of a family member. Your relatives will appreciate that you are making the effort out of a sense of duty, but they may also feel that you have no interest in seeing them for themselves. Moreover, visiting during a crisis may be more stressful to them than helpful.

You may not want to see relatives you have little in common with, but you could be pleasantly surprised by how a shared ancestry can forge a bond between you. You might also gain interesting new insights about your parents, siblings, or yourself.

A FAMILY MEDICAL TREE
If you look at past generations of relatives you may be able to learn about family illnesses that could be hereditary.

Grandmother, alive and well, age 70

Grandfather, died aged 60, of a stroke

Uncle, died aged 40, of a heart attack

Uncle, age 44, suffers from angina

Aunt, age 40, in good health

Mother, age 45, in good health
Father, age 47, in good health, but taking precautions due to a family history of heart problems among the men

Son, age 21, in good health

RELATIONSHIPS AFTER DIVORCE

A marriage breakup is highly stressful, not only for the individuals concerned but also for their immediate families; and it can have serious effects on the couples' wider circle, including colleagues and mutual friends. But the most profound effect of divorcing parents is on the children. Suddenly their world is changed completely as they lose all their former stability. Often the first emotion they experience is panic, swiftly followed by fear of abandonment, anger, and powerlessness. Even though the parents themselves are experiencing great emotional turmoil, they must allow their offspring to express their feelings without overreacting to them. Because children are often very sensitive during times of family upheaval, it is best to treat them as gently as possible.

Youngsters can become very trying as they come to terms with a divorce, engaging in behaviour that ranges from babyishness to aggression and rudeness, or withdrawal. If you understand that this is normal, and are patient but continue to set limits firmly, their adjustment will be easier. This phase can last for many months, and you too will be making adjustments, so it is important to have some support from friends or family, or even your family doctor.

Some children feel that the divorce is their fault, so it is extremely important that the circumstances of the breakup are explained to them in language they can understand. Children must be reassured that their sense of guilt has no basis in fact, and that you in no way blame them.

Except in the case of an abusing partner, the absent parent needs to maintain contact with his or her children. Some absent parents believe that their children are better off without them, but in fact parents have not only a personal value to their offspring but also a very important symbolic one. For children to be (or appear to be) rejected by a parent may deprive them of someone to receive hugs from, but it also signifies something even deeper and more hurtful. At the very least, a parent's absence should be explained to the children by the person concerned, and birthdays and other special occasions should be marked by sending cards and gifts. The parent who has full-time care of the children should encourage this contact, which will have great significance for the children.

When children are cared for by only one parent, it is common for them to lose touch with the family and friends of the other. But it is vital to maintain children's links with relatives and friends on both sides; otherwise they lose much more than a parent.

It will reduce your children's embarrassment if you tell other people, such as their friends' parents and perhaps their teachers, that you are getting divorced. This way the children do not have to break the news to others themselves.

REMARRIAGE

A second marriage can be a cause for joy, but it can also complicate an already overcharged emotional situation. For example, parents may have to learn to accept a son's new wife, even though his former one is still much loved and is the mother of their grandchildren. Brothers and sisters, too, may be hostile to the new partner and prefer the previous one.

Children may frequently feel that they are helpless in the face of remarriage, when they have to become part of an instant family with none of the familiarity and shared history of their past one. They may also feel jealous of their stepparent and any stepbrothers and sisters, possibly seeing them as usurping their place in their parent's affections. As a result, children may misbehave, disrupting efforts to form a new family bond. Children can also feel a conflict of loyalty between the parent they live with and the absent parent and his or her new partner. This can be exacerbated if either (or both) of the parents criticise the other to the child. Divorced parents need to talk to their children as positively as they can about each other, and obey the golden rule, which is never to speak badly of the absent parent.

The role of stepparent can also be daunting for adults who have had little experience in either living, or dealing with children. A relationship must be built gradually on mutual interests and trust, rather than trying to compete with the existing parent-child relationship. In any case, children need lots of understanding from the parents and their new partners at a time when the adults are trying to make their own relationship work. Even with constant reassurances of love and carefully negotiated rules, it may take time, patience, and hard work for the new state of affairs to be accepted.

Using positive reinforcement
If you have to reprimand your children, make it clear that it is their behaviour you are criticising, not them personally. Say, for example, 'I am unhappy that you broke the china plate', rather than 'How could you be so stupid?' Try to be rational and do your best to maintain a sense of humour.

MAINTAINING PERSPECTIVES Broken plates can be mended or replaced, but your child's damaged feelings cannot.

A Death in the Family

The death of someone you love – especially if it is unexpected – is a traumatic and stressful event. Dealing with it can be difficult if you don't know how to show your grief. Many health-care professionals believe that expressing your feelings is essential for good health, and that bottled-up emotions can manifest themselves as physical symptoms.

Forty-five-year-old Maureen was at work when her husband, Jim, was rushed to the hospital after a heart attack. She quickly realised that the attack was a serious one, and Jim died shortly after she reached his side. At first she felt only shock and disbelief. Both her daughters, Vicky and Clare, lived out of the area and during the first few hours after Jim died she felt too numb to contact them; the reality of Jim's death seemed unfathomable.

Soon after returning to their empty house Maureen felt strong enough to break the news to them, and after a sleepless night, she started dealing with funeral arrangements. She thought she was not doing this well, but was relieved to be busy. She imagined that people seemed embarrassed by her situation, so she kept conversations short.

Although they had travelled down especially to be with her, as the funeral approached, her daughters became withdrawn. Following the funeral, at which she cried very little, Maureen realised how angry she was with Jim for abandoning her. He had provided for her financially, but had left a chasm in her life. She felt guilty that perhaps she hadn't helped him to take care of his health, and she worried about her daughters, who remained distant from her. Maureen felt that life was not worth living.

Six months later, she was still feeling very depressed, was sleeping poorly, and had little appetite. She was also neglecting her physical appearance, was paying bills erratically, and was often ill with minor complaints. Her work was suffering and she often burst into tears. She knew this behaviour was upsetting to colleagues, which made her feel even more distressed.

WORK
It can help to have a job to go to when there is a crisis at home, but your concentration may not be good.

FAMILY
Communication can be difficult when everyone is unhappy, as family members are unable to share their grief.

HEALTH
Following a death in the family, the physical and emotional symptoms of grief can pose a health hazard for a year or two.

BEREAVEMENT
It can take a long time to recover from a partner's death, especially if you keep your grief and resentment bottled up.

FINANCES
Even when provisions are made, taking sole responsibility for future finances might suddenly seem overwhelming to the surviving partner.

WHAT SHOULD MAUREEN DO?

Maureen needs to move on in the grieving process, and help herself and her daughters to come to terms with their loss. The four stages of grief – shock, anger, depression, and acceptance – are not always clear cut. Maureen should understand that it is not only normal to switch between them, but also that the process of healing can take a very long time, depending on the nature of the relationship, the circumstances of the death, and the extent to which an individual can express grief.

It would help Maureen if she could find support from a trained outsider, such as a counsellor, her family doctor, or minister. She should also talk to her daughters, and encourage them to express their feelings to her. Showing how deeply you have been affected by someone's death is an essential part of recovering from that death, and the grieving process should not be rushed. Nevertheless, it is vital that Maureen starts to think about all the other aspects of her future, including her health, work, finances, and social life.

Maureen needs to explain to friends and work colleagues that she is still grieving. This will help them to understand and accept that she is not her normal self. A support group for the bereaved may also help.

Action Plan

BEREAVEMENT
Ask the family doctor to recommend a professional counsellor to help to deal with feelings. Consider joining a self-help group for the newly bereaved.

WORK
Talk with the boss – perhaps he or she might be willing to delegate some of her duties to others. Explain difficulties to colleagues so that they can appreciate and make allowances for any lack of concentration at work.

FAMILY
Talk to Vicky and Clare about their father, and try to bridge the gap that has opened up between them. Heart disease can have family implications, so the girls may need medical advice regarding dietary and lifestyle changes.

HEALTH
Seek help for long-lasting depression. Get some advice from a doctor on taking better care of health in general, and look into various relaxation therapies, such as yoga and meditation.

FINANCES
Gather together all bills, chequebooks, and bank statements to determine the financial situation. If necessary, make an appointment with an accountant to discuss handling affairs in the short term.

HOW THINGS TURNED OUT FOR MAUREEN

Maureen went to the bereavement counsellor recommended by her doctor. At the sessions, she talked about her anger with Jim for dying, how helpless she had felt at the hospital, and how inadequately she had coped with her daughters' grief. She and the counsellor discussed ways to put her life back together and improve communication with her children.

She invited the girls home for the weekend, and told them how she felt about what had happened; she also apologised for not having been as supportive as she thought she should have been. This opened the floodgates, and both daughters openly wept about their father and talked about their own emotions. Grieving together as a family proved to be therapeutic and brought them closer together.

Maureen found the idea of talking to her friends and colleagues about Jim's death daunting, but once she raised the subject, she discovered that most of them were extremely caring and sympathetic. Some also gave her useful advice,

putting her in touch with a support group for the bereaved, and also with an accountant.

Maureen began to eat properly for the first time in months, choosing foods to build up her strength. She and a friend began swimming once a week, and she also signed up for a yoga class. She found that the exercises relaxed her, and the meditation healed her mind.

Today, although she still misses Jim terribly, Maureen is seeing the future as less bleak and is feeling much more positive about life.

THE COUPLE

Building and maintaining a long-term relationship takes work, patience, and compromise. A major factor in this process is open and continuing communication to prevent a build-up of tension.

*INITIAL ATTRACTION
In a US survey* of factors that initially attracted 890 men and 928 women to their future spouses, the number one factor, personality, also turned out to be extremely important in sustaining that attraction.*

FACTORS	MEN	WOMEN
Personality	48%	43%
Looks	27%	16%
Warmth	13%	25%
Sexiness	8%	8%
Humour	1%	4%
Power	1%	3%

*The Janus Report on Sexual Behavior

The majority of people marry, and many do so more than once; fewer than 8 per cent of American women never marry at all, and only 9 per cent of British men remain unmarried by the age of 40. But these days people are divorcing readily – one in every two couples in the United States, the United Kingdom, and Germany (see page 78).

The reasons why some couples stay together while others divorce are complex. Physical attraction is important, but personality and circumstances also play a part. In *The Janus Report on Sexual Behavior*, both men and women rated personality as the most important factor in initial attraction. It also seems to be the glue that holds a relationship together. In 1985, two American researchers, Jeanette and Robert Lauer, found that both women and men attributed the success of their long-standing marriages to their spouse being their best friend.

Even within the happiest relationship, however, the potential for conflict always exists. After the wedding, the first hurdle may be coming to terms with differences in the couple's expectations of marriage versus the reality. Later, the challenge may be to try to devise an equitable way of living when children arrive; and all relationships have to contend with the different backgrounds, personalities, habits, work, and social lives of the two people involved.

MAKING IT WORK
Above all else, if a couple are to have any chance of a successful, lasting relationship, they need to communicate with each other. Unfortunately, it is all too easy to fall into a pattern where confidences and worries are not shared and solutions are not worked out to suit both partners.

It is important to 'reconnect' every day with your spouse. Even if you can manage

REFLEXOLOGY FOR COUPLES

Reflexologists treat ailments of the body by massaging 'reflex areas' of the foot. But couples can also use foot massage to promote relaxation and reduce stress by easing tense areas, and at the same time increasing intimacy.

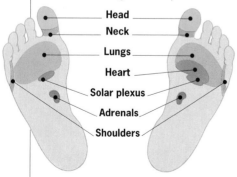

Head
Neck
Lungs
Heart
Solar plexus
Adrenals
Shoulders

*NECK POINT
Massage the ball of the foot up to the first joint of the big toe to relieve neck tension.*

*SOLAR PLEXUS POINT
Massage just below the ball of the foot in line with the second toe to ease emotional tension.*

*ADRENALS POINT
Using your thumb, massage the arch of the foot in small circles to relieve backache.*

only 5 minutes of focused conversation, this will help you to lessen any emotional distance that might have developed over the previous day. If both your lives are very busy, set aside a specific time at least once a week when you can sort through events and problems of the past few days and discuss the future. Try to do this away from your children, friends, and relatives.

Couples often shy away from discussing touchy subjects, just to keep the peace. For the sake of long-term harmony, it makes sense to deal with problems sooner rather than later, when they might be much more difficult to resolve. But it's important also to choose the right moment – no one wants to discuss difficult issues just after arriving home from work, or when everyone in the family is hungry and wants dinner.

When the time is right, tell your spouse what is bothering you. To set a tone of goodwill, preface your remarks with a statement such as: 'I want to bring up something that's not easy for me to talk about.' In fact, to avoid putting your partner on the defensive, always use 'I' statements, such as: 'I feel angry when you do not do the washing up', rather than: 'You make me angry when...'. Avoid sentences that begin with 'You never...'. or 'You always...'.

Remember that one of the joys of an intimate relationship is the freedom it gives you both to talk about anything. It also gives each of you more autonomy within your relationship, and provides a safe way to vent angry feelings that have nothing to do with the partner but can build up and lead to an explosion.

In modern Western society, it is common for couples to lead relatively separate lives, with both partners employed at different places or one taking responsibility for child care while the other works outside the home. If this is the case in your marriage, talk to each other about what you are doing and the people you come into contact with during the day. After all, what happens while you are away from each other – a car that will not start, for example – will undoubtedly have an impact at home. If this is too difficult, and you find yourselves drifting apart, try to find some activity that you can do together, such as playing tennis or bridge, gardening, or taking dancing lessons, that relieves some of the stresses and strains of both home and work.

THE GLUE THAT MAKES A MARRIAGE STICK

In a 1985 survey*, 315 couples who had been married longer than 15 years gave their views on long-term relationships. Significantly, the first seven reasons given by each for a successful marriage were identical. They are listed here in descending order.

MEN AND WOMEN

- ▶ My spouse is my best friend.
- ▶ I like my spouse as a person.
- ▶ Marriage is a long-term commitment.
- ▶ Marriage is sacred.
- ▶ We agree on aims and goals.
- ▶ My spouse has grown more interesting.
- ▶ I want the relationship to succeed.

MEN

- ▶ An enduring marriage is important to social stability.
- ▶ We laugh together.
- ▶ I am proud of my spouse's achievements.
- ▶ We agree on a philosophy of life.
- ▶ We agree about our sex life.
- ▶ We agree on how, and how often, to show affection.
- ▶ I confide in my spouse.
- ▶ We share outside hobbies and interests.

WOMEN

- ▶ We laugh together.
- ▶ We agree on a philosophy of life.
- ▶ We agree on how, and how often, to show affection.
- ▶ An enduring marriage is important to social stability.
- ▶ We have a stimulating exchange of ideas.
- ▶ We discuss things calmly.
- ▶ I am proud of my spouse's achievements.
- ▶ We agree about our sex life.

*Survey by J. & R. Lauer, published in *The Janus Report on Sexual Behavior*

LEARNING ABOUT YOUR SPOUSE

It is always worthwhile to keep up real communication with your partner. Talking, of course, helps, but if it only involves topics such as who is going to take the children to the dentist or how you are going to pay off that loan, you will not achieve the depth of intimacy that makes a truly satisfying relationship. Do not assume that you can read your spouse's mind; too many couples find out too late that they never really knew what each other wanted.

To learn another's innermost thoughts, it often helps to reveal some of your own first. This creates an atmosphere in which disclosure will feel welcome and safe. Something trivial, such as bringing up an embarrassing moment you had as a child, can then build up to more serious revelations.

It is important to listen actively to your partner when he or she begins to open up. Concentrate on what is actually being said,

TACKLING DISAGREEMENTS

A few practical changes in the way you communicate with each other can help to defuse conflict.

▶ *Encourage your partner to give his or her view of events.*

▶ *Try not to make your partner feel guilty, and do not dredge up past mistakes.*

▶ *Even if you believe that you are totally in the right, accept some of the blame for the problem.*

not on what you think about the statements or how you should answer. Don't tell your partner how to feel. Instead, just accept the other person's feelings.

If your spouse resists your efforts, respect his or her need for privacy. Some people find it extremely hard to talk intimately. You can, however, explain that the lack of intimacy in your relationship is difficult for you. Under such circumstances, you should make sure that you have someone you can confide in, because everyone needs intimacy in order to lead fulfilling lives.

Never try to find out more about your spouse's thoughts through such underhand methods as reading a diary, opening mail, or listening in on telephone calls. You may misunderstand what is written or said, and if you are discovered, you could justifiably be accused of betraying trust. This would

also be true if you were to use a confidence against your partner at a later date. If, for instance, a teacher confesses to her husband that she is having problems with the head of her department, and then during a later argument, he shouts: 'See, you can't get along with anyone!', she is not likely to confide in him about future problems.

BRIDGING THE LANGUAGE GAP

Studies have shown that in general men and women differ considerably in their communicating styles. Deborah Tannen, Professor of Linguistics at Georgetown University in Washington, DC, has pinpointed ways in which conversation between a man and a woman can cause conflict.

Many men believe that in most areas of life, including communication, they must win over someone else to get what they

ACHIEVING CONNUBIAL BLISS

Today it is common for both spouses to have careers. When work stresses are added to those of communicating with

each other and caring for a home and children, the result can be tension. Here are some ways to cope with the pressures.

ADD A ROMANTIC NOTE

No matter how busy you are with work and family demands, you should reserve some hours each week to be alone together. The goal is to enjoy each other's company, rather than spending all your time discussing everyday problems. Keep your romance alive by giving your partner a surprise kiss or hug, bringing home a bottle of champagne, planning a special dinner, or organising a weekend away.

PRIORITISE GOALS

Decide together what are the most important things in your lives as a couple, but also as independent people. That way, when you are overwhelmed by conflicting demands you will be able to prioritise accordingly. Remember, it is all too easy to let life control you, rather than you controlling your life. If you know what you want and what will make you and your partner happy, then go for it.

CHANGE FOR THE BETTER

All relationships have room for improvement – all you need is motivation. To do this, both partners should make lists of all the things that annoy them – these can be major, such as spoiling the children, or minor, like never putting clothing in the laundry basket. Compare lists, then draw up another list, this time of how things could be changed. Work your way through it slowly, reinforcing changes as you go along.

DIVIDE CHORES EQUALLY

Look at who is responsible for what in your household. The Social and Community Research 1991 British Social Attitudes Survey shows that although 75 per cent of couples believe both partners should share a task like washing up equally, only 37 per cent actually do so, and consistently fewer men performed chores other than repairs. It isn't surprising then that women may resent their partners. The ideal is to divide the work equally, or if you can afford it, hire outside help.

SETTLE MONEY MATTERS

Decide how much money you actually need in order to live comfortably. Together you may be earning a lot, but to achieve this you may have to work at jobs that keep you apart or bring intense pressures into your lives. If this suits you, fine. But you might want to consider a simpler way of life, with perhaps less demanding jobs, so that you have more time for each other. Job sharing is one option.

COMMUNICATE – ALWAYS

The stresses of modern life can often render us speechless – with exhaustion. For this reason, most partners barely have the energy to speak to each other or, if they do, and they are both under pressure, they usually snap in irritation. This is not communication! To express what you want to say in a nonhurtful manner, always think before you speak and consider what the impact of your words will be on your partner.

want. Those with this attitude usually feel more comfortable giving advice and orders than offering help and support, and they are frequently confrontational. Women, on the other hand, tend to regard communication as a means of achieving self-confirmation. They also desire intimacy, and usually prefer compromise to ordering people around or arguing with them.

These differing outlooks can cause unintentional hurt. Take the sentence 'Let's go to the cinema'. A woman will regard this simply as a suggestion to agree to or not; a man may see it as an order and become angry. Or how about 'Would you like to go to the cinema?' On the other hand, a man,

on being asked this question, might weigh up the pros and cons in his mind, decide that he would prefer to have a night in, and decline the offer. His partner, on getting this response, might become upset because she was in fact, in a roundabout way, stating what she wanted to do and now feels that her desires are not being respected.

Different conversational styles, therefore, can get in the way of honest communication, and so more directness on the part of women and more understanding on the part of men might go a long way towards bridging the communication gap. Without this, it is impossible for each to understand what they are getting at conversationally.

Achieving empathy

The power to identify mentally with others and understand them more fully takes conscious effort. The Native American saying, 'Walk a mile in another person's moccasins', helps you to see yourself through another person's eyes (or feet).

ANOTHER VIEWPOINT
It's important to put yourself in your partner's situation, so that you gain a better understanding of his or her opinion.

Nuts, whole grains, beans, and peas contain manganese, which may be involved in nerve function and fertility

Whole grains, liver, fish, bananas, avocados, eggs, and peanuts are good sources of vitamin B$_6$, which may relieve some of the discomforts of premenstrual tension, and boost fertility

Green vegetables, nuts, seeds, wheat germ, and whole grains are rich sources of vitamin E, which is helpful for relieving premenstrual tension and menopausal symptoms

Meat, beans, oysters, milk, wheat germ, and bran are rich in zinc, which stimulates testosterone production, and aids sperm formation, erection, and ejaculation

FOODS OF LOVE
Once the honeymoon is over, some couples find that sexual attraction wanes. Though oysters and champagne have been touted as the ideal food and drink for lovers, less expensive and more readily available ones may boost lovemaking and health even more.

Green, yellow, and orange fruits and vegetables are rich in beta-carotene, which plays a role in the production of all sex hormones

Sensuous Massage

Enlivening Relationships with

Passionate relationships can become routine and predictable, particularly when people have been together for a long time. The physical side is often the first to suffer, but you can rejuvenate it with the power of touch.

SCENTED OILS

Essential oils can increase the sensuality of a massage, but be sure to mix them with a base oil – never apply them directly to the skin. Add them to your massage oil to enhance its effectiveness. For best results, 20 to 25 drops of essential oil can be added to a small bottle that contains about 60 ml (2 fl oz) of base oil. This will usually be enough for one massage. To add atmosphere, heat oils in a vaporiser, or light an oil-impregnated candle.

An excellent way to enhance and bring new vitality to your sex life is to use massage for increasing feelings of warmth and intimacy. Massage also has the added benefit of helping to relieve physical and mental stress.

Simple massage strokes are easily learned and can be adapted to suit each partner's preferences. Seek feedback about the movements you use and listen to your partner – the massage is for his or her pleasure.

You do not need to make any elaborate preparations. The essentials are privacy, warmth, subdued lighting, a suitable massage oil, and a supply of clean, soft towels. You will also need a firm, towel-covered surface to lie on. Most beds and couches are too soft to give adequate support for a massage, so you will probably have to use the floor, but it can be made more comfortable by laying down an exercise mat, a blanket, or a quilt.

SETTING THE SCENE

Careful preparation can turn a simple massage into a wonderfully sensual and erotic experience for both partners.

▶ *Lay out your towels and massage oil (or lotion) and turn the lights down low.*

▶ *Check that your fingernails are short, smooth, and clean.*

▶ *Take off any jewellery that might come into contact with your partner's skin.*

▶ *Ensure that you have absolute privacy and that the room is warm and free of any draughts.*

▶ *Have some gentle, atmospheric music playing in the background.*

▶ *Perfume the room with incense or a vaporised essential oil.*

*Do not use if you are pregnant.

Clary sage* is used to treat fatigue, anxiety, and menstrual problems

Jasmine helps to relieve depression and is especially suitable for dry or sensitive skin

Lavender is a relaxant with mild painkilling and sedative qualities

Rose, a valuable relaxing oil, is frequently mentioned in ancient texts on the art of sex, including the *Kama Sutra* and *The Perfumed Garden*

Patchouli has a stimulating and sensual aroma which mirrors natural body scent

Joss sticks and incense help to create a relaxing atmosphere

Oils and lotions, which help to reduce friction and make a massage more sensual, are available from chemist's and body-care shops, or use grapeseed, sunflower, apricot kernel, almond, or soy oils. Use the oil by itself, or enhance its effects by blending it with an aromatic essential oil. For comfort, warm the oil by standing the bottle in a bowl of hot water. Rub a little oil between both hands, then smooth it onto your partner's skin.

EXPLORING TOUCH

Another effective way to create intimacy, in addition to basic massage techniques, is by simply caressing each other all over, using delicate, fingertip strokes. You can combine this approach with massage or use it as an alternative.

Explore new touch sensations by stroking each other with sensuous fabrics such as silk or velvet, with soft, long-plumed feathers, or with wooden massage aids.

CAUTION
Never give your partner a massage if he or she has: newly formed scar tissue; a skin infection, fever, or contagious illness; acute back or other pain; heart problems, thrombosis, phlebitis, or varicose veins; or any swelling or bruising.

MASSAGE STROKES

Take turns giving each other a massage. There is no correct sequence – just use any or all of the following basic techniques, either spontaneously or in a more planned massage session. You can repeat each stroke as often as desired, but make sure you try new techniques to keep massage sessions exciting.

NECK AND SHOULDERS
With your partner face down, place a hand on each shoulder. Slide your hands along them and up each side of the neck, gently squeezing and releasing the flesh.

BACK
Using opposing circular strokes, move your hands down the back to buttocks. With fingers pointing towards head, slide them firmly back up to shoulders.

FACE
Gently trace your partner's face with your fingertips. Place your thumbs at the centre of the forehead above the eyebrows; slide them out firmly towards the temples.

ARMS
With your partner face up and palms on the floor, stroke each arm from wrist to shoulder with cupped hands. Slide your hands back down inside of each arm.

HANDS
Moving your thumbs in tiny circles, gently massage the fleshy areas of each of your partner's palms and the base of each thumb.

FEET
Stroke along top of each foot with your thumbs. Massage soles, moving thumbs in circular strokes.

LEGS
With your partner face down, stroke the back of each leg upwards from ankle to buttock with cupped hands. Slide your hands back down the inside of the leg to the ankle. Ask your partner to turn over, and repeat strokes on the front of each leg.

PARENTAL CONCERNS

Being a parent is enjoyable and rewarding, but it also brings its own stresses. There are some things you can do, however, to reduce the strain and make parenting more pleasurable.

Fertility problems
For couples with fertility problems, anxiety can turn into anger, frustration, and a loss of self-esteem, especially when friends start families without difficulty. Their stress is compounded by the tests that have to be performed before the treatment begins, and increases during treatment, which not only disrupts their life, but also only has a 35 per cent success rate.

Changing from a couple to a family starts long before an infant arrives. Most babies today are planned, with couples often having numerous discussions before agreeing to go ahead. Some prospective parents make the decision easily, but then find pregnancy and the changes more problematic than anticipated. Still other couples, and in increasing numbers, find themselves unable to conceive. Both treatment for infertility as well as its failure can prove to be so emotionally damaging that a marriage may not survive.

Pregnancy itself is inherently stressful. A woman's body undergoes many changes – some are not always welcome – and the alterations in hormone levels can make her emotional. Many prospective parents may become anxious about the new baby, and wonder what life will be like after the birth.

THE EXPECTANT PARENTS
A woman's health, financial affairs, the stability of her marriage, and her job situation will work either for or against her ability to cope with the increased physical and emotional stresses of having a child. But whatever her circumstances, or those of her husband, learning more about the process of childbirth and child care will help prospective parents to worry less. Many maternity hospitals and health clinics hold antenatal classes, which include exercise and relaxation sessions for pregnant women, as well as classes that help her to prepare for labour, and there is a wide range of literature available on all aspects of pregnancy and child care.

Many men delight in their partner's pregnancy, while others find it hard to cope with. They may be alarmed by the physical changes or feel shut out of the entire process. This can have a detrimental effect on the woman, who may feel that she has been left to face this major life change completely on her own. If this is the case, she should try to talk things through with her partner. If this fails, she should broach the subject with her doctor, who may recommend the help of a counsellor.

GREAT EXPECTATIONS
During pregnancy it is vital that partners talk to each other about how they feel. Although many men express a desire to participate in pregnancy and childbirth, it is not mandatory and some women do not want partners to be involved. Each couple should come to an arrangement they're happy with.

IN TOUCH
A man can show his concern for his partner by minimising her discomforts. Massaging her feet and legs can be very soothing.

POSTNATAL DEPRESSION OR BABY BLUES

A few days after childbirth, about two-thirds of all new mothers experience feelings of depression, when they cry or feel anxious for seemingly no reason at all. Called post-natal depression or baby blues, these feelings are usually the result of hormonal changes and they disappear about two weeks after the birth of your baby.

Sometimes, however, these feelings last for much longer. In environments that are supportive and geared to helping parents during this major life event, prolonged post-natal depression is virtually unknown, but throughout Western society 10 to 20 per cent of all new mothers experience it.

There are certain stress factors that can increase the chance of a woman becoming depressed after childbirth. She may have had an unhappy childhood or difficult relationships with her family. There might have been considerable medical intervention during the birth of her child, or the pregnancy may not have gone well; as a result, the woman could feel she has failed in some way. Conflict with the baby's father, financial worries, or loneliness are also possible factors. Fatigue and lack of sleep, combined with a baby that is difficult to satisfy, can make things even worse.

Most depressed women find that talking to a sympathetic listener is an enormous help. For a woman who is severely affected, professional counselling, drug therapy, or even hospitalisation may be necessary.

BEING A 'GOOD ENOUGH PARENT'

Many people today have little experience of child rearing until they have their own children. And if, as is the case for many modern parents, they don't want to raise their offspring as they were brought up, there are even fewer 'rules' to follow. Consequently, many new parents seek answers from the multitude of how-to books that purport to

Homeopathy after childbirth

A number of natural remedies are suitable for new mothers. Discomfort from an episiotomy (cutting and stitching of the skin at the base of the vulva) may be eased by taking 30c *Arnica* four times a day until it subsides. The area can also be bathed in a solution, made by adding 10 drops of *Calendula* to 0.3 litre (½ pt) water.

A SOOTHING CREAM
A cream containing Arnica *and* Calendula *can be applied to sore nipples. Wipe cream off before breastfeeding.*

BABY MASSAGE

Massaging your baby from an early stage strengthens the intimate bond between parent and child and makes the baby receptive to physical touch. It also facilitates the relief of, and recovery from, many of the common illnesses that can afflict babies, including colic, constipation, coughs, and colds.

CHEST MASSAGE
Using both hands, gently stroke the chest from the centre outwards to the sides and back of your baby's body. Then gently stroke the diaphragm along the edge of the rib cage.

CRANIUM MASSAGE
With your palms, gently massage the crown in a circular motion. Then, using your fingertips, stroke down from the crown along the sides of the baby's face.

FACIAL RUB
With your fingertips, lightly stroke the forehead from the centre to the temples. Then, using a circular motion, massage the baby's temples.

A Single Parent

Single-parent families are becoming increasingly common in Western societies. Most single parents are women, the majority of whom have to raise children with limited financial resources. This is stressful enough, but if the father withdraws his financial contribution as well as his affection, the consequences for the entire family can be shattering.

Diane has two young children. A year ago, she and Eric, her husband of 13 years, divorced. Although she received regular maintenance and child support from him, the money – as well as his visits – has stopped now that he has been laid off. Diane has applied for welfare benefits, but it is not enough to feed and clothe two growing children, and cover the usual household bills or any extras. Diane's savings are quickly becoming depleted.

The children are suffering too: the young one has become withdrawn, and the older is becoming a bully. Diane always feels anxious and suffers from lack of sleep. She also lacks a social life and feels she will never enjoy herself again.

WHAT SHOULD DIANE DO?

To try to reduce the amount of isolation and helplessness she feels, Diane should seek assistance from her family and from other people in the community. To make her children happier and feel more stable, she must encourage Eric to see them and to cooperate with her for their benefit. At the same time, she has to try to make the children see that none of what has happened between them is their fault.

Diane also needs to obtain expert advice on getting the most out of her money, including all the benefits to which she and her family are entitled. Being able to relax would help her to sleep better and take a calmer view of her situation.

FINANCES
Welfare benefits rarely cover all of a family's needs; money worries can be the final straw to an overburdened parent.

PARTNERS
Many fathers stay away from their families after a divorce. This has grave consequences for the children as well as the mother.

HEALTH
Being on your own with no one to talk to or share problems with can cause a parent to feel desperate and to act irrationally. Not getting enough sleep can lead to illness.

Action Plan

PARTNERS
Visit or telephone Eric to let him know how his absence is affecting the children. Try to persuade him that seeing the children will benefit everyone.

FINANCES
Investigate free sources of advice. Ask social worker about benefits for which family is eligible.

HEALTH
Do something about feeling less anxious and getting more sleep. Join a single parents organisation to get emotional support.

HOW THINGS TURNED OUT FOR DIANE

A librarian put her in touch with a single parents group and a yoga class. The former enabled her to make new friends and meet potential baby-sitters, as well as providing advice on financial matters, benefits, and budgeting. The yoga class was free to mothers on benefit and was held during the children's lunch time. It took several phone calls to persuade Eric to see the children, but he has, and their behaviour has improved a great deal, as has life as a whole.

tell inexperienced parents the 'right' way to bring up their children. While offering much good advice, the authors of these books may differ in their opinions, often contradicting each other. There are really only a few basics required if you are to be what the psychoanalyst Bruno Bettelheim has called a 'good enough parent'. Your children need love, security, consistency in the way you treat them, a modicum of discipline so that they know the boundaries of acceptable behaviour, and most of all, they

UNDERSTANDING STRESSES ON CHILDREN

Stress can develop when youngsters covet certain material possessions that their parents can't afford or don't approve of, or when they feel pushed to achieve certain standards before they are ready. Parents should help their children to develop a healthy perspective on the criteria by which they feel acceptable to others.

FAMILY POSSESSIONS

A house in an affluent neighbourhood with a garden, pool, or an expensive car, can place stress on a child who may feel that there is too much to live up to.

ATHLETIC AND SPORTING SUCCESS

Being good at sports and winning awards and trophies can be gratifying, but it can also be a source of stress if a child feels pressure to repeat his or her success.

SUCCESSFUL PARENTS

Having parents in a prestigious profession, or who are pillars of the community, may pressurise a child to overachieve academically or professionally.

SPENDING MONEY

Earning one's own money is important but stress may arise if a child is not ready to take on the responsibility of a job, but desires the financial freedom.

TRAVEL

Exotic holidays are wonderful experiences, but children may feel that they need to have an expensive foreign trip every year in order to keep pace with their friends.

AUTONOMY

Feeling in control and being perceived as free to make choices is vital to a child's maturity, but this may lead to fears and anxieties about failure in the adult world.

Quality time

An increasing number of mothers now work outside the home – 46 per cent of those with children under the age of five and 69 per cent of those with school-age children. Most psychologists agree that children of working mothers do not lose out and have as good a chance of achieving scholastic success as their peers.

What is important is not whether you spend a great deal of time with your children, but how you use the time you do spend with them. Try to give your child your undivided attention on a regular basis – say an hour each day spent in talking, playing, or reading together.

need communication. This is not to say that it is easy to be a parent (it can be very hard, for example, to be patient with a child who continually throws tantrums), but parents who keep the lines of communication open eventually reap the benefits.

Every family is different, so the problems that arise and how you tackle them with your children will differ from those of your friends or relatives. Parents' manuals should be read for pertinent advice, not taken as gospel. Talking with an experienced friend, your family doctor, a professional child care worker, or even possibly a counsellor can help you to find solutions. You are not the first parent to have gone through these experiences, and this realisation may bring you a measure of relief.

COPING WITH TEENAGERS

Because babies and young children are dependent on you, they are usually easier to deal with as you have control of their discipline. (They are, for example, small enough so that you can remove them easily from a difficult scene to be dealt with in private.) Teenagers are a different story. They are nearly adult size and can verbally and physically make your life truly miserable in their search for independence.

As youngsters grow older, they gradually become less dependent on their parents, forming a set of different relationships outside the family. Children between the ages of 12 and 15 have reached a pivotal point. On the one hand, they don't want their friends to see their dependence on their parents, and they don't want their mothers and fathers to intrude on the identities they have forged for themselves among those of their own age group. On the other hand, their need for parental reassurance – even if it is mostly unspoken – is still very strong.

The type and extent of the parents' discipline become crucial at this time: if it is too authoritarian, it almost invites rebelliousness, but if it is too lax, teenagers may regard this as evidence of the parents' indifference. According to experts in child psychology and family therapy, the most successful parents are those who manage to communicate their love and concern to their teenagers without being intrusive or overbearing. Limits are set, but these are gradually modified to give young people a feeling of independence.

FAMILY VERSUS WORKING

Given that many of today's children grow up in dual-income households, the issue of child care can become a source of great stress in a marriage. Many mothers (and also fathers) worry that their children will somehow become emotionally deprived if cared for by others, yet research has shown that good quality care can actually make children more sociable and independent. According to American psychologist Alison Clarke-Stewart, quality day care can boost some children's educational levels. She found that children from poor backgrounds develop more quickly in day-care centres than they do when they stay at home, whereas affluent children develop at the same rate whether in day care or at home.

Often parents worry that by entrusting their child to a carer they will be losing touch during the important growing years, and that the children will be transferring their emotional allegiance to the carer. This is not so, because even if you work away from home, you will still spend more hours with your child in the mornings, evenings, and at weekends than any other carer. Children are aware, from a very early age, that their mothers and fathers have a special social status in relation to them, and they recognise that others only have authority over them because their parents have allowed it. Moreover, children have plenty of room in their hearts for a variety of close relationships; forming one with the person caring for them during the day can only give them an added sense of security.

But what kind of child care is best? In the UK at present, 50 per cent of preschool children of working mothers are cared for by grandparents and other relatives (21 per cent are cared for by their fathers). While this option is more flexible – and cheaper – than day-care provision, it may cost more in terms of conflict and resentment in the family. For example, grandparents often have different perspectives on childrearing, and they may feel exploited if their goodwill is imposed on too frequently. Parents need to accept that they have delegated a certain amount of control and show appreciation.

Additional child-care options include other mothers, day-care centres and nursery schools, and nannies. When you consider employing people to look after your children, be specific from the beginning about

SELF-ASSERTION
New mothers can be inundated with offers of help or unwanted advice. To prevent arguments, convey your needs clearly to over-willing friends and family.

what you expect from them in the areas of discipline, how the child should be occupied during the day, and how he or she is fed. It is also good to be very clear about the working hours, payment, what to do in emergencies, and so on.

Sharing the load

According to a survey carried out by the insurance company Legal & General, women in full-time employment spend an average of 49 hours a week doing housework in addition to their jobs. This imbalance can cause tremendous stress as many women feel torn between the responsibilities and duties that are required as a wife and mother and those as a worker, regardless of whether she has a career or a job.

It is therefore vital that you tell your partner as assertively as possible (see page 74) how you feel about this imbalance in the amount of housework being done by each of you. It may bring surprising (and beneficial) results. The same is true for children, who can be given increasing responsibility for small household tasks as they grow older. This is also excellent training for the time when they will leave home for good.

KEEPING SANE AS A WORKING MOTHER

Coping with the demands of both work and family is enough to daunt even the most capable mum. Here are some things that will make it easier for you.

▶ *When you get home from work, try to take 10 minutes to sit down and relax.*

▶ *Don't bring work home with you. Leave it at the workplace.*

▶ *Find leisure activities to share as a couple and as a family.*

▶ *Train yourself to become a less-than-perfect homemaker. 'Superwoman' simply does not exist!*

MANAGING TIME WELL

Dual-career families often find it almost impossible to complete all of their housework, errands, and chores in the time available, which means that the hours set aside for relaxation disappear in a flurry of activity. Try some of the following ideas to help you to organise your schedule, and give you time for a rest.

MEALS
To organise food shopping and preparation better, you should plan menus a week in advance. If possible, use labour-saving devices, for example, a microwave oven to defrost and cook food quickly and, to fill the freezer, double all recipes.

COMMUNICATION
To keep in touch with family members, get an answering machine. You can, for example, let them know about delays. Also, set up a bulletin board for schedules and memos.

TASKS
To save time in the morning, set the table for breakfast after dinner. Also, iron clothes in the evening before you go to bed, and lay out clothes needed for work the next day.

CLEANING
Distribute household chores to all family members; even small children can help to sort laundry. Do a quick daily cleaning of bedrooms and living room, leaving larger tasks for the weekend.

A Family Divorce

The breakup of a marriage is one of the most traumatic experiences that anyone can go through, and when children are involved, the problems multiply. Children often feel responsible for the split and need reassurance that they were not at fault. Parents must make an effort to deal calmly and fairly with what is at issue, so that a bad time can be made more bearable for all concerned.

During the last few years of their 16-year marriage, Joan and Bob have been seeing less and less of each other and rarely talk of anything other than the children or the house. Both have careers, but Bob's takes him away from home so often that Joan has almost begun to see herself as a single parent and to resent what she sees as Bob's jet-set lifestyle. Bob can't understand her anger: after all, it is his salary that allows them to live in such a big house and want for nothing.

Everything comes to a head when Bob suddenly announces that he has to go on an unplanned business trip and breaks his promise to see his son's play. As a result, Joan is not able to attend a weekend management seminar that is vital if her career is to advance.

This is the last straw. Bob must cancel the trip for the sake of both his son and his wife, or that will be the end of their marriage. When Bob refuses and flies off on his trip, Joan has the locks changed and contacts a lawyer.

Joan feels both relieved and tense. She knows that it is hard to be a single parent, but she is almost one anyhow. The future, however, seems very uncertain. She doesn't earn enough to pay the mortgage and support the boys and herself.

Bob is outraged and bewildered. He had thought that his marriage, while not great, was more or less happy. He sees all that he has worked for going down the drain, and he is surprised to find how much he misses his sons. He decides to apply for custody of the children, as well as to keep the house.

Richard and Daniel, their sons, are shocked by this turn of events. They are used to their father's absence but still feel close to him. However, they recognise that their mother's complaints against their dad are justified, although they are worried that they themselves might be the cause of the breakup.

CHILDREN
If consulted, most children never want their parents to divorce. They often react badly, becoming withdrawn or aggressive.

HEALTH
Divorce is a traumatic emotional experience that can sometimes result in mental and physical breakdown. The changed circumstances can cause the whole family to suffer.

FINANCES
Divorce – and its aftermath – is always expensive: legal fees can soon mount up, and two households have to be created from one.

PARTNERS
Whether one or both parties want the marriage to end, divorce usually leads to feelings of failure, a sense of betrayal, and great anger.

WHAT SHOULD JOAN AND BOB DO?

To settle their divorce with a minimum of bad feelings, Joan and Bob will have to put their emotions to one side while they sort out the legal and financial aspects of their future relationship. Anger and resentment can make sensible property, financial, and custodial arrangements difficult, if not impossible. Clear thinking and reopened lines of communication may not be a possibility without help from an uninvolved person (see box, below left), but they must agree that such help would be useful before they can progress.

Joan and Bob should stop arguing over the children and find a solution that takes into account their sons' points of view. It is imperative that they don't put the boys on the spot by making them choose one parent over another to live with. Joan and Bob must also make every effort to reassure their children that the divorce is not their fault; rather it is a result of their own relationship breaking down. The goal is for the boys to maintain a good relationship with both of their parents so that they feel secure in their love.

Action Plan

CHILDREN
Make legal agreements about custody of the children, living arrangements, and visiting rights. Bob must decide if he is really committed to working less so that he can look after his sons. Consult the boys about the situation and try to deal with their emotions as compassionately as possible.

FINANCES
Come to an agreement on child support and payments on the family home. Joan needs to ask Bob to help her to manage the mortgage or else she should consider moving somewhere more economical.

PARTNERS
Joan and Bob should talk individually to a close friend or relative who is a good listener. They should also attend mediation, or ask the family doctor to recommend a professional marriage guidance counsellor.

HEALTH
Joan and Bob each need to consider some method of relaxation to minimise stress, such as yoga or meditation. They should eat sensibly, resist smoking too much, and try not to bury hurt feelings in alcohol or food.

MEDIATION

Independent mediation services are available in most areas for divorcing couples, and they are often recommended by experts in the divorce field. An impartial third party – a mediator – will meet both partners and their children separately to discover their feelings and needs. The object is for the partners (and, if they are old enough, the children) to discuss these matters together in an informal and non-legalistic setting, so that they can come up with acceptable solutions. Mediation is not intended as a means of reuniting couples, but instead to help them to make considered decisions.

HOW THINGS TURNED OUT FOR JOAN AND BOB

Joan and Bob contacted a mediation agency and met, with a mediator, for six months. They found the process painful, but as they discussed their marriage, they realised that it really was at an end. They gradually found that they could express their regret and sense of failure.

After lengthy discussion, Bob realised that for practical reasons he would not be able to care for Richard and Daniel, but he did want to see them frequently. He and Joan agreed to sell the family home and share the proceeds; Joan would buy a less luxurious house and Bob a flat nearby. He would pay child support for the boys, but she would carry the mortgage on the new house and support herself. The boys would have two homes: they would visit Bob at weekends, but would live most of the time with Joan. Bob told his sons that he thought it would be good for the three of them to take up a hobby; they decided to go windsurfing together.

To relieve anxiety and tension, Joan and Bob each tried a variety of relaxation techniques, including meditation, aromatherapy, and massage. Although initially very traumatic, the divorce eventually had some long-term beneficial effects for all of the family.

Family Therapist

All families encounter problems from time to time. These may relate to one individual or to events over which the family has no control. Many can find solutions on their own, but some can benefit from the help of a trained outsider.

THE FAMILY AS A SYSTEM

Family therapy is also known as systemic family therapy because it holds that the emotional and psychological relationships of a family act as a dynamic system. Although a single member of the family may often appear to be the 'affected' individual, he or she is in fact simply acting as a scapegoat for disturbances in the whole family system. Thus a problem child's behavioural disorder (a common reason for families to attend therapy) is viewed as the expression of the whole family's problem.

Family therapists, or counsellors, are trained in psychotherapy or counselling. They take a holistic approach – everything that happens to one member of a family must be considered in relation to the whole family, and everyone's opinion should be sought to find the best solution. They also believe that if traumatic or stressful events are not dealt with openly, family members will hide their feelings, which may erupt later in negative behaviour that will ultimately affect the entire family.

What problems do family therapists deal with?

Therapists deal with a wide range of problems. The most common are relationship problems between family members; stress resulting from dual demands of home and career for adult partners; financial pressures; children who bully or are being bullied; children – often adolescents – who have other behavioural problems that affect the whole family; bereavement, separation, or divorce; the trauma of child abuse.

STAGES OF FAMILY THERAPY

Seeing the results of family therapy usually takes time and more than one meeting. Most therapists prefer that the whole family attend, because any family problem affects all of its members. Sometimes, those who initially refuse to take part change their minds once they see that the others are benefiting.

1 *All family members feel nervous and uncomfortable. The therapist starts the discussion.*

Father, reluctant to participate, has arms and legs crossed

Mother, anxious, sits on edge of her seat

Son looks at the floor to avoid eye contact

Daughter has uncrossed her legs and is taking more interest in what is being discussed

Son begins to communicate with the therapist

2 *Trust is established and the therapist hears comments from all of the family members.*

What happens in family therapy?

During sessions, each person has the opportunity to state his or her viewpoint to the therapist in front of the rest of the family, and no one is allowed to interrupt. Some of what is said may seem ridiculous or be extremely hurtful; however, on reflection, many people find that the feelings expressed during these sessions have helped them to understand things that previously had puzzled or worried them about the relationships within the family.

What is the role of the therapist?

The role of the therapist is not to sit in judgment but rather to ensure that everyone has his or her say, to guide the family towards tackling problem areas, and to control the situation if it becomes emotionally tense. The therapist will also try to help the family to look for solutions, come to their own conclusions, make compromises where necessary, and then will be supportive of whatever decision is reached.

How long will each session last?

A session will normally last from 45 to 50 minutes. This is usually sufficient time for each person to speak and for the therapist to initiate discussion, but not so long that the participants, particularly children, become emotionally exhausted.

How many sessions will be needed?

This varies with the type of problem. One session may be sufficient to open the floodgates for discussion on a previously taboo subject, such as the death of a loved one. For more long-standing problems, it may take time to unravel the emotions involved and to deal with them. Some sessions may seem painful or confusing, but it is important to continue, even if difficult. You should attend at least four sessions before making an assessment of their worth.

How does the family benefit?

During the therapy sessions, each member has the opportunity to speak freely and be listened to with respect.

Often, this is not possible at home, where only the person who is the most assertive or who has the loudest voice or the greatest authority is heard. Additionally, family members begin to gain perspective on their own role in the family; this insight helps them to improve interaction.

How do I go about finding a family therapist?

Ask your family doctor to recommend someone who is properly qualified. Once you have checked a therapist's credentials, ask for a preliminary meeting to find out how the therapist will run the sessions, what the charges are, the sort of psychological philosophy he or she holds and – most important – if you feel comfortable with him or her.

WHAT YOU CAN DO AT HOME

Knowing how your behaviour affects the members of your family is the first step to improving relationships and creating a happier and more harmonious atmosphere. It is very important that you gauge your response before you communicate it to others. This should help you to avoid unnecessary and potentially hurtful confrontations.

3 *All family members have expressed their opinions and the therapist has guided them to some conclusions, thus helping to resolve the problem. Everyone is happier and more relaxed.*

Father and daughter are smiling, gesturing, and actively participating in the conversation

Mother displays physical affection towards her son

SPENDING TIME TOGETHER
A child who feels neglected by his or her parents, or a parent who experiences alienation from the family group, should try to find things of mutual interest to do together.

THE CHILDREN

Children under stress are often unable to express what they are feeling and may show that they are upset in indirect ways. They might become aggressive, for example, or physically ill.

ACCEPTING A NEW BROTHER OR SISTER

Although a new baby in the family is a joyful event, it can also make an older child feel threatened. To help to smooth the way:

▶ *Before the birth, start the older child in a play group or nursery school – something that only 'big' children do.*

▶ *When the baby is born, give the older child a present from the baby, and devise special treats that are appropriate only for big boys and girls.*

▶ *Have a relative make the older child his or her special concern, to replace the temporary loss of the mother's attention.*

BEING A BIG BROTHER
Allow the older child as much contact with the newcomer as possible.

A child's relationship with brothers and sisters is immensely important, and often very rewarding and pleasurable. It can also, however, be a source of jealousy and rivalry. Some children become very clinging when a sibling arrives, so parents need to consider how to keep this to a minimum. The birth of a new family member frequently makes older children feel displaced, and they may respond by regressing to babyhood, perhaps wetting their beds, or becoming destructive as they play out their anger, or showing aggression towards the new baby or other children.

They need reassurance that they are still loved, and their feelings should be appreciated, not dismissed. If parents are disapproving or critical – saying, for example, 'Don't be such a big baby' – children will hide their anger. This feeling could later emerge as intense rivalry towards, or even hatred of, the newcomer.

Another source of stress for children can be the way their families sometimes label them, calling them, for example, 'the smart one' or 'the pretty one'. Parents should understand that children are more likely to thrive if they feel that all options are open to them for as long as possible, and they may feel stress if they have to fulfil other's expectations of them. Anxiety can also be caused if parents compare one child with another. If one child is less gifted than another, remember to praise him or her for something more general, such as good behaviour or being helpful, and be careful to distribute hugs and kisses evenly.

SCHOOL DAYS
Children spend, on average, six hours a day at school, which for them can be a potentially stressful environment. A positive attitude on the part of their families will help them to settle happily in school. Parents

---

IS YOUR CHILD UNDER STRESS?

Any of the signs below may indicate that your child is under stress, especially if such behaviour is prolonged. You can help by trying to get your child to talk

▶ *Exhibiting regressive behaviour, such as bed-wetting, demanding to be bottle-fed, and throwing tantrums*

▶ *Refusing to go to sleep or having nightmares*

▶ *Being aggressive, unusually naughty, unruly, or destructive*

▶ *Stammering*

▶ *Refusing to eat*

▶ *Lying or stealing*

▶ *Being weepy, fearful, or clinging*

▶ *Refusing to go to school or skipping classes*

about his or her feelings. If, despite this, the unacceptable behaviour continues, you should consult your family doctor or consider seeking professional help.

EXAMINATION HELL
The stress of taking exams can, in extreme cases, lead older pupils to commit suicide.

DEALING WITH SOME COMMON CHILDHOOD PROBLEMS

AGE	CHILDREN WILL BE	PARENTS MAY BE	PARENTAL SOLUTION
0-1 (BABYHOOD) 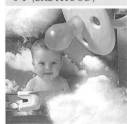	Learning to make sense of the world. Being sweet, charming, yet incredibly demanding. Crawling, with its potential dangers.	Exhausted from giving constant care and attention, compounded (in early months) by lack of sleep.	Take a nap or rest when your baby does. When crawling starts, baby-proof the house as much as possible by moving dangerous or breakable objects out of reach.
1-3 (TODDLER)	Learning to express themselves and be more independent, but feeling constant frustration. Having screaming fits and temper tantrums.	Stressed out in private and embarrassed in public by 'terrible twos'.	Develop organised routines so that your child has only a few new things to cope with. During a tantrum, distract him or her with an activity, toy, or story.
3-5 (PRESCHOOL)	Venturing out. Anxious about starting school and making friends. Perhaps learning to accept a new baby in the family.	Concerned for the child, wanting the best for him or her. Worried about his or her capabilities and whether you have provided good ground-work for learning.	Try not to overreact because you are worrying about your child's future. Believe in your child's ability to do whatever he or she wants, and provide lots of encouragement.
5-9 (SCHOOL AGE)	More independent. Taking no notice of you, rudely saying that you do not know anything. Playing up in school and hard to discipline.	Frustrated by children's growing independence but continual immaturity. Worried about children's adjustment to school and social life.	Listen to your child and consider his or her views seriously; try to deflect anger with humour. Be consistent and firm in your own views and behaviour.
9-13 (ADOLESCENCE)	Embarrassed and confused about physical changes and feelings. Finding difficulties in trying to cope with the opposite sex on a social level.	Nervous and shy about discussing their children's body changes and also sex. Perplexed by their children's moodiness and desire to be by themselves.	Talk directly to your children about puberty and sex. Be prepared to answer questions, even on disconcerting topics. Above all, be open and honest with them.
13-17 (YOUTH)	Considering the future. Feeling anxious about school work, college, or employment. Struggling against parental and school restrictions.	Apprehensive for the future and safety of youngsters. Hurt and angered by disagreements and disruptions to family life.	Encourage your child to talk about his or her future. Emphasise studying but without pressure. Increase amount of freedom, with reasonable limits.

Getting children to sleep

Bedtime can become a battle of wills between parents and children, especially if the children are overexcited or overtired. Pouring a few drops of lavender oil in the children's bath before bedtime will help to calm overstimulated children and ease their sleep.

SOOTHING LAVENDER
A lavender-filled pillow, or one impregnated with lavender oil, can be a helpful remedy for insomnia.

Bullying

Bullying has become a major problem in schools. Children who are repeatedly harassed, verbally or physically, by other children lose their confidence and sense of security. Bullying also causes great concern for the parent. In extreme cases parents have been known to move so their child can attend a school in a different area. Bullying should always be reported to school authorities, many of whom are now developing policies to combat this problem.

PLAYGROUND FEARS
The stress on a child caused by bullying can make school a place to be feared, and have a negative impact on behaviour at home.

should expect everything to be fine; if they show signs of anxiety that they think their child may be frightened without them, he or she will fulfil their expectations by becoming worried, too. Children can succeed at school when they are encouraged to regard it as a place where their parents are happy to send them.

Even so, your children are bound to suffer some stress from school. They may have problems getting along with teachers or classmates. Friendships may be quickly made and then hurtfully broken, signs of individuality might be rebuffed by classmates, and, once a child reaches secondary school, the competition for girlfriends and boyfriends results in as many losers as winners. In addition, difficulties in keeping up with their course work and sometimes obsessive worry about exam results can make school a harrowing experience.

Parents should let children know that they are always on hand, ready to offer a sympathetic ear. They must be careful, however, not to interfere unless asked, as an intrusive parent can damage a youngster's standing among his or her classmates and seriously affect their self-esteem.

It is also important that children be appreciated for themselves and their own abilities even if their achievements at school are only modest. Encouragement will ensure that

they make the most of themselves, although there is a fine line between this and burdening them with unrealistic expectations that they cannot fulfil; parents need to be careful not to push too hard.

SERIOUS ILLNESS

When very sick, young children appear especially vulnerable but in fact they often handle serious illness quite well. It is more frequently the parents who become traumatised. It will be helpful if you hide your own worries. Your child is likely to be frightened by unpleasant symptoms, and your calmness and control can be reassuring. You must be truthful, however, so the youngster will feel free to talk to you about any worries or fears he or she may have.

If a young person has to be admitted to a hospital and you have time to prepare, find books (picture books for the very young) that describe life in a hospital. You can use these to start a discussion about what is going to happen, which will go a long way towards allaying a child's fears. Some hospitals will agree to visits before the admission date so that a child can become at least a little familiar with this new environment, and many also allow one parent to stay with the child throughout an illness. These visits can be reassuring for both yourself and your child during what can be a stressful time.

THE ROLE OF FAIRY TALES

Small children tend to see the world in black and white, ignoring the confusing grey areas that are often beyond their comprehension. For example, a child may find it hard to reconcile the loving behaviour of the parents with the anger and aloofness that they can exhibit, particularly when the child has been naughty. And even small children are not immune to the talk of violence and death that permeate every news broadcast.

Fairy tales offer a safe area in which children can work through scary notions such as being abandoned by their parents or attacked by strangers. The stories also allow them to be frightened of something outside their own small world, with the knowledge that in these special scenarios there is almost always a happy ending.

REASSURING RED RIDING HOOD
Children easily identify with the 'good' and 'bad' characters in popular fairy tales. You can use stories to help your children to confront and overcome their own fears.

CHAPTER 6

A STRESS-FREE HOME

---

*Your home should be the place where you
rest and recuperate from life's pressures, where
you can close the door against external stresses.
Many factors contribute to this haven – colours,
furniture placement, appropriate lighting, pleasant
aromas, and more. Vital, too, is safety within the
home and the know-how to keep intruders out.
Here we show you how to create a safe and
relaxing environment in every room,
and a welcoming atmosphere for
your family and friends.*

MAKING YOUR HOME A HAVEN

When your home is pleasing to the senses and is kept in good order, it can be a haven from stress, a place where you can relax and recharge your batteries in comfort.

To make your home a calm centre to your busy life, consider the effects not only of colour and lighting, but also of sound, air quality, and odours.

COLOUR AND LIGHTING

The colours in rooms can do much to create a certain mood (see box, opposite page). They also affect your perception of warmth and coolness, and can be used to offset the climatic condition which results from a room's position. For example, if you want to cool down south-facing rooms, which are normally sunny, furnish them in blues and greens. To warm up north-facing rooms, which are in shade much of the day, use reds, oranges, and yellows.

Your own reaction to certain colours is significant, too. Those you like will make you feel good, wherever you use them. But you can have too much of a good thing. Rooms are generally more soothing if you keep the walls and flooring in light to medium neutral tones and use favourite colours in upholstery, draperies, and accessories.

Lighting has a major effect on a room's colour scheme (it can enhance it or make it seem drab) and on its mood. Each room in a home needs a variety of lights to achieve a pleasing effect and to suit different purposes

PET THERAPY
Some pets require more space and attention than others, but all of them can provide relief from anxiety, loneliness, and stress (see page 110).

and activities. Background lighting, usually from a ceiling fixture, should illuminate the whole area with a low level of light. If there is no ceiling fixture, then you need two or three lamps to get a similar effect. Task lights must provide enough wattage to do a particular job, such as putting on make-up. Accent lights are used to call attention to a particular decorative element, such as a painting, tapestry, or sculpture.

Dimmer switches allow more flexibility in lighting. For instance, a dimmed ceiling fixture can set a soft mood for dining. The colour of bulbs is important, too. Pink bulbs give a much warmer light than white; blue, even the light blue of some fluorescents, will create a subdued feeling.

SOUND

Not just your sleep but your mental state when you are awake can be disturbed by unpleasant external noise. If you live in a noisy neighbourhood, consider investing in very thick curtains and double- or triple-glazed windows. If this is not effective, try to negotiate with neighbours about keeping noise levels down.

Some noises that bother you might be within your own control. For example, if your refrigerator is buzzing loudly, it may need repairing. If excessive noise emanates from your plumbing or central heating system, have an expert inspect it. And for noise that you cannot control, a good sound system playing your favourite music can mask much of the irritating background clatter.

AIR QUALITY

The air quality in your home can have a great effect on how you feel. If you are cold, your muscles will become tense; if you are hot, you may feel sleepy and lethargic much of the time. Experiment with various heating levels: altering temperature by just a few degrees can make a big difference.

If central heating has been drying out your skin and breathing passages, installing a humidifier is one solution. Another, less expensive way to solve the problem is to place shallow containers of water on radiators or hang them over heating vents. Potted plants also help to keep humidity levels more comfortable. Where high humidity is common in summer, hot weather can be unbearable. If you do not have air conditioning, one solution is to install a dehumidifier; another is to use fans. An attic exhaust fan is very effective for drawing out hot air.

SMELL

One sense often overlooked in a home is smell. The connections in the brain for it are closely linked with the circuits of the limbic system, which deals with emotion. This is why some scents bring childhood memories flooding back, and why a room, although perfect in every other respect, may feel uncomfortable if the smell of it is somehow wrong. Estate agents sometimes suggest that their clients bake bread or make fresh coffee when prospective buyers are coming as these aromas create an agreeable atmosphere.

There are many other ways to give your house an appealing smell. First, go outside

continued on page 110

COLOUR IN YOUR HOME

Psychologists, artists, and decorators all know that colour can be used to influence mood. For example, blue is the colour of peace and communication and is suitable for rooms where you normally relax and converse. Green, which enhances concentration and creativity, may be a good choice for a workroom or study. Yellow and orange are welcoming, while red is sensual and stimulating. The more intense a colour is, the more strongly its effects will be felt. Also, paler tints make a space seem larger, darker shades, smaller.

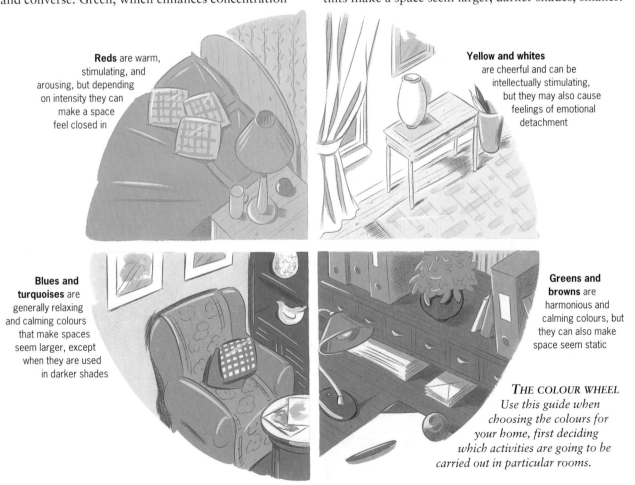

Reds are warm, stimulating, and arousing, but depending on intensity they can make a space feel closed in

Yellow and whites are cheerful and can be intellectually stimulating, but they may also cause feelings of emotional detachment

Blues and turquoises are generally relaxing and calming colours that make spaces seem larger, except when they are used in darker shades

Greens and browns are harmonious and calming colours, but they can also make space seem static

THE COLOUR WHEEL
Use this guide when choosing the colours for your home, first deciding which activities are going to be carried out in particular rooms.

Feng Shui

Feng shui is an ancient Chinese art that evolved from the observation that human beings are affected – positively or negatively – by their surroundings. Recognising and respecting this can result in a harmonious and prosperous environment.

THE POWER OF FENG SHUI
Feng shui can be used to create a home where harmony reigns and beneficial energies are free to flow.

According to the masters who practise it, the aim of feng shui is to ensure that correct choices are made concerning the position of structures and objects. This, in turn, will alter the environment and harmonise it in a way that will improve the well-being and prosperity of those living and working in the space. The term feng shui means 'wind' and 'water', and it is held that these forces are responsible for determining health, wealth, and good luck.

While most people recognise that a badly designed room, insufficient space, or a visually unpleasing shape may make them feel ill at ease, or

that a poor choice in lighting or furniture may be uncomfortable, the exponents of feng shui carry this concept one step further. They believe that more than being just an issue of aesthetics or physical comfort, the design, combination, and positioning of objects creates a physical force in its own right, one that may act for good or for ill.

Who uses feng shui?
Feng shui can be applied to any size living or working space – from something as small as an office desk to an area as large as an entire country. The practice has many branches

FENG SHUI REMEDIES
Once feng shui masters have made their assessment of a space, they will suggest changes to remedy situations that are unharmonious. The following are frequently recommended:

Plants are positive symbols of health and attract good chi

Wind chimes and musical sounds disperse bad chi and attract good fortune

Weights and statues stabilise an unsettled influence that may be disturbing

Bright, shiny objects, carefully placed, deflect hostile chi

Hollow pipes in a confined space channel chi and release its flow

Origins

Feng shui evolved from the agrarian way of life in China during the Shang dynasty (*c.*1766–*c.*1123 BC). Because farmers lived in an environment that was often hostile, they had to find ways of coexisting with nature in order to survive. Siting a farmhouse halfway up a south-facing hill might provide shelter from harsh winds and floods, and at the same time ensure enough sun for crops to grow. The Chinese in ancient times recognised the power of nature and the importance of harnessing it without interfering with or exploiting it. If nature is treated respectfully, they believed, it will yield power and prosperity.

and a wide range of applications. Masters train for a number of years, and their expertise is employed not only in private homes, but also in industry and government.

How does feng shui work?
The art of feng shui is based on the observation and understanding of chi, the life force that – practitioners believe – exists in all living things. Positive chi is said to be responsible for good health and spirits. For this reason, much of Far Eastern philosophy and medicine is geared towards balancing chi. A feng shui expert looks at the ways in which the impact of a space can be enhanced to produce more positive chi.

Feng shui's goal is to tap the earth's chi, just as the role of acupuncture is to tap a person's chi. According to the feng shui masters, buildings, trees, even sunlight affect the quality and flow of chi. Their aim is to create a place where chi flows smoothly and the principles of yin and yang are balanced.

What do feng shui masters do?
Central to feng shui is the idea of position. When choosing a site on which to settle, the ancient Chinese studied the landscape for sacred symbols, represented by the presence of water, for example, the shape of a lake, the smell of the rain, the appearance of the leaves on the trees, or the way in which wind rushes through a valley. Feng shui experts have adapted this concept to the modern landscape, both urban and rural. They also incorporate astrology and Taoist principles into the making of their assessment, and use all of their senses – not just touch, taste, smell, sight, and hearing, but also latent ones.

With these they pick up atmospheric signs and energy patterns similar to those detected during dowsing (seeking underground water by using a divining rod).

When is feng shui used?
Sometimes feng shui is employed at the design stage of a building to ensure that the location is ideal and that the best construction techniques and layout are used. More often, however, a feng shui master is asked to remedy existing problems. This is particularly true in towns and cities where space is at a premium.

How can feng shui reduce stress?
When you use colour, light, plants, textures, and furniture in a way that will promote a feeling of harmony with your surroundings, you create a space that will increase your sense of well-being.

WHAT YOU CAN DO AT HOME

USING FENG SHUI
Use this example of a house's layout, room by room, to help you to position furniture and plants in order to obtain the most propitious force for your life.

The bed should stand against a wall for stability, and it should also face the entrance to the room

A bead curtain prevents chi rushing from room to room

Windows should open outwards to allow the maximum amount of chi to enter the room

Mirrors should be hung high enough for the tallest person in the house

The toilet should never face the door

Flowers and water bring energy into a room and allow chi to circulate

The stove must have plenty of space around it so the cook's chi is not restricted

The front door must open easily – squeaking doors will unbalance chi

Colours must be chosen carefully to enhance the flow of chi in the house

Home Health Spa

Giving yourself the benefits of a relaxing and refreshing spa in your own home is neither difficult nor necessarily expensive. Sometimes the smallest comforts, such as warm towels or sweet-smelling bath oil, can make a world of difference.

WHIRLPOOL BATHS
The benefits of warm water can be further enhanced by the massage action of water jets, which channel water into a fine or coarse spray. A similar effect can be achieved by spraying a handheld shower against your body.

Water has been used for relaxation and therapy in many different cultures. An essential part of life in ancient Rome was the bathhouse, where Romans went to relax and socialise. You, too, can make your bathroom a refuge, where you can soak away your cares.

Fill your bathtub with water that is just hand hot. This temperature will reduce your heart rate and promote a calming effect. If the water is too warm, your blood vessels will dilate and your heart rate will increase, putting additional physical stress on your body. For extra relaxation, add some essential oils or fragrant herbs to your bath (see page 68). Once you are in the bath, practise relaxation techniques (see page 39) and soak for 15 to 20 minutes. Add more hot water if necessary to keep the water temperature comfortable.

Follow your soak with a shower, starting with hand-hot water to continue the calming and relaxing effects of your bath. After a few minutes, switch to cooler water, then finish with a brief and invigorating cold shower. This should leave you pleasantly glowing. When you are dry, you will be ready for a massage.

THE POWER OF 'NATURAL' BATHING

There are many ways to enhance the revitalising and relaxing effects of a bath. Many natural products can help to ease tired muscles, relieve tension, or invigorate you. You can experiment with oils and salts in your bath water, or use natural applications directly on your skin.

NATURAL BEAUTY
A wealth of natural preparations are available which can be tailored to your requirements.

Soft towels can be used to rub your body down, invigorating and stimulating you after your bath

To moisturise dry and flaky skin, add 1 or 2 tablespoons heavy cream and a few drops fresh lemon juice to the bath water

To exfoliate skin, mix together 1 tablespoon oatmeal and 1 tablespoon honey. Apply to face. Allow to dry before washing off

Pumice, loofah or exfoliating cream can be used to remove dead skin cells

A few drops of bath oil added to the water will ease tension and induce sleep

Epsom salts in the bath will rid the skin of impurities and reduce swelling. After you bathe, rinse off under a warm shower

Essential oils can enhance a massage by relaxing and uplifting you

Wooden foot and leg massagers can be used for a relaxing massage

Cucumber slices or an eye mask will help to soothe tired eyes

MASSAGING THE FACE

Stroke across the forehead to the temples

Make a large 'O'

Pressure should be firm but gentle

Use circular movements

FOREHEAD AND TEMPLES
From the centre of your forehead, stroke outwards to your temples with gentle soothing motions of your fingertips. After a minute or so, press gently on your temples to complete this calming massage.

AROUND THE MOUTH
With your index and middle fingers, make small circular motions over your chin and mouth. Exercise the muscle around your mouth by making a large 'O' shape, keeping your lips pressed against your teeth.

NECK AND SHOULDERS
Using your left hand and starting under your ear at the base of your head, stroke down your neck, right shoulder, and right arm. Keep the pressure firm and smooth. Repeat three times, then massage your left side.

BACK OF NECK
Press gently but firmly on the muscle on either side of your spine with the fingertips of both hands. Using circular movements, gently work up your neck to the base of your head and back down again.

MASSAGING THE LEGS

Massaging tired leg muscles will not only relieve aches and tension but also stimulate circulation. Done regularly, it can improve the appearance of your legs as well. You can achieve the best results by completing the whole sequence on one leg before beginning on the other.

KNEAD THE CALF
Squeeze the muscle away from the bone, then release it. Stroke gently from the ankle to the back of the knee, one hand following the other.

STROKE EACH LEG
Working from the ankle to the hip, stroke the leg, as shown at right, pressing firmly and smoothly. Repeat three times.

Relax your shoulders

Press firmly with your fingertips and thumbs

Towels make good padding so you can sit comfortably

PUMMEL THE THIGH
With loose wrists, work the front and sides of your thigh. This will ease any stiffness in your muscles.

RECIPE FOR A ROOM SPRAY

Choose your favourite fragrance or tailor one to match your mood, and create your own refreshing room spray, using the following recipe:

▶ *10 drops of an essential oil of your choice*
▶ *7 tablespoons of water*
▶ *1 tablespoon of pure alcohol or vodka*

Mix all the ingredients together and pour into a clean spray bottle. The alcohol will help to preserve the essential oil.

CHOOSING A SCENT
Geranium and orange oils are an effective combination. Geranium is a sedative but it is also uplifting, and may help to ease nervous tension and relieve depression. The scent of oranges adds an energising note to the blend.

and take a few breaths of fresh air, then go back in and sniff the rooms. Your ability to smell specific things lasts a short while, so try to identify anything unpleasant as soon as you come back inside. You may find that you have become accustomed to an odour that you would now rather do without. Then take steps to eliminate it – for instance, by improving the ventilation, repairing any areas of plaster or wallpaper where mould may have taken hold, repairing damaged drainpipes, or removing a strong-smelling potpourri.

Using essential oils

After eliminating unpleasant smells, you might want to add some pleasing ones to your home. Prepare a room spray, using the recipe (left), pour it into a metal or glass sprayer (a plastic one may disintegrate), shake well, and spray it around your rooms. You can also place a drop of an essential oil on a piece of cotton wool and put this behind a radiator or inside a heating vent.

Another approach is to release the fragrance of an oil by gently heating it, either in a saucer of water, to which a few drops of the oil have been added, or with a candle. To create an exotic, intimate atmosphere, use sandalwood or patchouli; to unwind in the evening, try geranium or lavender or ylang-ylang. For a lighter touch, orange, lemongrass, or neroli are popular choices. Lavender is often recommended for bedrooms, and will always make your guest room inviting to visitors.

Potpourri, joss sticks, incense, and air fresheners are good alternatives to essential oils. Potpourri that has faded can be revived by adding a few drops of aromatherapy oil. A herbal pillow or scented wooden blocks and paper lining for shelves or drawers can also be pleasing.

PLANTS AND PETS

House plants can transform a living space, making it more appealing and attractive. They can add interest to a dull area, divide up spaces, or soften awkward corners. And certain plants have the ability to enhance your environment in more specific ways. The scented leaves of pelargoniums, for example, release a powerful fragrance when their leaves are touched or pressed. The weeping fig (*Ficus benjamina*) is a great general air freshener; Boston fern (*Nephrolepis*

exaltata bostoniensis) is good for removing noxious fumes; and pothos (*Epipremnum aureum*) can remove carbon monoxide.

Even when limited to a terrace or window box, gardening can be very soothing and satisfying. Just seeing the plants that you have tended grow and flourish can provide immeasurable pleasure.

Pets in your household can also enhance it; they are surprisingly effective in reducing stress. Studies have shown that animal owners have less anxiety, lower blood pressure, and generally better health compared with non-owners. Some doctors in Great Britain have been giving out unusual prescriptions to patients suffering from mild depression or stress, or who are recovering from heart attacks: twice-weekly visits to a charitable trust that cares for donkeys and ponies. Just being with the animals and helping with their care has made it possible for these patients to reduce the amount of medication they are taking.

You might not be able to keep pet fish, but they, too, are excellent stress reducers. Researchers have found that dental patients who waited in a room with fish swimming in a tank had far less anxiety than those who had no fish to watch. Many institutions for the elderly and the mentally ill have also noted that individuals who keep fish seem to be less lonely and much calmer.

REPAIRS

Allowing household repairs and maintenance tasks to pile up can add unnecessary stress to your life. An annoyance such as a squeaking door or dripping tap may keep you from relaxing at the end of a hard day. Clogged plumbing or a malfunctioning boiler could become a full-blown emergency. To keep on top of things, make a list of all maintenance jobs that must be done regularly, such as changing a filter or cleaning a chimney, and tend to them at the scheduled times. Set aside at least an hour each week for small repairs; you will get instant satisfaction every time you draw a line through a completed task.

For larger problems, such as a leaking roof, make a plan showing how you can save up to have the repair done, when doing the work will be possible, and who will do it. This way you can stop worrying aimlessly, do what needs to be done, and get on with the more enjoyable aspects of your life.

HOME SAFETY

By making sure that your home is accident proof and can't be broken into by burglars, you will be able to reduce considerably your levels of anxiety and stress.

Your home may be a refuge but it also has potential hazards – fire, bodily injury, asphyxiation, and poisoning. Every year in the UK, 3 million people are injured in home accidents and 5000 die. Here are ways to make your home safer.

You can greatly reduce the risks of fire and electric shock by taking note of possible dangers, such as articles left near an open flame, a carelessly extinguished cigarette stub, or the fraying lead on an electrical appliance. A sensible measure is to have

COMMON HOME HAZARDS

Falls, burns, scalds, and electrical shocks account for most injuries at home. By taking a few simple precautions, you can minimise the risks to yourself and your family.

▶ *Flooring: Use nonslip rugs, or secure loose rugs to the floor. Take care when walking on wet or highly polished surfaces.*

▶ *Stairs and hallways: Keep these well lit and clear of obstructions such as toys, bicycles, and pushchairs. Make sure stair carpets are securely fitted. Install safety gates at the top and bottom of stairs to protect young children.*

▶ *Electrical equipment: Do not overload outlets or extension leads as this creates overheating that can cause fires. Do not use appliances such as space heaters, radios, and televisions in bathrooms.*

▶ *Water heater: Set the thermostat no higher than 50°C (120°F); above that temperature, water can scald people.*

MAKING THE HOME SAFE FOR THE ELDERLY

A decline in their agility can leave elderly people particularly vulnerable to household accidents. The bathroom, kitchen, and stairs are the most hazardous places, but with a little care all areas in the home can be made much safer.

IN THE BATHROOM
Slippery, hard surfaces are hazardous and need special attention.

Install hand rails

Have long-handled taps for bath, basin and sink, which are easier to use by those with weak hands

Use a nonslip mat on the floor

Place a suction mat inside the bath.

THE LIVING ROOM
Keep the area free of clutter, such as electrical leads and small rugs, which may cause falls.

Be sure to have ample light

Use a chair that gives good support.

THE BEDROOM
Provide for the possibility of having to get out of bed during the night.

Install a telephone within arm's reach

Keep a torch on the bedside table, and a plug-in night light.

smoke alarms installed on each floor of your home, and change their batteries regularly (usually about twice a year). Make sure that there are at least two possible ways to escape in an emergency. If the house has more than one storey, consider keeping a rope ladder upstairs, and have family members practise using it. Buy an all-purpose fire extinguisher and store it in an easily accessible place in or near the kitchen, where most domestic fires occur.

If you have a gas boiler, make certain that it is properly ventilated, and install a carbon monoxide detector close by (convenient battery-operated types are available).

Store all medicines, cleaning materials, and toxic chemicals in their original containers, with adequate labelling, and out of the reach of children.

Keep a comprehensive first-aid kit on hand, remember where it is, and make sure you know how to use its contents.

CHILDPROOFING THE HOME
By following the suggestions on these pages and ensuring that your children live in the safest environment possible, you will help to reduce the worry and stress that can accompany the joys of bringing up a family. Making your home safe for a young child is not difficult or expensive; it simply requires a few precautions, so that natural curiosity and the urge to explore do not put him or her in danger of injury.

CRIME PREVENTION IN THE HOME
While crime of any sort is distressing, the invasion, however slight, of our own 'inner sanctum', the one place where we and our loved ones are supposed to be inviolate, has a special power to shock and horrify us. The psychological consequences of a burglary usually far outweigh the material loss. But you can protect your possessions and create a greater sense of security in your home by

THINGS TO WATCH OUT FOR
Medicines should be kept in childproof containers and stored in a cabinet out of reach.

Pins, needles, scissors, sharp knives, matches, lighters, and other dangerous items must be kept in a locked cupboard

Poisonous substances, such as cleaning fluids and bleach, should be stored in their original containers in a childproof cupboard

A first-aid kit should be kept on hand for use in the event of an accident

Boiling food should never be left unattended. Use back burners if possible, and turn saucepan handles towards the back of the stove

Childproof catches should be fitted to the inside of all cupboard doors and drawers, or they should be locked

Short, coiled leads should be used for electrical appliances, and they should be unplugged when not in use

THE IDEAL KITCHEN
Most home accidents take place in the kitchen, because it is a place full of hazards and a supervising adult can easily become distracted. Taking extra care when cooking or cleaning up can help to prevent unfortunate mishaps.

taking a surprisingly small number of pre-cautionary measures (see box below). At the same time, you should check your home insurance policy to be sure that it covers your valuables sufficiently, and make an inventory of them, including photographs if possible. If something is stolen, you'll have a good record for the insurance company.

MAKE YOUR HOME YOUR CASTLE

Burglaries and other crimes are not the only threats to privacy and security at home. Many types of intrusion can occur, often without a foot being set in the home or any recognised offence being committed. Such intrusions create their own, often equally disturbing stresses, and it helps to build up defences against them. For instance, most of us have suffered from telephone cold calling at inconvenient times or the unwelcome attentions of door-to-door salespeople. Some people are constantly irritated by neighbours who are insensitive (permitting unreasonable noise from cars, motorcycles, stereos, or dogs); inconsiderate (allowing trees, hedges and overgrown plants to encroach on others' property, or taking up too much parking space); or just downright unpleasant (taking every opportunity to voice the smallest grievance in the most aggressive manner). The only way to deal with these intrusions effectively is by being assertive (see page 74). When you give a clear, public definition to your personal space, you may avoid some of the disputes that often occur in daily life.

CRIMES IN THE HOME
Although the media provides lots of scare stories, increasing people's fear of burglary, in reality the likelihood of it happening is small. Figures have been coming down in the US, and are still quite low in the UK.

HOME BURGLARY		
YEAR	UK*	US*
1982	2.1	7.8
1987	2.5	6.2
1992	3.7	4.9

*Percentage of households

PREVENTING BREAK-INS

Most burglaries take place during daylight hours. They increase during the summer, when open doors and windows are an invitation to would-be burglars. The majority of break-ins are not the work of professional criminals but of opportunists taking advantage of someone else's carelessness. Compare this model home with yours to see what you can do to deter casual crime and make your home more burglarproof.

TAKING PRECAUTIONS
A few simple steps can make your home more secure and perhaps prevent a burglary.

Curtains or blinds should be drawn when you are out during the day

A shed should not provide a step up to windows in the house, and ladders and tools should be locked away

Lights should be left on in a downstairs room, as well as the hall and front porch when you go out at night

All windows should have locks

A light by the door makes it difficult for an intruder to gain access unnoticed

The front and back doors should be fitted with a deadlock (a double-cylinder type if there is glass in the door), a safety chain, and peephole

A 'beware of the dog' sign on the gate might deter some prospective intruders

CELEBRATIONS AND ENTERTAINING

Social get-togethers can be sources of great joy, but hosting them puts extra demands on time, energy, and money. Realistic expectations plus careful planning can help to limit the stress.

STRESS-FREE FAMILY GET-TOGETHERS

Tensions between family members and unresolved childhood feuds can come to a head at family reunions. To avoid unpleasant scenes:

▶ *Speak to family and relatives well in advance and ask them to make a real effort to bury the hatchet.*

▶ *If people are travelling long distances to the event, suggest that a 'difficult' family member, who often upsets others, stays in a hotel or with friends rather than in the family home.*

▶ *Try to remain calm if any tensions do arise. Getting upset will only make things worse, and it will spoil the party for everyone.*

Human beings are social animals who like to entertain and be entertained by others. But the process is not effortless. A pleasurable event takes thoughtful planning and preparation by the hosts, and consideration on the part of the guests in giving a prompt answer to an invitation, arriving on time, taking an active but not domineering part in conversation, and leaving at an appropriate time.

Successful party-givers manage to gather a lively blend of guests. A way to do this is to mix people who have interesting things to say with others who are good listeners, and make sure that the company share some interests but not all are in the same line of work (persistent shop talk can make for a very dull event). If a newcomer is included in a group of people who know each other

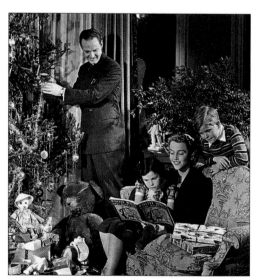

A HAPPY CHRISTMAS?
Christmas is usually a time of family togetherness, but holiday preparations and expectations often put extra stress on relationships.

well, it is considerate to have at least one person there whom the outsider knows or at least has mutual interests with.

If you are reluctant to entertain because of limited time and/or money, consider sharing the hosting duties with friends. Have dinner at one house, and dessert and coffee at another. Or you might want to share the cost of hiring outside caterers, or of taking mutual friends out.

When you see a bargain joint of meat or some other food that you would serve for dinner guests, buy it and put it in the freezer for your next party. The same applies to special offers at a wine merchant. You may save money by preparing food yourself, but if time is limited, it might be better to spend more and include some take-away food in the menu. For whatever you cook, select recipes you can prepare ahead of time, saving the hassle of last-minute preparations.

FAMILY GET-TOGETHERS

Wedding receptions, 18th birthday parties, New Year's Eve and Mother's Day, these are among the special occasions that afford opportunities to be with people you feel close to. But there can be pitfalls. Family members will usually want to participate in the planning and preparations. If there are differing views on who should be invited, what food to serve, what music to play, and so on, diplomacy is called for.

When the event is in your home, you have the right to do it largely your way, but you still need to consider others' suggestions, especially if you expect them to help with the preparations. Encouraging everyone to contribute something will usually be more satisfying than having a perfect combination of foods or exquisite decorations. If any members of your family are feuding, or if there is a relative who often creates confusion or irritates others, you might assign special tasks at the party that will keep them too busy to cause tension. You could perhaps allay your fears by speaking to them ahead of time about your concerns. You may find that they are willing, for the sake of the occasion, to modify their behaviour or perhaps even bury the hatchet.

CHILDREN'S PARTIES

Children's parties present special challenges, but they can be the most rewarding events. As a rule, it is best to limit the number of guests to a few close friends, especially if you live in a flat. However, if your child wants to invite a larger group, consider renting a hall in a church, community centre, or day-care facility, or using a nearby park, and hire a couple of teenagers or ask another parent or two to help out.

Appropriate activities are the keys to a successful party. For preschool-aged children, simple games such as Simon Says, or a treasure hunt for sweets or simple toys are fine. Primary school children usually enjoy memory and guessing games. This is also a good age for an outing to a zoo, ice skating rink, or the cinema.

When planning a party for teenagers, set firm rules about attendance (invited guests only), alcohol (none will be allowed), and music (decibel levels will be limited). It's probably a good idea to notify neighbours of the coming event and tell them what time the party will finish. Be sure to have plenty of food and soft drinks on hand and, if you can, provide some activity, such as ping-pong. Also, plan to be at home. You can help to greet the young people, then retire to another part of the house.

PARTY PLANNING

Be realistic about how long preparations will take. Experience, of course, is the best guide, but if you are planning a large event of a sort you've never done before, consult a friend who has, or consider using a party planner. You may be surprised at how far ahead you must start (see box, page 116).

Break down tasks into manageable units. Consider offers of help, but accept them only from those who can be relied on to do what they promise. Be clear about what you want, how you want it done, and by when.

Passive smoke

Nowadays, an increasing number of people have never smoked or have stopped, and those who continue to do so find that their habit is far less acceptable than it once was. In fact, just as fewer public places allow smoking, many households have banned it altogether.

If you are having a party and you know that a few guests are smokers, you don't have to allow them to pollute your home. However, you don't want to make them feel unwelcome either. A sensible compromise is to tell guests beforehand that you don't allow smoking in your home, and then give them somewhere relatively warm and dry where they can smoke if they want to, such as a garage or conservatory with plenty of ventilation.

STRESS-FREE ENTERTAINING

Some hosts and hostesses are so busy and stressed that they have little time to spend with guests or enjoy the party. These tips may help to make your next social event fun for everyone.

TIPS FOR A SUCCESSFUL PARTY

▶ *Select a theme for an event. Telling guests that you are planning an Italian dinner or come-as-you-are house party sets a mood of anticipation.*

▶ *Keep things simple. The goal should be to put guests at ease and for them to have fun, rather than to impress them with elaborate food and decorations.*

▶ *Allow yourself plenty of time for preparations, so that you are calm when guests arrive. Make a list of everything to be done, see if you can delegate any tasks, and prepare as much as possible in advance.*

▶ *If you are serving alcohol, be sure to offer a reasonable selection of soft drinks as well.*

▶ *Try to remember what you forgot the last time you held a social gathering, and check that you have remembered it this time.*

▶ *Steer guests clear of topics that you know they might strongly disagree upon. Political discussions may be all right for some gatherings but not for others.*

▶ *Feel free to serve some ready-cooked foods. Today, people accept the fact that those who lead busy lives don't have time to prepare every meal from scratch.*

▶ *Serve dishes that you have made and enjoyed before. There is nothing more stressful than trying to cope with a disappointing or failed recipe in front of company.*

A drink or two

Social gatherings often include alcohol, but today many people do not drink. Below are two festive fruit punches, to which you can add alcohol if you choose, or you can serve them as non-alcoholic alternatives.

RASPBERRY FRUIT PUNCH
Mix together in a large bowl 225 g (8 oz) raspberry fruit purée, 3 cups pineapple juice, 2 cups fresh orange juice, 3 tablespoons fresh lemon juice, and 1 tablespoon sugar. If you like, add 2 cups rum.

CITRUS FRUIT PUNCH
Bring to a boil 8 cups water, 1½ cups sugar, 1 teaspoon each ground ginger and cinnamon; simmer for 5 minutes. Add 2 cups fresh orange juice and 1 cup grapefruit juice; stir well. Add 2 cups gin if you like. Decorate with mint and fruit.

How far ahead should you invite guests? If people must make travel plans, three to six months is not too much notice, but the formal invitation may go out six weeks in advance. For a Saturday-night dinner, three weeks' notice is usually sufficient. Many people don't mind being invited at the last moment for casual come-as-you-are events. Sometimes these are the most fun.

Include time in your plans for relaxation before the party begins. You might listen to favourite music, have a soak in the bath, or just spend 15 minutes with your feet up. Or you may want to break away completely, perhaps by going for a walk. Include it in your schedule though, or you may be working on preparations even as guests arrive.

Once the party is under way, concentrate on making the company feel at home rather than fussing over details, and bear in mind that you and your family are responsible for guests for only a few hours, not a lifetime.

A 50TH WEDDING ANNIVERSARY

George and Mavis Brown celebrate their Golden Wedding anniversary in six months' time. Their daughter, Elizabeth, wants to give a big party for family, friends, ex-colleagues, and neighbours. Because she lives in a flat, she has decided the party should be held in the hall that is run by the church her parents attend regularly. Elizabeth and her son, Paul, live some distance from her parents' home, so many of the arrangements will have to be done with the help of others.

THREE MONTHS BEFORE

Make a preliminary booking for the church hall.

Investigate hotels and guesthouses in the area where the out-of-town relatives can stay.

Ask parents for names for invitation list. Buy or make invitations and send them out. Ask people to arrange their own hotel bookings; enclose a list of places.

Book railway tickets for herself and Paul to travel to her parents' home two days before the celebration.

TWO MONTHS BEFORE

Contact Suzanne (an old friend in her home town) for help. Ask her to put together some tapes of music from the era when Elizabeth's parents got married.

Order the cake, deciding with the cake shop on the type, what is to be written on it, the size, and the price. Send a deposit.

Contact one of the women at the church about organising a few others to make coffee and punch and to serve drinks and the cake. Find out if they can provide a punchbowl, coffee maker, and music system. Offer to make a donation to the church fund.

ONE MONTH BEFORE

Hire a photographer to record the event.

Arrange for her parents' wedding photograph to be blown up, for use as part of the decorations.
Order flowers and special anniversary table napkins.

Write lists of the things to buy and do when she arrives in her home town.

Decide what she and Paul are going to wear.

Contact a relative or close family friend and ask him or her to make a speech at the party.

TWO DAYS BEFORE

Travel to her parents' town.

Contact the hall secretary and her friends to make sure that all the arrangements have been carried out.

Arrange for the cake to be delivered to the hall.

Visit the church to check the hall.

Buy decorations for the church hall, and glasses, cups, plates, and cutlery for the refreshments.

ONE DAY BEFORE

Buy a variety of buffet foods and drinks for the party.

Spend the afternoon calling hotels and guesthouses in the area to make sure that all the relatives have arrived safely and that they have organised a way of getting to the hall.

Arrange for one of the relatives to take her parents to the church.

Write out the place cards for the guests.

Arrange for the flowers to be delivered to the hall.

THE DAY OF THE CELEBRATION

Get up early and check list of things to do.

Go to the church, put up decorations, and set up the music system.

Pay for the cake and flowers on delivery and make sure that the tables are set out as planned.

Decorate the tables and set out the buffet and drinks.

Leave enough time for a relaxing bath before changing into party clothes.

Celebrate!

CHAPTER 7

STRESS AT WORK

People under a great deal of stress at work are more likely to suffer injuries and poor mental and physical health. For companies, the consequences of this are absenteeism, high staff turnover, and reduced productivity. Some firms have set up wellness programmes to teach employees how to stay healthy and reduce stress through diet, exercise, and relaxation. In this chapter you'll learn how to spot the signs of job stress and discover ways to cope with it effectively.

IS YOUR JOB MAKING YOU STRESSED?

Job stress is a major adult health problem in the UK. There are many ways to cut down on job stress, but first make sure there is a good match between your personality and your job.

ARE YOU UNDER STRESS? *Work can induce high levels of tension in even the most easygoing people. It can also create stress-related health problems, such as headaches and stomach disorders. There are steps you can take to make even the worst jobs more enjoyable.*

In the wake of increasing competition and big demands on individual performance, employed people everywhere are experiencing rising levels of stress. Job stress takes a heavy toll on industry, and costs thousands of pounds in absenteeism, lost productivity, and work-related accidents. Increasing numbers of workers are winning large compensation claims against their employers for illness and loss of earnings resulting from stress in the workplace.

Job stress is not confined to managers and executives. In fact, it affects workers at all levels regardless of their job title or the amount of responsibility. In a recently completed 10-year study of civil servants, researchers found that men and women in the lowest levels of work, who worked for overbearing and difficult bosses, were three times more likely to become ill than similarly employed workers who had some degree of authority or control over their job.

What is job stress? It is difficult to define, but in essence it occurs when workers have a lot of responsibility but little authority. It's important to remember, however, that what is unbearable stress to one worker is an exciting challenge to another. While some people thrive in a hectic work environment, others feel overwhelmed. It depends on the worker's personality. In fact, most cases of job stress could be avoided if an individual's personality was better matched to the appropriate job. For instance, putting an energetic go-getter on an assembly-line will soon lead to job stress, as would placing a quiet, unassuming person in the role of spokesperson for a high-profile company.

TOP 10 CAUSES OF STRESS AT WORK

In a May 1984 study by *International Management* of over 1000 executives in five countries, work pressures were ranked on a scale of 1 to 10, with 1 as the most stressful. Time pressures and work overload were the most highly rated.

STRESSORS	UK	US	GERMANY	SWEDEN	JAPAN
Time pressures and deadlines	1	2	1	2	1
Work overload	3	1	2	1	2
Too much travel	2	8	7	6	7
Long hours	4	4	3	3	5
Taking work home	7	6	8	4	9
Lack of power and influence	6	3	5	10	8
Keeping up with technology	5	10	10	7	3
Inadequately trained subordinates	9	7	4	5	6
Bad interpersonal relations	8	9	9	8	4
Incompetent boss	10	5	6	9	10

Here are some of the major elements of job stress: inadequate time to complete a job, lack of control or pride over one's work, little recognition or reward for a job well done, unpleasant working conditions, such as noise or overcrowding, not being able to use one's abilities, and a lack of clear objectives or support from management.

Other aspects of job stress have to do with the hours and logistics of the job, such as excessive shift work, long hours, extended periods of monotonous or repetitive tasks, constant change in work patterns, too much work-related travel, and having too much or too little to do.

Job stress typically results from a combination of circumstances that are unique in each industry. A study at an American car production factory, for instance, identified four key factors that led to job stress: a heavy workload, restrictive company rules, conflicts with colleagues and superiors, and having no control or influence on the work being carried out. What appears to upset workers most is the loss of dignity and pride resulting from management's indifference to workers' comfort and satisfaction.

Other frustrations and anxieties are connected to job insecurity. Rumours of layoffs cause job stress, as does talk of one's company transferring employees to another part

Pathway to health

A few simple tips can help make your workday a little more pleasant. If you are desk-bound most of the time, remember to do stretching exercises every hour or so. A five-minute walk around the office every few hours will refresh you for your next task.

Find an aerobic exercise class to go to at lunchtime or right after work. Far from tiring you, such exercise is more likely to invigorate you and relieve mental stress.

Keep your food intake constant from day to day. A regular breakfast and lunch will stop you from feeling lethargic in the afternoon, while skipping breakfast or eating a large lunch will reduce energy levels.

Keep a bottle of mineral water nearby; drinking water will reduce your intake of coffee and tea, which can overstimulate the nervous system.

Do not take your troubles home with you. When you have finished work, try to switch gears. Read a novel on the train ride home or take a route home that will make you feel relaxed. Then enjoy your leisure time.

Perfume for the mind

To stimulate mental alertness, add a few drops of rosemary, basil, or peppermint aromatherapy oil to a piece of damp cotton wool. Place the cotton wool in a saucer or container near a radiator or a patch of sunlight or under your desk lamp – the heat will release the oil's aroma.

MASSAGE IN THE WORKPLACE

Massage is one of the best forms of stress relief, and workers in high-stress jobs are increasingly using it as a way to relieve tensions induced by the pressures of their work. Some Wall Street traders now employ massage therapists who give them neck and shoulder massages at their desks. Take a leaf out of their book and use the simple techniques below to relax you and recharge your batteries at work.

FOR RENEWED ENERGY
Straightening your upper back lifts the rib cage. This expands the capacity of your lungs and increases the amount of oxygen in your bloodstream.

A massage therapist will apply pressure to your back to help release tension in your spine.

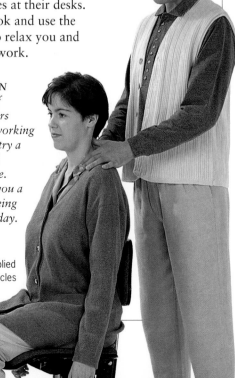

FOR RELAXATION
To help ward off rounded shoulders caused by long working hours at a desk, try a regular neck and shoulder massage. It will also give you a feeling of well-being that will last all day.

Firm, consistent pressure will be applied to taut shoulder muscles by a therapist.

HIGH, MEDIUM, AND LOW-STRESS JOBS

Using a 10-point scale, psychologists at the University of Manchester carried out a general assessment of the degree of stress inherent in a range of occupations.

High stress

Miners	8.3
Police officers	7.7
Construction/ building workers	7.5
Civil airline pilots	7.5
Prison warders	7.5
Journalists	7.5
Advertising executives	7.3
Dentists	7.3
Actors	7.2
Broadcasters	6.8
Firefighters	6.3
Ambulance personnel	6.3
Personnel officers	6.0
Social workers	6.0
Public relations officers	5.8
Lawyers	5.7
Military personnel	4.8
Secretaries	4.7

Medium stress

Photographers	4.6
Pharmacists	4.5
Veterinary surgeons	4.5
Market researchers	4.3
Hairdressers	4.3
Accountants	4.3
Physiotherapists	4.2
Opticians	4.0
Architects	4.0

Low stress

Computer programmers	3.8
Laboratory technicians	3.8
Beauty therapists	3.5
Church personnel	3.5
Bank cashiers	3.3
Nursery teachers	3.3
Biologists	3.0

of the country. Sexual harassment and age discrimination cause a great deal of job stress – a fact that law courts and industrial tribunal panels consider when determining compensation awards.

Stress and different occupations

Stress is very much an individual concept. Some people might describe a demanding job as 'exciting' and 'stimulating' while others would call it 'exhausting' or 'draining'. Researchers have found, however, that certain occupations involve a more or less consistent level of pressure and are able to group all occupations under the broad categories of high, medium, and low-stress (see left). Within these categories, however, it will be both the individual's response to the job and the actual working conditions that will influence personal stress levels. Some people whose job calls for them to face physical danger for which they have been trained and equipped, for example, may have lower stress levels than others in relatively safe occupations.

Other jobs may have certain built-in stresses, such as unpleasant confrontations with the public, but have other pleasant aspects that may often help to offset this. Hairdressers, for example, deal with people all the time, but the job that they are doing is creative and involves touch, two factors that help to counteract stress. Certain occupations, such as that of a market researcher, computer programmer, or bank cashier, consist of routine work, which may be quite skilled but does not involve a lot of decision making. These types of jobs, too, are less stress inducing.

Occupations that usually involve well-established routines and little responsibility, such as factory work, however, are often boring and poorly paid, and provide few real challenges. This lack of pressure may suit those who have a low threshold for stress, or have no interest in establishing a career. To a more ambitious person, such a job may cause intense frustration, and he or she will move on quickly to another job to avoid the stress of repetitive work.

Combating stress at work

Although it is now universally acknowledged that businesses suffer when their employees are under stress, many companies are still reluctant to deal with the problem. This means that people in the workforce, including the growing number of self-employed, must pay serious attention to their own symptoms of too much stress,

WHAT IS THE POTENTIAL STRESS RATING OF YOUR JOB?

A good salary and job satisfaction often involve some work pressures, which may affect your health. To find out your level of job stress, think back over the past three months and check all the questions that apply to you. Add up the points. If you have more than eight points, then you are clearly under pressure at work. If the stress is more than you can handle, then you should consider getting a different type of job, or making changes to the one you have to alleviate some of the stress.

QUESTIONS	SCORE
Is your job poorly paid or insecure?	1
Do you have to work in unpleasant conditions?	1
Are you responsible for the mistakes of others?	1
Are you responsible for your own mistakes?	2
Are the consequences of any errors you make likely to cause financial loss or danger to others?	2
Are you solely responsible for your own workload?	2
Do you have strict deadlines or sales targets to meet?	3
Do you have to work long hours to cope with your workload?	3
Do you have to face arguments or confrontations?	3
Do you have to face dangerous situations?	4
TOTAL	

THE POTENTIAL STRESS IN DIFFERENT OCCUPATIONS

The degree of anxiety you feel in a particular occupation depends not only on the stresses inherent in the work but also on you as an individual. Jobs can be of low, medium, or high stress (see page 120) or only stressful at certain times. Some people would characterise a particular job as pressured or exacting, while others would see the same position as challenging and rewarding. Below are descriptions of six different occupations, together with some of the reasons why they are potentially stressful as well as how they offer satisfaction.

DOCTOR

Although a respected and well-paid profession, the hours can be long and there can be unrealistic demands on the individual. Responsibility for other people's lives, plus the risk of claims for medical negligence, make the job very stressful.

TEACHER

A potentially rewarding job, where there is a high degree of control. However, the level of stress can be very high if you are not supported by your superiors, if your pupils are not motivated, or if there is a lack of resources.

SELF-EMPLOYED WORKER

As long as there is plenty of suitable enjoyable work available, being your own boss can be rewarding. Stress increases when work is scarce, and there is a lack of contact with colleagues which can give rise to feelings of loneliness.

SENIOR EXECUTIVE

Job satisfaction and benefits are high. Working at this level involves taking responsibility for many others, but there is scope for delegating. Stress arises from long work hours, a great deal of travelling, and knowing that mistakes can be costly.

OFFICE MANAGER

Taking responsibility for work done by others can be stressful – poor performance by a subordinate reflects badly on you. But you will have some control over your conditions of work, and you can delegate tasks you dislike.

SALES ASSISTANT

Shop work is often boring and poorly paid, but it is relatively undemanding and carries little responsibility. Dealing with the public can be stressful, but problems can normally be passed on to a manager.

Dentists' dilemma
A study published in the *Journal of Occupational Psychology* in 1978 found that American dentists suffer from high levels of stress. The dentists attribute their high stress levels to the conflict caused by their perceptions of themselves as fulfilling a caring role, and the public's perception of dentists as 'inflictors of pain'.

***PUTTING IT ALL
TOGETHER***
*Consider all aspects of
your personality, as well
as practical matters,
when choosing a career,
and you will lessen your
chances of experiencing
job frustration.*

namely sleeplessness, headaches, stomach problems, or excessive irritability, and develop their own strategies for coping.

The first step to stress reduction is to determine what is really bothering you. Be specific. Vague statements such as 'I hate my job', are not helpful. Analyse what it is about the job that is making you unhappy. One common cause of anxiety at work, for example, is not knowing exactly what is expected of you. If this is true in your case, you might ask your boss or personnel manager for written guidelines and schedules. If the problem is a personality conflict with another worker, try to resolve the problem with the help of the personnel department or a senior staff member. You might even consider a heart-to-heart with the individual involved. Serious worries should always be referred to a more senior member of staff or to your union leader.

Changing jobs

You may find that no matter what you do – talk to your boss, come up with plans to reduce stressful working practices, sort out differences with colleagues – you are still unhappy and tense at work. Often the only answer is to find another, different type of job, one that has the potential to provide

---

TAKING STOCK OF YOUR ABILITIES

Employment consultants conduct interviews and tests to find out what type of work will suit their clients, but you can create your own personal profile. The self-knowledge you will gain may give you an idea of where you would best fit in, or explain why you are not happy in your present job. You can also use the information to construct a CV or to prepare for job interviews or assessments by a consultant. The list below may help you to present your talents, qualifications, leanings, and interests in the best possible light. Read it through, and then write down on a separate piece of paper the statements that apply to each section.

APTITUDES

▶ Verbal: includes the ability to express yourself and to persuade others, and to read carefully and write clearly.

▶ Numerical: ability to calculate with figures and formulas, to understand statistics, and to present them clearly.

▶ Conceptual: includes the ability to construct and follow an argument, and to determine the relationships and sequences within a variety of data.

▶ Practical: level of manual dexterity; ability to plan in two dimensions and to visualise in three dimensions.

▶ Creative ability: attitude toward innovation; ability to arrive at new ideas and concepts; artistic and design sense.

▶ Organisational skills: ability to create order, both mentally and practically; reliability in following tasks through to completion.

▶ Interpersonal skills: ability to coordinate with and influence others.

INTERESTS

▶ Activities that you currently engage in.

▶ Activities you would like to pursue.

▶ Consider how they reflect your personality, and how they relate to and complement your work.

PERSONALITY

Establish your personality type by deciding where you fit between each of these extremes:

▶ Are you sociable or self-contained?

▶ Are you excitable or unemotional?

▶ Are you a leader or a follower?

▶ Are you rigid or flexible?

▶ Are you tough-minded or sensitive?

▶ Are you conforming or independent?

QUALIFICATIONS

▶ Academic qualifications: examinations, degrees, training courses.

▶ Professional attainments: range of tasks you have undertaken, depth of experience gained in each, achievements at work.

ASSESSMENT

Look at what you have written and try to find a single thread that runs through it. You need to see the big picture before you can draw conclusions and limit your job choice and field. For instance, if you find that you describe yourself as independent, methodical, and good with numbers, a career in accounting, or perhaps laboratory work or another scientific endeavour might be worth considering.

fulfilment and stimulation. In today's economic climate, however, it would be unwise to remove yourself from one set of problems only to subject yourself to other stresses, namely, financial insecurity. So make your decision to leave, but do some hard thinking; if possible secure your next job before you say good-bye to what you have.

To find out whether your work is suited to your background and abilities, first complete the questionnaire on the opposite page.

Once you have done this, think about what you want from a job. There are a number of questions to consider. Could you work at a desk job or do you need to be able to get out and meet people? How much travel are you willing to do? Do you want a job that has a path to promotion? How do you feel about responsibility? Do you need to have complete control over your work, for example, managing projects from start to finish? Do you want a job that calls for managing people? Are you comfortable delegating tasks? Do you like to work alone or do you want to be part of a team? Do you like working with the public? Does job satisfaction mean more to you than financial reward? How hard do you want to work?

Also, think hard about the 'package' you would like. Some companies offer more than just a salary, for example, pension and health insurance, as well as in-house training programmes come with many jobs. Consider the type of work environment you feel most comfortable in and the amount of time you want to spend commuting to and from work. Also, think about how much overtime you would be willing to put in.

INTERVIEW SUCCESS

Good preparation gives you confidence, thereby reducing anxiety. Keep the following in mind:

▶ *Read the job description carefully. If there is not enough information, phone the company and ask if further details are available.*

▶ *Find out about the company. Check the financial press or any relevant trade journals. If possible, speak to someone who works (or has worked) there. Secure a company brochure or a catalogue of their products.*

▶ *Prepare a list of questions in anticipation of being asked 'Do you have any questions about the job or the company?'*

▶ *Try visualising the interview (see page 135) the week before it happens. Run through the entire procedure, from the moment you arrive at the company to when you leave.*

▶ *Look the part. Self-expression through clothing is fine, but if you want the job, dress appropriately (see left).*

▶ *Arrive on time!*

▶ *Take along a copy of your CV (in case the original has been mislaid) and, if relevant, samples of your work.*

▶ *You are likely to be asked 'So, why do you think you're suitable for the job?'. Be ready with an answer in terms of work experience, education, relevant interests, and special strengths.*

DRESS THE PART FOR YOUR JOB INTERVIEW

First impressions are crucial, so make sure you are appropriately dressed. If you can, spend five minutes outside your prospective workplace the day before your interview, and observe the people who work there. You will quickly get an idea of the right clothes to wear.

PUBLISHING
An informal, relaxed style of dressing is acceptable; good grooming will ensure you are taken seriously.

Hair should be short, or swept up

FINANCE
Subdued colours and conservative styles are essential.

Neckline needs to be high and unfussy

Scarves and jewellery for women will have a softening effect on businesslike attire

Long hair is acceptable but a good cut is critical

SALES
Crisp, bright colours are good for making you look approachable, but styles should be classic.

Body Language

The way you move – or do not move – can reveal a lot about you. If you learn to use gestures and posture to your advantage, it will boost your confidence and help you cope more effectively with stressful situations, both at home and at work.

STRESS-FREE SITUATIONS

The following tips will help you to negotiate successfully any stressful situation.

▶ *Visualise anxiety-producing events in advance so that you can desensitise yourself to them (see page 135).*

▶ *If you have something important to say, practise it in private first.*

▶ *Breathe deeply and evenly before a particularly stressful encounter.*

▶ *Think positively – negative thoughts will affect the way you speak and hold yourself.*

Most of us use our bodies as aids in communication – just try talking without making any facial expressions or moving your hands. Body language is a powerful method of communicating, and people often make judgments about each other based on it, especially on eye contact, smiles, and frowns.

The most revealing gestures are those that we make deliberately.

When you greet someone, you can let your actions 'speak' your feelings: a vigorous handshake and a shoulder touch tell people you like them.

At interviews you will give a better impression if you walk confidently into the interviewer's office, rather than sidling in. Folding your arms across your stomach is often a defensive gesture whereas avoiding eye contact indicates a lack of confidence.

USING BODY LANGUAGE

If you are aware of the impact your body language has on others, you can use this to great effect, but first you must become aware of any unconscious gestures and learn to control them. Pay close attention to how you respond when you meet a friend. Notice how you move your hands, hold your head, or use facial expressions. Does your body language match what you are trying to say?

GOOD SITTING POSTURE
Sit straight in your chair, with shoulders relaxed and head up.

Fingers should not be used to point; this is seen as aggressive.

Hands should be used to convey and clarify meaning.

BAD SITTING POSTURE
Slouching gives the impression that you have a negative view of the world.

Feet and legs should be close together, not splayed or crossed.

USING PERSONAL SPACE

How near or far people place themselves in relation to you tells you a great deal about how they feel about you. A person who encroaches inappropriately on another's space is seen as threatening, but if someone you consider a friend withdraws too far, you may feel he or she no longer likes you or is trying to distance themselves from you for a particular reason.

Tolerable nearness varies with each individual, and is also influenced by cultural factors. If you are from Latin America, the Middle East, or the Mediterranean region, for example, you may feel comfortable within closer limits than someone from northern Europe.

In this crowded world, people often have to move into the space of others, for instance, during a rush-hour bus or train ride or even standing in line at a supermarket checkout or post office. If you are tired, nervous, anxious, or in a hurry, these ordinary situations can become stressful. To make them less so, keep your arms loosely by your side and avoid eye contact. Try to remain relaxed by finding something restful to focus upon.

HOW CLOSE CAN YOU GET?
Studies have defined four levels of body space that people use in their dealings with others. Each is appropriate for a different level of relationship.

Intimate space is reserved for very close friends, lovers, family 15–46 cm

Personal space is where only friends and close colleagues are tolerated 46 cm–1.2 m

The social zone is for formal relationships and casual acquaintances 1.2 m–3.6 m

The public zone is the province of complete strangers over 3.6 m

READING THE BOSS

To gain important information during meetings, pay attention to the body language of the participants. For example, you may notice your boss touching his or her face a lot. This often demonstrates nervousness. What are the subjects that cause this?

When listening to anxiety-provoking subjects, show as much openness as possible. Sit with your legs uncrossed and lean forward a bit. Using relaxed body language when someone else is anxious or aggressive may help to dispel negative feelings.

NEEDS CONVINCING
Her tilted head indicates interest, but strong arguments are needed to win this boss over.

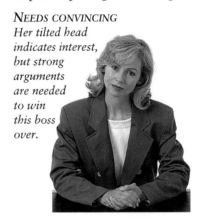

EVALUATING
If your boss is looking at you directly, with his hand on his chin, he is taking your viewpoint seriously.

STALLING FOR TIME
Taking off glasses is a ploy to gain time. Clearly what you have said has made him think.

LET YOUR BODY SPEAK FOR YOU

Many people rely on their reading of another person's body language far more than on the words that are spoken to them. For instance, if the body language of a person conflicts with his or her verbal message, that person is less likely to be believed. By following the tips below, you can influence what your own body reveals to others, and use gestures to make positive rather than negative statements.

BODY PART	DO	DON'T
Head	Keep your chin up.	Look at the floor.
Eyes	Make eye-to-eye contact. Use your eyes when you smile.	Hold eye contact for so long that it becomes a stare.
Mouth	Relax the muscles; tension often shows in the mouth.	Smile constantly, clench your teeth, or keep your jaw rigid.
Shoulders	Hold them down and back slightly. Keep them relaxed.	Hunch over – it's a sign of insecurity.
Hands	Use hands for emphasis, but keep gestures small.	Fiddle, play with rings, crack your knuckles – it indicates nervousness.

THE ENVIRONMENT AND THE WORKPLACE

Most of us spend at least half our waking hours at work. No matter the type of workplace – office, factory, or home – we all benefit if it is as healthy and free of stress as possible.

WORKPLACE STRESS

The physical situation and layout of a building can give rise to stress. Factors that promote it include:

► *Dirty surroundings.*

► *Inadequate or outdated equipment.*

► *Bad lighting.*

► *Uncomfortable room temperature.*

► *Overcrowding and lack of privacy.*

► *Poor hygiene and refreshment facilities.*

► *Noise.*

► *Stuffy, badly ventilated atmosphere.*

► *Inconvenient or dangerous location.*

Medical authorities have come to recognise that people do seem to get sick more often while working in some buildings than in others; this phenomenon has been labelled the 'sick building syndrome' or SBS.

A World Health Organisation committee has estimated that up to 30 per cent of new and remodelled buildings may have some problems relating to air quality. A 1992 report from Britain's own Health and Safety Executive stated that up to 55 per cent of people who worked in air-conditioned buildings could have been adversely affected by poor air quality.

People working in 'sick' offices and factories can develop nose and throat irritation, wheezing, headaches, a feeling of lethargy, and eyestrain. Typically, these symptoms appear at work, and are relieved only when the sufferer gets home.

According to the USA's Environmental Protection Agency, SBS is usually caused by three major factors: air pollution from noxious substances, such as cleaning fluids or pesticides; poorly designed ventilation systems; and problems arising from a building being used for purposes for which it was not intended, as when a residential building is used for commercial purposes. Moreover, in an effort to make buildings more energy efficient, architects have made offices and other workplaces sealed units, so that the heating and air-conditioning systems are out of the employees' control.

To tackle the major causes of SBS, company employees need to present a united front to management, and point out that an unhealthy workforce is much less productive than a healthy one. At the very least, you should ensure that 'no smoking' policies are enforced, and that work environments are free of noxious chemicals. Also, ask for environmentally friendly office and factory supplies; they are becoming cheaper and easier to find.

Studies have found that people who work in an office environment where they can see something of nature, such as trees and water, have higher productivity and lower absenteeism rates than other workers. These findings have brought about changes in

*AN OFFICE OASIS
Well-watered plants on your desk can provide much-needed humidity in an air-conditioned office.*

THE POWER OF PLANTS

NASA scientists working on the US space programme have decided that plants are a sure way of cleaning the atmosphere of an enclosed space such as a space station or an office. The human body exhales the waste product carbon dioxide, which can accumulate in poorly ventilated buildings, causing wheezing, breathlessness, and fatigue in people who work there. Plants, however, absorb carbon dioxide, and convert it to oxygen, which is then released into the air, thereby purifying it.

But plants provide other benefits. For instance, just looking at them is refreshing – a reminder of outdoors and a relief from the office environment. But if you need more than a reminder, go out at lunchtime for some fresh air and rest your eyes on some natural greenery.

THE BENEFIT OF IONISERS

The air you breathe contains electrically charged particles known as ions, mainly created by radiation from the sun and outer space. The ions can be positive or negative and in the 'best' air they are in equilibrium. But storms and pollution encourage a buildup of positive ions, leaving negative ions in short supply, which can make people feel unwell. After the storm has passed, people often feel uplifted, due to the return of negative ions in the atmosphere.

IONISERS
Available as large and small machines, ionisers emit a stream of negative ions, thus improving the balance in the atmosphere.

design: fountains and waterfalls can often be found in the reception areas and atriums of many large new office buildings. If possible, most offices should overlook graceful scenes, such as a pond or flower garden. The movement of water will also reduce the amount of pollution in the air.

FENG SHUI IN THE OFFICE
The Chinese art of feng shui makes the best use of the forces of nature by carefully positioning buildings and the objects that are within them in order to promote health, wealth, and happiness, and business success (see page 106).

OFFICES THAT BREATHE NATURALLY
Today's architects aim to design naturally ventilated structures. Cool air entering a building is warmed by occupants and equipment and moves toward a central atrium where it is drawn up through a wind tower and expelled.

BAD FENG SHUI
A cluttered, untidy and cramped office, with little space and closed windows, obstructs the flow of chi, causing disharmony.

GOOD FENG SHUI
A spacious, tidy office, with carefully placed furniture, channels forces which promote efficiency and harmony within the work environment.

Plants with rounded leaves create good energy and allow it to circulate

Mirrors are said to help distribute good energy

Clutter creates disharmony, so papers should be stored in an orderly manner

Spiky plants create an environment with bad energy

The window should open outwards allowing the maximum amount of chi to enter and circulate in the room

A chair facing away from the door means that the person who sits in it will be blocking the flow of good energy

The telephone should be easily accessible to aid communication

The desk should face the door so that no-one can enter unnoticed and surprise you

Keys to success

Networking – making contact with others in a similar field or work situation through electronic mail or social events – can put you in touch with others in organisations relevant to your work, and also self-employed people who live near you. In addition to the social aspect, you may also find job opportunities or information valuable to your work. Networking can be essential for home workers or those who are training in fields where the technology or area of expertise changes rapidly, such as in educational CD-ROM development.

When the Bank of China built a new office in Hong Kong, opposite the Hong Kong and Shanghai Bank, it was believed to have created bad feng shui for all the surrounding firms. A master of the art of feng shui said that the new building's sharp edges acted like daggers, slicing at neighbouring buildings. The master ordered many design changes so that good feng shui returned and the bank and its neighbours felt secure.

Masters help to provide good feng shui in workplaces by advising on where particular functions should be carried out, how and where desks should be positioned, and how to block the path of bad feng shui by the judicious placing of objects such as plants, mirrors, and goldfish bowls. The masters claim that a properly sited aquarium with goldfish is an effective way of combating negative influences, but only if there is an odd number of fish in the tank.

A SUCCESSFUL HOME OFFICE

Many people dream of being their own boss, leaving behind office politics and having flexible time for themselves and their families. One way to make that dream come true is to work from your home.

Starting a home office is appealing, especially when you think of all the hours you would save if you no longer had to commute. Other advantages include the freedom of choosing your own working hours (as long as your deadlines are met), and wearing clothes that please you, unconstrained by formal dress codes. While many of these benefits can lead to less stress in your life, working at home can create a whole new set of stresses unless you plan carefully.

To ease yourself into working at home you might consider a situation where you work exclusively for a company or client who provides you with all the necessary equipment, such as a computer, modem, and fax machine. Telemarketing is just one example, but the range of occupations is increasing rapidly.

Problems may arise if, instead of doing a full day's work at home, work takes over all of your home life. It is very easy to lose sight of the importance of free time. With most jobs, when you leave the premises, your time is your own. If your office is in your home, there is nothing to stop you from spending every moment of the day working. Even when you are just starting out, it is important for your health and well-being that you allow a reasonable amount of time for yourself to relax and unwind.

Learning how to schedule your workload is essential. Use a calendar to keep track of when work is coming in, how long you think it will take, when you should make an invoice for it, and when you have received payment. Keep careful records. A paper trail of a project completed on time can be a template for the next one. It will also come in handy when you prepare your tax returns.

THE PROS AND CONS OF STARTING A HOME OFFICE

There are many factors to consider when you contemplate working from home. In addition to the listed advantages, tax breaks may be possible. It is a good idea, therefore, to consult an accountant before setting up a business at home.

ADVANTAGES	DISADVANTAGES
▶ *The sense of liberation that comes from being your own boss.*	▶ *You can feel isolated from the world.*
▶ *If you have a variety of clients, any trouble with some may be outweighed by good relationships with others.*	▶ *A lack of contact with people in your field can lead to worries of being out of touch and left behind.*
▶ *The extra flexibility means you can work when you want, and run the odd errand when it suits you. Child care is made easier, and illnesses cause fewer problems.*	▶ *Family and friends can prevent you getting work done, unless you set clear limits.*
▶ *If it is your own concern, it will be satisfying to know that your hard work results directly in cash in your own pocket.*	▶ *Without a clear division between your work life and your personal life, you may find it hard to settle down to work.*
▶ *Not having to commute to work.*	▶ *Work can dry up for no reason, and clients can be slow in paying or default altogether.*
	▶ *Many self-employed people take on too much work, and exhaustion can result.*

Also, because there are a number of tax issues involved when starting a home office, you should consult an accountant or solicitor. And don't overlook such essentials as health insurance and pension plans.

To help you prioritise your work, use time management strategies (see page 133), and have a clear idea of what tasks need to be tackled first. It is also important to communicate with your clients. While nobody likes being told about major setbacks, you should inform clients of important problems, especially if you have solutions.

Despite some negative aspects, there is certainly a future for home office workers, thanks to advances in modern technology. Advocates have high hopes that the benefits of working away from a central office will come to outweigh possible problems.

The stress-free home office

It is important to create a working environment that is conducive to both your health and productivity. Pay special attention to protecting yourself from the distracting noises of the household. Before you start up your home office, talk with your family about the noise factor, and negotiate with them. For instance, music may be played only after certain hours or far away from your office. However, you may have to recognise that there is nothing at all you can do about certain noises, like a dog barking in your neighbour's garden. Consider buying a fan or a machine that makes white noise (see page 143). Locating your home office in a basement or attic may be the answer. Or, if you live in a particularly noisy area, you can soundproof your office.

You should also make sure that your office is well stocked with office supplies. You don't want to have to run out for paper or staples in the middle of an important project – this is not cost effective.

Another skill you will need to acquire is the art of saying no. Family and neighbours will make demands on you once they know you are at home; you will have to be clear about how flexible you can be because, after all, you are working. If you do not set limits early on, you will find yourself getting stressed at yet another interruption.

(see page 133)

BUSINESS PLANS

Business plans are essential if you want to borrow money from a bank to start or expand your business or upgrade your equipment. They will clarify where you are in terms of your career, what you want to do, and how you might go about achieving it. The following are some of the crucial questions you will have to consider when making your business plan.

▶ *What are your products or services?*

▶ *What is your market and what is your place in it?*

▶ *What is the competition like?*

▶ *What progress has your business made over the past three years?*

▶ *How do you see your business developing?*

▶ *What plans have you made to improve or replace your current production or services?*

▶ *What financial goals have you set?*

▶ *What is your financial forecast for next year? For the next five years?*

WELL-BEING FOR HOME OFFICE WORKERS

For those who work at home, it is all too easy to remain with your nose to the grindstone hour after hour. Therefore, if you want to remain sane and healthy, you should make a conscious effort to take a 15-minute coffee or tea break every morning and afternoon and eat a nutritionally balanced lunch. If you use a computer, take regular short breaks and do the stretching and flexing exercises shown on the right.

At least once a day, leave the house, if only to mail a letter. You should take this opportunity to move around, getting some fresh air and a change of scenery, as this will refresh you and keep you mentally alert.

When you take your breaks, turn on your answering machine, and once you have finished for the day, close the door to your office, physically and mentally. Although it can be very difficult, you should make an effort to separate your work life from your home life.

Keep shoulders relaxed throughout

SHOULDER STRETCH
Lift your left arm, and gently bend it back and down. Repeat with your right arm.

ARMS AND FINGERS STRETCH
Lift your arms, with fingers stretched. Using your left hand, touch your right thumb with each fingertip in turn. Repeat.

Keep arms at shoulder height

Computer Work

Many of the physical stresses caused by using a computer, such as bad backs, eyestrain, headaches, and upper limb strains, can be avoided or at least minimised by using a properly designed workstation.

CAREFUL LIGHTING

Good lighting in a work area is essential in order to prevent both eyestrain and headaches, and to enable you to work well.

▶ *Windows and lamps should be to one side of the screen only.*

▶ *If glare from sunlight is a problem, fit vertical blinds to the windows (venetian blinds will focus sunlight into pencil-thin beams).*

▶ *Buy special louvres to counteract the glare from light fixtures.*

Millions of people around the world spend most of their working lives at computer terminals. This has resulted in a widespread increase in the range of occupational illnesses, especially repetitive strain injuries or RSI (see opposite page).

These health problems can be prevented if you take a little time and effort. For instance, you will need to assess such things as the height of your workstation and chair, the placement of your computer terminal, and the position and type of your lights. Additionally, correct sitting positions and special exercises may help ward off strain in your hands, arms, and shoulders.

SETTING UP THE IDEAL WORKSTATION

To work efficiently and comfortably, you should be able to make adjustments to your desk, chair, and computer screen to suit your height, build, weight, and arm positions.

Your screen image should be stable, with no flicker

Your chin should be tucked in

A wrist rest will prevent you straining your wrist

Your shoulders should be relaxed

Your screen should be adjustable by tilting it up or down, or moving it to the left or right to reduce glare

Your backrest, at belt level, will give support to your lower back

Your desk should be sufficiently low so that your computer screen is at eye level. If you can't lower your desk, raise your monitor by placing it on top of your computer

Your knees should be bent at right angles

Your chair should be fully adjustable and allow forearms to be horizontal when using the keyboard

A footrest will assist your circulation if you cannot keep your feet flat on the floor

PROTECTING YOUR EYESIGHT

Working on a computer does not in itself harm the eyes; however, many people who do intensive work using a computer screen often report having problems with their eyes. Because of this, it makes good sense for anyone who is contemplating or already working on a computer to have his or her eyes examined at regular intervals.

The heat generated by a computer can make the surrounding atmosphere so dry that wearing contact lenses can become difficult for some people. Additionally, computer users tend not to blink as much as other workers, which can also make eyes feel dry. Blinking more often and using eyedrops can help.

Strained eyes can redden, water, or cause headaches. Alleviate such symptoms by exercising your eye muscles. Focus on a spot far away, if possible through a window to the horizon. Next focus on a spot a few feet from you, and then look at something close, like the tip of your nose. Reverse the process, and do the exercise whenever you can. Two more useful eye exercises you can try are illustrated below.

RESTING THE EYES
Cover your closed eyes with your cupped hands for five to 10 minutes, concentrating on pleasant and restful thoughts. Do not let your cupped hands touch your eyes.

NEAR AND FAR FOCUSING
To exercise the eye muscles, focus on each of two pencils in turn, one 15 cm (6 in) from your nose, the other at arm's length. Repeat 10 to 12 times.

REPETITIVE STRAIN INJURY (RSI)

This is an umbrella term that covers various injuries of the hands, arms, and shoulders caused by repeated movements. Some examples are carpal tunnel syndrome (compression of a nerve within the wrist) and tenosynovitis (inflammation of a sheath that covers a tendon).

Repetitive strain injuries can strike anyone who does work that requires excessive hand movement, such as assembly-line workers, musicians, typists, meat packers, and chicken pluckers.

RSI usually starts with a tingling in or numbness of the affected part of the body, or a slight pain that goes away at night but returns when the individual starts to work. If nothing is done, the pain gets worse until it prevents virtually all use of the hand, wrist, arm, or shoulder. This aggravated condition may last for months. If you suspect you have RSI, seek medical treatment immediately.

PLAYING THE VIOLIN
Any activity that involves constant repetitive motions has the capacity to cause RSI.

Learn to relax wrists, neck, and shoulders to prevent RSI

STRESS-BEATERS FOR YOUR MIND AND BODY

Follow these tips to avoid some of the mental and physical strains that commonly arise during work.

▶ *Take regular breaks from your work. Experts recommend taking one every hour, for 5 to 10 minutes; they believe that frequent, short breaks are better than longer, less frequent ones. If your boss objects to you taking a break, then do a completely different type of work at these times.*

▶ *Avoid holding yourself in static, awkward positions for long periods, and adopt a relaxed position whenever possible. Stretch and flex your hands, arms, shoulders, and neck regularly.*

▶ *Keyboard operators should consider using a padded wrist rest, and look into getting an anti-RSI keyboard (one that is split into two parts so that the hands can be held in less strained positions).*

131

MANAGING THE JOB

Too much to do and too little time to do it in – this is a sure recipe for job-induced stress. But an enormous amount of frustration can be avoided by managing time and people wisely.

TIME MANAGEMENT
Sensible scheduling of your time is the key to working efficiently and cutting out unnecessary stress.

KEEPING INFORMED
You will work better if you communicate well with colleagues both above and below your job level.

Stress-management experts have identified four qualities in those people who cope best with a difficult work situation: commitment to chosen tasks, viewing problems as challenges rather than difficulties, believing in one's competence to cope in any crisis, and positively welcoming change. You can reduce a large amount of the work pressure you face by altering your attitudes toward your job to match these qualities, but more important you can also adopt certain practical measures to make your working life easier.

Some common stress factors at work are time related, for instance, setting unrealistic targets and therefore missing deadlines. Others are people related – disagreements with your colleagues or differences with your boss, for example. By tackling these two areas alone, you could transform what might be a runaway disaster into a controlled, fulfilling experience.

COMMUNICATION

In one study, it was discovered that 48 per cent of industrial employees were unsure of their responsibilities. The researchers attributed this to a lack of proper communication with their superiors. These employees also derived less satisfaction from their jobs than those who felt they understood what was expected of them.

A lack of communication can happen anywhere within a company hierarchy. For a business to achieve its goals, those in possession of needed information must pass it on to others, whether superior or subordinate in the work situation.

Managers are responsible for providing essential data and assigning achievable goals to their subordinates. If you find that you are not being given the information you need by your superiors, try suggesting regular meetings, with a circulation of memos

and minutes. Meetings help keep everyone informed of developments and can provide opportunities to define roles and assign tasks. They can also provide open forums to discuss problems. A newsletter and bulletin board can also make developments public.

Asking for help and saying no

Many people hate asking for help; they believe it implies that they cannot cope, but requesting help does not need to be embarrassing. In fact, your status in the eyes of your colleagues can be enhanced by how you enlist help. Often, the person being asked feels flattered, as your request indicates a belief in his or her abilities. And it is productive, since you do not waste a lot of time struggling on your own. A well-timed request for assistance can nip a potential problem in the bud.

The same sort of beneficial response can be gained by learning how to say no constructively. The art of refusing to take on extra work, while avoiding being seen as 'difficult', is one that demands a certain amount of skill. The best method is to decline the proposal gracefully but then to offer an alternative solution.

PLANNING AHEAD

When looking at the weeks and months ahead, pencil in about 10 per cent of your schedule as free time, so that you can cope with extra tasks that may arise. If there are things that your daily routine currently does not allow for – like impromptu meetings – make time by marking off hours or days in your diary. You should do the same for leisure activities; they are just as important as work. Also, inform those you work with of their deadlines well in advance so that they can manage their time effectively and avoid the need for asking for extensions to complete their tasks.

Setting priorities is another key to time management. It may be pleasant to discuss matters face-to-face with your clients, but is the time-consuming travel involved really worth it? Can the subject be discussed on the telephone? It may be valuable to attend a seminar, but will it fit into your schedule? Are other matters more pressing?

Organising daily tasks

Set aside some time first thing in the morning to plan your day. List the things that you want to achieve by the evening. Look at them in terms of how much time they will take and how much time you have, and decide what you can reasonably accomplish during the working day. Those jobs that must be carried out should be assigned a high priority and done at the earliest opportunity. If you see that there are too many tasks to do in one day, determine which are less urgent and tackle them later, or delegate them to a subordinate.

Schedule big or important jobs for times when you are most likely to feel fresh and energetic. (You can do less vital jobs at other times.) For example, if you are a morning person who often feels sleepy after lunch, then get your most difficult tasks over with early in the day. Save routine jobs such as filing or making phone calls for your afternoon slump time. If possible, intersperse boring or tiring jobs with interesting or easy ones.

As often as you can, complete each task before going on to the next one. Similarly, you should not avoid making decisions; unresolved problems are a source of tension. To aid your concentration, you should remove all papers from your desk except those that refer to the task at hand – you do not want to remind yourself of all the other things that need to be done.

Managing people

Even when you have learned to manage your time and have control of your workload, you still need to learn how to manage your boss, colleagues, and subordinates. Learning to get the most out of your co-workers will make your job easier and much more rewarding.

Bad working relationships increase stress and real efforts should be made to repair them. If you allow extra time for talking through problems with colleagues, you may improve matters. Good relationships provide tremendous support and confidence and should be nurtured. Looking after work relationships – both good and bad ones – is hard work and can be time consuming.

To get your work done you may need to 'train' others to stop wasting your time. For although you may be well disciplined and hardworking, others may not be. These people can steal time from you, either by distracting you with their problems or just by stopping by to talk.

One way is to convince inconvenient visitors that meeting them at another time would be of mutual benefit to you both. Dealing with 'chatterers', who can be the bane of any office, requires courtesy and resolve. Politely say you do not have time to talk now, but you will get back to them. Then get on with some work. If they keep talking, pick up the telephone and make a call (it does not matter to whom); they will not hang around long. So that you do not hurt their feelings, make time to talk when it is more convenient.

TIME MANAGEMENT

If you arrive at work early, leave late, and still take work home, you are likely, if it goes on for too long, to become stressed out. This could lead to a physical illness, a mental breakdown, or total burnout. Learning to manage time correctly can help you avoid these problems.

▶ *Organise your timetable well ahead. If certain events such as meetings are a regular thing, record them weeks or months ahead in your diary.*

▶ *Allow space between projects in case they take longer than expected, and to give yourself time to recover physically and psychologically.*

▶ *If your work piles up, ask your boss to remove or reschedule something from your workload.*

▶ *You could also suggest that it would be possible for you to do the job, but only with additional time or resources. Or you could nominate someone else who has a particular interest in that area. At all times, you should emphasise that you do not want to risk jeopardising the work you have in progress.*

Tasks to do:

'TO DO' LIST
Write down all the tasks you must complete and by when, and keep an ordered account of the point you have reached during the day.

Public Speaking

There are numerous techniques and skills you can acquire to achieve clear, impressive, and successful presentations without any visible signs of nervousness. If you take the time to practise these simple skills, it will be time well spent.

MARTIN LUTHER KING
The greatest public speakers often strike a chord with their audiences by sharing personal experiences.

For most of us, the mere thought of giving a speech is enough to cause numerous symptoms of stress. Instead of running from the anxiety, channel that adrenaline into preparing your speech. Good preparation and a lot of practise are the keys to more confident and competent speech making.

In order to ensure a smooth presentation, you should do the following. Be sure that you cover all the necessary points in your speech. Rewrite any difficult or untidy phrases – you don't want to appear to stumble over your words. Your cards or notes must be legible and in order; if they're not, rewrite and reorganise them. Check that all your visual aids are working; slides or charts should be correctly positioned.

BE YOUR OWN AUDIENCE

If you go through your presentation in front of a mirror you may soon see certain areas of your approach that others could find distracting. Do you slouch, or lean to one side? Do you scratch your chin too often, or frown, or sniff, or stumble over a particular phrase? Do your clothes hang untidily? Are these aspects that need to be worked on, or are they slight enough to be ignored?

GOLDEN RULES OF PUBLIC SPEAKING

For a successful presentation, follow the three golden rules of public speaking, devised by Dale Carnegie, author of the classic book *The Quick and Easy Way to Effective Speaking.*

▶ *Tell them what you are going to talk about (give a brief overview of what your talk is about).*
▶ *Tell them (give your speech).*
▶ *Tell them what you told them (summarise the key points).*

USING PROMPTS
Practising often enough will help you memorise most of what you want to say so that you can use your cue cards solely as prompts.

Compose your face to look relaxed and comfortable

Stand up straight, but do not tense your shoulders or neck

A POINTER
Use your hands to draw attention to your visual aids or to underline certain statements.

A COMMUNICATOR
An open hand is very reassuring and it also indicates trust, reason, and simplicity.

SPEAKING IN PUBLIC

Try to talk on a subject you know well or one you feel comfortable with. Knowing your material well is essential to building your confidence.

Some people find public speaking much easier if they are talking on behalf of others, such as their company or fellow employees, and not about themselves. Always keep your audience in mind. The majority of speeches are designed to pass on information, so be sure you know who your audience is and their information needs.

BREATHING EXERCISES

Stressful situations can cause breathing to become fast and shallow, making effective speaking all but impossible. To combat this, do these breathing exercises a few minutes before your speech. They will help you to relax and to keep your breathing steady and even throughout.

INHALING
Place your right hand index and middle fingers on your forehead. Close your left nostril with your ring finger. Inhale through your right nostril.

When giving a speech, maintain eye contact with your audience. Note cards are useful, but be sure that they are in order. Visual aids like charts, slides, and overhead projectors relieve you of some of the attention, but too many images can be confusing and too much equipment can be distracting.

For good voice projection, practise speaking slightly louder than usual, but do not shout. Talk at a slower pace so your audience can follow you more easily.

EXHALING
Release your left nostril and close your right nostril with your thumb. Exhale through the left nostril. Repeat the sequence.

VISUALISING SUCCESS

Visualisation involves making a mental movie of all the various steps involved in a potentially stressful task (see page 41). The goal is to imagine all the steps being performed perfectly. Many athletes use visualisation to prepare for competition, but it can be tailored to help in any situation. In one sense, visualisation offers you the chance of a dress rehearsal where no one will spot any mistakes except you. At the same time, a positive vision can give you the confidence to take things further. If you visualise your audience enjoying your speech, for instance, it may help you over an

awkward moment in your speech. Here are some guidelines for using visualisation.

▶ *Sit in a comfortable position in a place free of noise and distractions; shut your eyes and relax. See yourself breathing deeply and evenly.*

▶ *Imagine yourself standing in front of your audience. In your mind's eye, try to see as many details as possible. If there will be people that you know and like, concentrate on them.*

▶ *Imagine successfully giving your speech. See the audience enjoying it, and feel your own pleasure at how well you did.*

▶ *Repeat the process until you feel completely confident.*

PREVENTING ANXIETY

Some people become acutely anxious when asked to give a public presentation, and suffer from excessive blushing, rapid heartbeat, shaky legs and hands, and tightness in the chest. Stress-reduction techniques can help to relieve these symptoms.

Behaviour therapy can sometimes also help allay the fear of public speaking. Here, anxious people are first taught relaxation techniques and then encouraged to use them while imagining what they most fear: giving a speech. Once they gain confidence, therapists urge their clients to give a real speech.

Homeopathy can provide treatment for acute anxiety. A homeopath may prescribe *Gelsemium*, a remedy derived from the yellow jasmine. Among the symptoms it is said to relieve are nervousness, fears and phobias accompanied by trembling and the need to pass urine, and the inability to sleep because of excitement.

TREATING ANXIETY

For severe anxiety attacks, your doctor may prescribe a beta-blocker, a drug that blocks some of the effects of adrenaline. It can be taken for a very brief time, but it is not suitable for asthmatics. Tranquillisers can also be prescribed for relief from anxiety.

POISON IVY
A remedy made from Rhus toxicodendron, *a North American species of poison ivy, is used by homeopaths to calm nerves, ease restlessness, and reduce irritability.*

WORK UPHEAVALS

A job provides an income, status, and often a social life. Unless handled skilfully, taking a leave of absence or losing a job can upset your financial security and sense of purpose.

Most men and an increasing number of women spend a great proportion of their waking lives at work. (Almost 100 000 hours if you start at the age of 18 and retire at 65.) Studies have shown that people who have supportive relationships at work are less anxious, less depressed, and ill less often than those who do not work or have no similar supportive relationships. How then does loss of work affect people? Does it matter if the decision not to work was made by the worker?

MATERNITY LEAVE

More and more women are going back to work after having a baby. For many it is not an option; they have to work to support their families. Other women, who are more financially secure but committed to their careers, are faced with a dizzying array of child-care choices (see page 94). In the UK a woman is entitled to a minimum of 14 weeks maternity leave whether employed full or part time. If she has worked for the same firm for at least two years up to 15 weeks before the baby is due she is entitled to 40 weeks leave. If she returns to work within six months of the birth her employer must give her her old job back or offer a comparable one. Many women are also entitled to 18 weeks Statutory Maternity Pay (SMP). The amount received depends on current salary. Those who do not qualify for SMP (including the self-employed) may be entitled to Maternity Allowance.

Having a baby is a major milestone that affects every facet of your life. For a start, there is the physical ordeal of giving birth and caring for a newborn. There is also the emotional impact a baby can have on a marriage and other family members. Finally, there are the added financial concerns of raising a child and paying for child care. Taking care of a newborn in the first few weeks requires tremendous stamina. For many new mothers, the world of work is all but forgotten in the joy of their new duties. To others, working is sorely missed.

TO RETURN TO WORK OR QUIT

Ideally, before the birth of a child, mothers and fathers need to assess their priorities. Can the family get by on a single income? Does the mother want to take time off from her career to care for the child? Does the father? Would her company let her work part time? Would his? What type of child care do they want? Is there good day care nearby? Before parents answer any of these questions they need to consider how stressful their work is. If the mother's job calls for long hours and lots of deadlines, then caring for a new baby will add a great deal to the family's already high stress levels. This is especially true if the baby needs special attention because of a health problem. It might be wise to ask for less taxing assignments for the first few months after returning to work. If the mother's job is fairly low-key, then managing a new baby, even a difficult one, will be easier. The important thing is to get as much support as possible from your family and employer. Taking care of an infant is very hard work. Ask for help before the stress gets too high.

Choosing when to return to work can be difficult. Most experts advise new mothers to wait until they feel securely 'bonded', that is attached to their baby. Bonding is a mysterious process. For some mothers it occurs at the moment of birth, for others it takes a little longer.

STAYING AT HOME

Most women usually feel guilty about working instead of remaining at home and taking care of their children. Planning can help to ease a woman's return to work and

PARENTS AT WORK Working while caring for young children demands organisation and determination. When managed well, it can be beneficial to everyone.

ensure that both the baby's and mother's needs are met. Do not overestimate your capacity to perform logistical miracles; keep in mind your own personal needs as well as those of your child. Consider joining a group of other mothers to share problems and discover solutions. Negotiate with your partner so that housekeeping duties can be divided equally.

It is reassuring for parents to know that, according to research, the children of working mothers grow up to be confident and well adjusted as long as their parents give them love and attention at predictable times and leave them in charge of carers who make them feel secure.

Some women choose to stay at home full time so they have more time and energy for their families. Some choose to wait until they feel that their children are old enough

LEADING WORK-RELATED DISEASES AND ILLNESSES

According to a study by P.L. Bolakoff in *Issues and Trends in Health*, the greater number of work-related diseases and injuries arise from blue collar jobs, but there has been an increasing shift to white collar stress-related disorders. Work-related disorders include:

▶ *Occupational lung diseases: asbestosis, byssinosis, silicosis, pneumoconiosis (coal workers), lung cancer, occupational asthma.*

▶ *Musculoskeletal injuries: disorders of back, trunk, upper and lower extremities, neck, injury-induced Raynaud's phenomenon.*

▶ *Occupational cancers (other than lung): leukaemia, cancers of nose, liver, and bladder.*

▶ *Amputations, fractures, eye loss, lacerations, and fatal injuries.*

▶ *Cardiovascular diseases: hypertension, coronary artery disease, heart attacks.*

▶ *Disorders of reproduction: infertility, miscarriages, birth defects.*

▶ *Neurotoxic (nerve poisoning): peripheral neuropathy, psychoses, extreme personality changes related to toxic exposure.*

▶ *Noise-induced hearing loss.*

▶ *Dermatological (skin) conditions: scalds, dermatoses, chemical burns, contusions.*

▶ *Psychological: neuroses, personality disorders, alcoholism, drug dependency.*

to manage without them. For these women, being out of touch with the working world can be stressful. Self-esteem issues can arise, especially if the woman defined herself by her job. Joining a mother's group is a good way to off-load that stress. If possible, arrange to have a sitter for a few hours each day or week. This will give you some time to yourself and allow the baby to learn how to interact with others.

RETIREMENT

After even a few years of hard work, the idea of endless free time for yourself can be very appealing. For many, however, retirement is the long-awaited reward for the years spent working. As with any major life change there are a number of stressful issues to resolve. Decision making is in itself always stressful, and when it comes to one's retirement, there are a great many to make, such as when you want to retire (this is the first and perhaps the most difficult decision), where you want to live, and finally, how you will live.

The key to successful retirement is financial planning. The quality of your retired life will depend to a large extent on how much income you have, and that will depend on what provisions you have made regarding your pension and investments. Ideally, financial planning for retirement should begin years before you leave work. If financial arrangements are left too late, your income may be severely limited. This may require a deep cut in spending or perhaps a move to a smaller, more economical home.

Before you leave the routines of employment behind, it is important to think about what you want to do, if anything, during your retirement. One of the great benefits of retirement is the flexibility it offers, allowing people to take advantage of off-season travel, good weather, special treats that crop up unexpectedly, or simply having time to sit and think. For some retired people, however, the idea of unstructured time can be very unsettling and stressful. If you are worried about how you will spend your days, make a list of each day's activities and note the time to be spent on various jobs around the house, sporting events, or volunteer work. Keeping a calendar simulates old work habits and can make the transition to retirement easier.

continued on page 140

KEEPING WELL AT HOME

Many people let good health habits slide when they are not working, leaving themselves open to illness. Use these strategies to help you to maintain yourself physically and mentally.

▶ *Avoid living on a diet of convenience foods.*

▶ *Use the extra time you have to shop carefully, choosing the freshest fruit and vegetables and the leanest meat you can find.*

▶ *Take vitamin and mineral supplements, if necessary.*

▶ *Take a brisk 20-minute walk each day – it's good for the heart and for the circulation.*

An Out-of-Work Executive

Losing your job can be devastating. The emotion it generates is often compared with bereavement. People who have been laid off report feeling a loss of self-worth. Some see it as shameful and blame themselves. Others are hardier and use their time while unemployed to finish personal projects and explore new and different types of work.

Tom is a 50-year-old executive who has worked for an international computer company for the past 20 years. He is European manager in charge of marketing and runs a staff of 15. His job is very demanding: it requires long hours and a great deal of international travel.

Eighteen months ago his company merged with another computer company and Tom lost over half his team. His remaining staff were put under pressure to maintain the group's output. Morale plummeted. Tom felt he had let his staff down and buried his guilt in the job. He felt compelled to work harder and increased his time on the road. To ease some of the pressure he felt, he began to eat more – usually unhealthy foods. He started smoking again and his alcohol consumption also increased.

Within a few months, Tom's health started to suffer. He began to have difficulty sleeping and complained of headaches, chest pains, and a constant stomach upset. A medical examination revealed that he had both high blood pressure and high cholesterol levels.

His home life was also affected by the strain. Except for the few weekends when he was not overseas on business, he rarely saw his wife Jean or his two sons, aged 12 and 15. Jean, who also worked, had to take on his parenting duties, which caused even more strain in the marriage.

Three months ago, the school psychologist called to say that their younger son was becoming argumentative in class and bullying the younger children in the playground, and urged he be given counselling.

Last week Tom returned from a long trip overseas and learned that his job was to go and his remaining staff were to be laid off – 'effective immediately'. He was completely devastated by the news.

FAMILY

Parents' anxieties can be transferred to their children, who then feel insecure about their own lives. These worries can lead to behavioural and psychosomatic problems.

EMOTIONAL HEALTH

Being laid off can bring on self-doubt, just when you need confidence to begin reassessing your skills and abilities.

CAREER

It is common for both partners in a marriage to have careers. Often, too little consideration is given to the conflicts of interest this can sometimes cause.

FINANCES
Job loss inevitably brings anxiety over finances, especially if you have a family. Advice from financial experts is essential at this stage.

HEALTH

A demanding job, combined with insecurity about employment, can be dangerous to health.

WHAT SHOULD TOM DO?

Tom is in a state of shock and must not make any quick decisions. His company has hired an outplacement firm to help Tom and his staff cope with the dual tasks of dealing with the loss of their jobs and help them look for new ones. It is important that Tom make an appointment with the outplacement counsellor immediately. He would also gain some peace of mind if he talked to a financial adviser and found out how much his being laid off will affect his family's material security.

Jean's views and suggestions should also be considered. Tom needs to recognise that she, too, has suffered from the demands of his career, and that it has taken a heavy toll on their family life.

Tom must try to understand how much his self-esteem is linked to his job, rather than to an inner sense of worth. Instead of viewing being laid off as a tragedy, he could see it as an opportunity to escape from a highly demanding way of life and begin to consider his family's needs and his own well-being.

He also needs to consider some activities, not connected with work, that will build his self-esteem, such as sports or volunteer work. Once he pays some attention to his health, peace of mind, and the happiness of Jean and his sons, he and his family will be able to get back on track.

Action Plan

FAMILY
Recognise that neglect of your family can often lead to tension in a marriage and to problem children. To foster family togetherness, set aside certain evenings in the week for family-only activities.

EMOTIONAL HEALTH
Accept that employment with lower status can be just as fulfilling as a high-pressure job, especially if your personal life is given greater emphasis.

CAREER
Visit head hunters and employment agencies to discuss chances of finding new employment. Be clear about what you want from your new job, for instance, working shorter hours. Explore the possibility of becoming self-employed.

HEALTH
Start regular exercise, reduce alcohol consumption, and eat a healthier diet to reduce blood pressure and cholesterol levels. Ask family doctor, or family and friends, for ideas for beating insomnia and giving up smoking.

FINANCES
Visit a financial adviser. Discuss the implication of living on a reduced income for both the short and long term. Find out if any grants are available for retraining, or for setting up your own small business.

HOW THINGS TURNED OUT FOR TOM

Tom had four sessions with the outplacement counsellor, and many discussions with Jean. At first he was too anxious to focus on anything, and Jean suggested he join a group of unemployed workers who met at the social club once a week.

Over time he realised that he had never considered whether he actually liked his job. He discovered he enjoyed marketing computers, but he hated all the travelling. His financial adviser pointed out that with his redundancy package and his wife's income, he was financially secure for at least a year. After considering a number of options, he decided to go into partnership with one of his laid-off staff members. They set up a computer consultancy, and soon had their first client. Initially, they worked from Tom's home. This meant Tom could be flexible with his working hours and see more of his sons and his wife.

Although Tom now earns a lot less than previously (partly because he sometimes turns work down), his health has improved considerably. His headaches and chest pains have stopped, and he realises that they were directly related to all the stresses of his old job.

Tom now enjoys his life and gets immense satisfaction from volunteering at a local charity. He is determined never to allow work to dominate his life again.

Yin and yang balls
Made in China for many hundreds of years, these metal balls are thought to promote good health and a feeling of well-being. They are hollow, and give off a high or low-pitched ringing sound when rotated in the hand. They are available in a variety of sizes, and as you become practised at manipulating them, you may progress to larger ones, or put three or four in the palm of your hand at the same time.

STIMULATING YOUR ACUPRESSURE POINTS
Using one hand at a time, move and stretch all your fingers in sequence to make the balls revolve in your palms. This will stimulate acupressure points connected to vital organs, which, it is said, will help relieve fatigue and reduce anxiety.

Conflicts at home

Retiring usually means spending more time at home. This can be especially stressful if your partner considers the home his or her domain. Retired people in this situation worry that they will suddenly be under the feet of their partners who, until now, have regarded the home as their own kingdom.

It is important to come to some workable arrangement so that your retirement is not marred by your partner's conflicts with your new lifestyle. If your home is large enough, perhaps you could mark out your own 'territories'. Or you might try sitting down once a week and planning the following seven days so that your partner knows when you will be out of the house and can get on with some of the routine tasks he or she used to do alone.

SUDDEN UNEMPLOYMENT

While people can plan for retirement and the positive as well as negative stresses it engenders, finding out that you have been laid off or being forced to take early retirement usually comes as a shock.

These days layoffs or forced retirements are usually the result of a economic problems or poor management and not anything an employee might or might not have done. Still, human nature dictates that even if you are one of those who are laid off, it is common to think that you are responsible for your unemployment and blame yourself. By incorrectly taking on the responsibility of your job loss you gain a sense of control over the event, but the price is very high, for you are often left with feelings of despair and self-loathing.

Self-blame is debilitating and cuts away at your self-esteem. For this reason alone, counselling is a good idea. Your company may have hired the services of an outplacement firm to help those recently laid off to find other work. Be sure to take advantage of this service. Also consider joining a 'job club' to share information with other unemployed workers.

If you have been in the same job for some time, you will probably need to hone your interviewing skills (see page 123). You will also need to learn how to write an effective CV (see page 122). It's a good idea to create two CVs – one should be chronological for job agencies to review, the other organised around your skills. The latter is particularly useful if you are returning to work after a long absence.

While you are looking for work, you should get in touch with any financial institutions to whom you owe money – most will be sympathetic to your plight. By doing this early on, you may be able to reschedule loan and mortgage payments while you look for employment.

Try to take each day as it comes. Don't let any job rejections discourage you from your goals. Use your free hours to learn new skills. If you have always wanted to change careers, take this opportunity to retrain. Or you could use your spare time to help others by doing volunteer work.

One easy way to earn money and discover whether you are interested in pursuing a new line of work is to register with a temp agency. You can request to work only in industries of your choice.

Some of these agencies offer training in certain skills, such as word processing or bookkeeping, which will help boost your marketability. Temporary employment is an excellent way to supplement fixed incomes with extra money and get a glimpse at how different businesses work. The retired are finding that temporary work meets a number of their needs. They can choose to work when and where they want, keep a hand in the business world, meet new people, stay active, and earn extra income too.

Pathway to health

There are a number of things to try at home to maintain a positive mental attitude when coping with a change in your work status.

To improve your concentration and ease tension, consider taking a class in yoga (see page 56) or tai chi (see page 36).

Try visualising (see pages 41 and 147). Not only will it refresh you from the stresses of suddenly being at home, but you can also use it to help you achieve new goals.

Be kind to yourself, and set aside time each day to devote to your needs. Practise meditation (see page 42) or simply indulge in a soothing bath with aromatic essential oils (see page 68).

CHAPTER 8

STRESS AND THE ENVIRONMENT

*The frantic pace of modern living can
keep stress levels at a fevered pitch. Add to
that an ever-increasing rate of crime and the world's
troubles brought every day into our homes through
the media, and the fight to reduce stress may seem
hopeless. But there are a wealth of strategies
available to help deal with everyday life.
In this chapter, you'll find helpful tips
to reduce your level of stress.*

THE WIDER WORLD

Noise, bad weather, pollution, natural disasters – all of these environmental factors create stress, but you can mitigate some of their effects by taking simple, commonsense precautions.

How noise can damage hearing

Sound vibrations funnel into the outer ear and then are registered by the cochlea in the inner ear. The cochlea, a tiny organ shaped like a snail's shell, is lined with some 20 000 groups of delicate hairs that move in response to sound vibrations. This movement is picked up by the auditory nerve, which then conveys the information to the brain. Impaired hearing, even total deafness, can result when sounds are too intense and damage the hairs lining the cochlea.

AVOIDING LOUD NOISE Whenever possible, steer clear of places where there is a sustained high volume of noise, such as on a building site where drills are in use.

People have always been at the mercy of political and social change as well as threats from the natural world around them. But today, the plethora of noisy vehicles and machines, industrial water and air pollution, coupled with the sheer pace of modern life, contributes to keeping stress levels very high. Add to these the barrage of worldwide wars and disasters, and it seems that people in contemporary society are subject to more stress-inducing situations than those in many previous ages.

ENVIRONMENTAL FACTORS

Sometimes the impact of the environment on the health of the body's systems is obvious. For example, we now recognise that there are direct links between asbestos and lung disease, and between air pollution and asthma attacks. But the effects of high noise levels seem to be more insidious and take place over a longer period of time.

In the Western world, where many older people show significant hearing loss, it has long been assumed that the decline in the ability to hear was a normal result of ageing. But evidence for the contrary has been provided by studies of several preindustrial tribes, such as the bushmen of southern Africa, whose old people show no appreciable loss of hearing. Excessive noise in the modern industrial world is taking its toll. In 1991, scientists at the Harvard Medical School wrote that 'a significant amount of hearing loss may be a consequence of a lifetime of exposure to noise rather than an inevitable by-product of growing older'. If what they say is true, it makes sense to take

DECIBEL VALUES

Around 80 decibels is the maximum safe limit for hearing (about 130 causes pain in most people). Rock concert music can reach 120 decibels, but sustained noise from common appliances such as vacuum cleaners may pose as much of a risk.

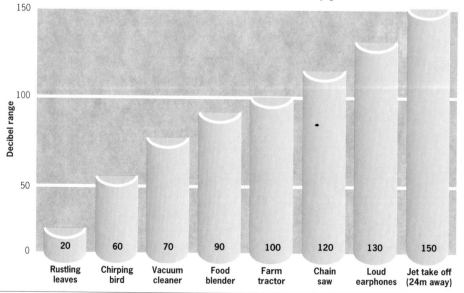

20	60	70	90	100	120	130	150
Rustling leaves	Chirping bird	Vacuum cleaner	Food blender	Farm tractor	Chain saw	Loud earphones	Jet take off (24m away)

precautions against unnecessary exposure. If you are using a personal stereo with earphones, for example, keep the volume low. If you are outdoors at an airport when a jet is landing or taking off, cover your ears. When operating a vacuum cleaner or hair dryer, wear earplugs.

The indirect effects of noise

Continual loud noise can cause other problems besides hearing loss. The incessant sounds of sirens and heavy traffic or power mowers and leaf blowers keep a person's body in a constant state of arousal. Just as visible danger provokes a heightened awareness response, noise acts on the autonomic nervous system, raising levels of adrenaline and noradrenaline and increasing heart and breathing rates. These effects continue even when you become so used to certain noises you sleep through them. Research shows that people who live close to airports suffer more than average from such stress-linked ailments as anxiety and high blood pressure, and their use of sedatives is higher.

Fortunately, many government agencies are now monitoring sound levels in problem areas, setting restrictions, and taking action

against offenders. You can do your part by supporting and adhering to local ordinances against excessive noise. You can also limit the amount of noise entering your home by installing double or triple-glazed windows and heavy curtains. Consider, too, buying a white noise machine, which modifies the effects of intrusive noises by adding a soothing overlay of sound, such as ocean waves.

Weather and natural disasters

Gloomy skies can mean depressed moods, and for some people, the reduced number of daylight hours during winter can lead

Caught in a storm

If you find yourself caught in a thunderstorm while outdoors, look for a sheltered hollow away from trees. If you are in open country, lie flat on the ground. Never shelter under trees because they are excellent conductors of lightning. If you are in a car, you are safe, because if lightning does strike it flashes over the surface of the car – which is virtually a metal cage – and runs harmlessly to earth. If you are at home, unplug the television and avoid using the telephone.

SEASONAL AFFECTIVE DISORDER (SAD)

The depression that many people suffer during the winter months is due to the activity of the pineal gland, which is located deep within the brain. It responds to daylight through nerve fibres connecting it to the eyes. As the sun goes down, it begins to release the hormone melatonin, stopping again when the sun comes up. Melatonin is believed to affect the body's circadian (daily) rhythms. Because there is less sunlight during the winter, melatonin levels are at their highest, and high levels suppress some of the body's functions. In some people, this results in depression, anxiety, and lethargy – symptoms which make up the syndrome known as seasonal affective disorder, or SAD. Women suffer from it four times more often than men, although the reason is unknown.

Most sufferers find that their symptoms can be relieved by spending a few hours each day sitting in front of a special light box. This box emits a bright, white, full-spectrum fluorescent light with enough intensity to imitate summer daylight. This tricks the pineal

Pineal gland

THE PINEAL GLAND
The body's circadian rhythms, also known as biorhythms, are governed by secretions of the pineal gland.

LIGHT THERAPY
Light boxes can trick the pineal gland into producing less melatonin, and provide relief for SAD sufferers.

gland into producing less melatonin and most people improve within a few days of treatment. Doctors also suggest that sufferers spend as many daylight hours as possible outdoors during the winter. In extreme cases, sufferers have moved to sunnier climates.

The 'Big One'

Earthquake tremors are experienced not only directly – as when overhead lights sway or cracks appear in walls – but also indirectly. The tremors produce sub-sonic vibrations that can have unsettling effects on the brain, resulting in feelings of anxiety and foreboding even when there is no physical evidence of earth movement.

UPHEAVAL
The loss of family, community links and property in a natural disaster is catastrophic, but the shock, stress, anxiety and depression arising from the aftermath can be even more devastating. Many people benefit from a 'debriefing' session with a counsellor or psychologist in which they talk in their own factual terms about the details of their disaster experience, particularly any mistakes they feel they made during it. This method was first used to assist Second World War American soldiers to cope with post combat depression and can now provide a release at a time when the usual social support networks are broken down.

to seasonal affective disorder (SAD), more commonly known as winter depression (see page 143), a medically recognised condition that affects up to one in five people.

Hurricanes, floods, earthquakes, and volcanic eruptions exact dramatic tolls of death and destruction. The predictions of an impending disaster can cause many people to feel helpless and can place them under additional psychological stress. Knowing emergency procedures and taking sensible precautions can go far towards helping them to regain a sense of control.

If you live in an area that is at risk from extreme weather conditions such as gales, flooding, blizzards, or snow drifts, keep at hand a battery-powered radio and torch with spare batteries, safety matches, candles, nonperishable foods, bottles of water, camp stove, extra warm clothing, and a first-aid kit. Sandbags – and a supply of sand – are useful in flood-prone locations.

Prepare a survival strategy so that you will know what to do if disaster strikes. For example, plan how to prevent floodwater entering. Work out the best way to move furniture and carpets quickly to upper floors, and how to keep you and your family warm and dry until help arrives.

Pollution

Air pollution is a concern in many nations today. Heavy car and lorry traffic, for example, seriously affects air quality in urban areas, and problems are compounded in industrial cities. In some places, up to 40 per cent of school-age children who live near major roads suffer from asthma or other chronic respiratory problems. Stringent emission standards and lead-free petrol plus the limiting of coal burning have all helped to improve the air in some regions. You can play your part by adhering to the air pollution bylaws in your area.

The quality of tap water varies from one region to another. Industrial and domestic waste products and detergents and nitrates that are used in agriculture get into water courses through seepage from leaky pipes and uncontrolled runoff into streams and ditches. The dumping of chemicals into lakes, rivers, and oceans plus accidental oil spills from tankers have resulted in major ecological disasters. Some situations are improving because of effective fines for large-scale polluters or mandates that they finance a cleanup. Individuals can also help by not using toxic chemicals in their gardens or dumping refuse from their boats.

PURIFYING YOUR WATER

If you are concerned about the quality of your tap water, you can call your local water company for a free test, or ask them for the latest monitoring results. If your water comes from a well, you will have to pay for testing.

One of the first things to look for is coliform bacteria, which would indicate pollution from sewage. If it is found you must boil all drinking and cooking water until the situation has been corrected. High levels of copper, iron, chlorine (a by-product of chlorination), or nitrates can be harmful. The presence of *any* lead, mercury, or arsenic is dangerous. Consult a water-treatment expert for a solution.

A pH test is also a good idea. If your water is found to be acidic (pH below 7), it can corrode pipes and leach metals, such as those listed above, into the water.

A carbon water filter (see right) will remove chemicals, odours, and a bad

taste, but not lead. Filter cartridges are available for lead removal; a distiller will remove lead and microorganisms as well, but not ordinary chemicals. These devices must be regularly maintained.

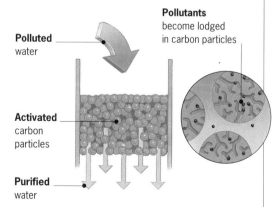

Pollutants
become lodged
in carbon particles

Polluted water

Activated carbon particles

Purified water

FILTERED WATER
Carbon water filters work by passing water slowly through charcoal permeated with tiny channels, to which the pollutants will stick.

THE WORLD STAGE

The media reports of wars, hostage taking, and famines around the world are more graphic and immediate than ever and help perpetuate negative images and attitudes. This continual assault on people's sensitivities can lead to what is known as compassion fatigue as well as depression about the state of the world and an increased sense of helplessness in the face of all of these horrors. Nevertheless, by maintaining an awareness of what is happening in the world around you and by learning to appreciate improvements where they do occur, you will develop a greater ability to retain realistic expectations and to avoid stress-making disappointments.

Bad news

Crime statistics are often among the most worrying kinds of news. The sensationalist reporting of relatively rare cases, such as those concerning serial killers or kidnappers, sells newspapers and increases television audiences. It also results in these crimes appearing to be much more of a risk than they actually are.

In 1990, for example, a total of 67 children were killed in the UK – a disturbing figure, but not high enough to constitute a wave of infanticide in a population of more than 50 million. In the US the percentage was higher, but the reported 888 child murders took place in a nation of more than 250 million people. As a consequence of largely unwarranted fears, many children today are more restricted and monitored than in the past, despite the fact that child-related crime has shown little increase.

The evidence for any real increase in the rate of crime is not necessarily supported by the rise in reported cases. In recent years the apparent escalation in rape, for example, is to some extent the result of the larger numbers of courageous women who are now reporting it to the police. The statistics may simply be reflecting a truer picture of what was actually happening before.

Although the tables of facts and figures are scarcely much comfort for those who have encountered or fear to suffer the effects of crime, it does put the true issue into a less perilous perspective. Violent crime, which primarily affects young males, is mainly recorded among groups on the shadowy fringes of law-abiding society.

Statistics for nonviolent crimes against property tell a similar story of fear outrunning the peril. Older people are particularly prone to worries about burglary, leading them to feel that they are prisoners in their own homes. Yet elderly people are not high on the list of victims among the thousands every year who suffer break-ins. In fact, the figures demonstrate that the most vulnerable groups in the community – women, children, and the elderly – are statistically the least likely to be affected by crime.

They also show that the lion's share of statistics is taken up by the less mysterious or sinister aspects of criminal activity. The majority of people are more likely to deal only with crime that involves no violence or confrontation (car theft and pickpocketing, for example). Violence, or the threat of it, is almost universally domestic – generally the result of open and long-running conflicts between spouses or members of the same family, in which emotional antagonisms spill over momentarily into a more physical form of expression.

It is sensible not to expose yourself to unnecessary dangers, and any precaution you take is good. But becoming aware of the myths as well as the facts about crime will help you to assess the real risks you face so that you can make better decisions about how to deal with them. Listed on page 146 are a number of steps you can take to make yourself less vulnerable and reduce your risk of becoming another crime statistic. It is better to be safe than sorry.

Pathway to health

Psychotherapists and others who work with people under stress suggest that the degree to which individuals feel in control of their lives significantly affects how they react to stress. People need to believe that they can influence their environment. If you feel bothered by things that appear to be out of your control, you may find that it would be beneficial to consult a psychotherapist. He or she will help you to come to a clearer understanding of why you are feeling this way, and enable you to put your troubles in perspective.

Is your child safe?

With so much crime being reported in the media, parents no longer feel secure in allowing their children the freedom they themselves once enjoyed. A child cannot always be under the protecting supervision of a parent, however, so make sure yours understands the danger of strangers offering a ride or sweets. All children should also know their own address and telephone number as well as the name and telephone number of a family friend or relative.

SAFETY MEASURES
As early as possible in your child's life, show him or her how to use the telephone, and particularly how to make emergency calls.

SAFETY OUTSIDE

Safety on the streets is everyone's responsibility; we should all be alert and prepared to take action to prevent crimes and the stresses they induce.

Face-to-face with potential violence

Because one of the most effective deterrents against assault is to make the assailant feel you might be able to ward off an attack, looking self-assured can help reduce your vulnerability.

Enrolling in a self-defence class will give you the confidence and ability to walk, talk, and behave in an assertive, purposeful manner.

Some people who have escaped attack have spoken of the value of 'dissipating the atmosphere' of potential violence. This is done by keeping calm and avoiding sudden movements when menaced by an assailant. If possible, try to maintain eye contact, and talk in a matter-of-fact voice. Should the encounter escalate into violence, it is best to comply with the demands of the attacker.

While violent assault is a rarity, the fact is that most people will eventually have some experience with a minor crime such as theft or vandalism. Being a victim can cause you to have less self-confidence and harbour bad memories for weeks, perhaps even months afterwards. It is therefore wise to consider realistically and carefully what you as an individual can do to keep feelings of helplessness from spilling over into your daily life. A good start is to contact your local police station and ask them to advise you on any risky areas in your neighbourhood that you should avoid. The police should also have information on local groups such as Neighbourhood Watch and women-only taxi services. In addition, many police forces have a crime prevention officer who is available to discuss security measures.

You should also think about what actions you can take to protect yourself and your family outside the home, whether you are on foot (see below) or in your car. When driving in a risky neighbourhood, especially at night, lock the doors, keep windows shut, and stow valuable items, such as purses and mobile phones, out of sight. If you suspect you are being followed, drive to a well-lit area, where there are people around, and ask for help. Also, if you see what appears to be an accident or someone tries to flag you down, consider the situation very carefully before stopping. It might be safer to drive on until you find a convenient phone from which to report what you have seen.

Campaigning for improved street lighting can also contribute to building collective responsibility for security with neighbours and increasing your personal sense of safety.

BECOMING STREETWISE

One of the most effective ways to prevent yourself from becoming another crime statistic is to think strategically and avoid presenting an open invitation. Being aware of your surroundings can help you to steer clear of trouble.

▶ *If you carry a handbag, use one with a long strap and wear it slung across your body.*

▶ *When shopping, take only as much cash as you expect to need and handle it discreetly.*

▶ *Travel on busy, well-lit streets. Plan your route to avoid empty underpasses and dark streets and alleys.*

▶ *Be sure of your route before setting out, so you won't have to ask for directions.*

▶ *When travelling by train or tube, avoid sitting in an empty carriage. If the one you are in empties, move to another.*

▶ *If you think someone is paying you too much attention, do not acknowledge the person but move to a place where there are other people.*

▶ *If somebody is following you, cross the road and, if necessary, go into a shop or knock at a house.*

▶ *Walk facing the flow of traffic so that a car cannot pull up behind you unnoticed.*

▶ *If you carry an alarm or whistle, be sure to hold it in your hand. It will be of no use buried at the bottom of your handbag.*

▶ *Always have your key ready as you approach your home or your car.*

▶ *Take a self-defence course to increase your confidence.*

Visualisation

The ability to free your mind of distracting thoughts in order to achieve a goal or cope with a stressful situation is a vital skill in combating the pressures of life. It works by letting your imagination take you to calm and restful places.

You can greatly enhance the effects of progressive relaxation (see page 39) by visualising an idyllic haven and then placing yourself in this imaginary picture. The exercise will bring mental calmness and further reduce physical tension.

   After progressively relaxing all your muscles, start saying the words 'serene', 'safe', 'calm', 'relaxed' over and over again in your head. Focus on them, and when other thoughts try to enter your mind, gently push them away. Then imagine an appealing place; it could be a favourite room, a forest glade, lush island, lake, beach, or mountainside. It may be a location that you know or just a product of your imagination. The key is that it should be a spot where you can feel happy and secure.

   Perform your visualisation in a comfortable position in a place where you will not be disturbed.

PRACTICAL VISUALISATION EXERCISE

Take a relaxing mental holiday with these simple steps. Close your eyes and imagine that you are eating a ripe peach. You will find that your mouth waters, such is the power of imagination to affect your body. Now choose a pleasant haven where you would like to relax, and visit it in your mind. Smell the smells, feel the air, hear the sounds, notice all the sights. Make a practice of visiting your retreat regularly and you will reap the benefits.

Your mind should focus on a simple image

Your eyes should be closed

Your body should be relaxed

1 *Once you have chosen your haven, begin examining it in your mind's eye. If you have selected a tropical island, you might see expanses of sandy beach fringed by blue sea, and perhaps a palm tree outlined against a cloudless sky.*

2 *Then look at the scene in more detail. There may be a few puffs of cloud, flecks of white foam on the waves, or perhaps a boat on the horizon, some shells along the shore, and possibly a colourful parrot perching in the palm tree.*

3 *Listen to the sounds of your sanctuary. These might include the splashing of the waves against the shore, the squawking of the parrot, the chirping of other birds, or the whisper and rustle of the palm fronds in the breeze.*

4 *Now feel the fine sand run through your fingers, the warm sun on your skin, and the silkiness of the ripples of water tickling your feet. Imagine you can pick up a beautiful shell, and when you hold it to your ear, you can hear the sound of the sea.*

MANAGING TRAUMA

In the event of a crime, accident, or full-scale disaster, knowing what the most common human reactions are can give you and those you love emotional protection.

HOW TO SURVIVE A TRAUMA

Traumas are deeply personal experiences and reactions to them differ, depending on the nature of the event and the personality of the individual involved. But there are some practical steps that can help.

▶ *Allow plenty of time for sleep and rest.*

▶ *Don't bottle up your feelings: talking or crying can bring relief.*

▶ *Let the event work itself through a little at a time. Allow yourself to think about it, and do not be afraid of any bad dreams that you may experience.*

▶ *Keep to your usual daily routine as much as possible, but take special care when driving or carrying out difficult or stressful tasks.*

▶ *Don't isolate yourself; be with family and friends when you can.*

At times of major crises, reactions of shock, fear, and anger are very common, and they are often followed by feelings of sadness, helplessness, and guilt. But less obvious consequences – physical as well as psychological – may also follow, even after some delay. Such symptoms may be indicators of post-traumatic stress disorder, or PTSD.

PTSD can be triggered by any distressing traumatic event outside the normal range of experience. A natural disaster, war, or, more commonly, a serious assault, near-drowning, or a fire or traffic accident may cause anyone who experiences the event, and even those witnessing it, to develop PTSD.

Consequences of PTSD

The event may be reexperienced in the form of unprompted memories. There may be disturbed sleep or nightmares, or even vivid flashbacks during waking hours, when sufferers feel and react as if the events were taking place all over again.

Sufferers sometimes undergo an emotional numbing as well. They may lose interest in their hobbies, their work may deteriorate because they find it difficult to concentrate, and their memory might become poor. The traumatic events could become unreal to them, seeming to be like dreams, and they may begin to feel detached from the rest of the world. Personal relationships can suffer, often as a result of the victims' desires to avoid anything that symbolises or recalls the traumas they have endured. As a consequence, they may begin using or increase their consumption of alcohol or drugs.

Unpleasant physical sensations, such as headaches and abdominal pains, are common, too. In addition, there may be periods of palpitations, trembling, breathing difficulties, dizziness, tightening in the chest, menstrual disorders, nausea, or diarrhoea.

As symptoms can occur some time after the actual events that trigger them, the link between the symptoms and trauma may not be obvious. If they remain unrecognised and untreated, these symptoms have the power to destroy lives by changing the sufferer's personality and damaging social and family relationships. It is important to seek immediate help from health professionals and support groups when symptoms of stress from a traumatic event first begin to surface.

Treating trauma

At the heart of all prevention and treatment of PTSD is the sharing of the traumatic experience with others. One approach is to talk through the pain with people who have undergone a similar trauma. While much relief can be gained by discussing a trauma with fellow survivors, complex psychological issues such as survivor's guilt or blaming oneself can arise. If this occurs, one should turn to a psychologist or psychotherapist trained in treating PTSD as soon as possible.

One approach used frequently is debriefing, in which sufferers are helped to counter any instinctive feeling to shut the event out, because of fears that they may have of losing control. Instead, they are encouraged to let the reality of the event work itself through, by talking about the experience with sympathetic listeners. The debriefing may take the form of individual or group discussions, and is usually carried out as soon as possible after the event.

If the shock and trauma are deep or the victim is particularly vulnerable, then more intensive counselling may be necessary. As well as going over the events of the traumatic experience in great detail, the counsellor and sufferer investigate how these events have been affecting his or her physical and emotional responses and ways of thinking, reacting, and coping with things in general.

Post-Traumatic Stress Victim

The effects of a traumatic event are not always felt immediately. Both emotional reactions and physical symptoms can occur weeks or months later, and their link with the crisis may not be clear. Yet if symptoms of post-traumatic stress disorder (PTSD) go untreated, they can be more incapacitating and longer lasting than a physical injury.

Nick, a young engineer, had just been promoted to a more responsible position, when he was attacked by a gang of drunken youths after a night out. While the attack was violent, and he sustained severe bruising, he escaped before suffering any major injury. A couple of weeks later, however, he had trouble getting to sleep and began to experience disturbing flashbacks. As the days passed, feelings of anxiety, accompanied by palpitations, sometimes overwhelmed him. To escape these feelings, he is now drinking heavily, which is having a bad effect on his relationship with his girlfriend, Anna. At work, he is irritable with colleagues and is finding it hard to concentrate, so he makes repeated mistakes.

WHAT SHOULD NICK DO?

Nick must accept that he has a problem and seek professional help. Simply making the decision to do this will boost his confidence.

During debriefings by his counsellor, Nick should resist the temptation to bury the experience. By going over the events of that evening in detail and facing up to what he felt during the attack, he will realise how natural his reactions are. When he has understood how the experience has affected him, he should talk to his girlfriend and explain the reasons for his antisocial behaviour. He should also take steps to reduce stress levels by taking on less work for the time being, looking after himself physically, and having some time off to relax.

Action Plan

EMOTIONAL HEALTH
Contact a support group to find out what kind of help is available and share the experience with others who have suffered similarly. Temporarily adopt a slower pace of life, with plenty of time for rest.

PARTNERS
Stop burying the crisis, allow feelings to surface, and talk to Anna. Ask for her understanding and support while recovering from the effects of the attack.

WORK
Ask for time off work or to have his workload reduced temporarily.

EMOTIONAL HEALTH
A refusal to face up to feelings of anxiety may result in severe depression and destructive patterns of behaviour.

PARTNERS
Lack of communication about distressing issues can cause misunderstandings and result in the breakdown of relationships.

WORK
The feelings that arise from a traumatic episode may interfere with the ability to carry out a job.

HOW THINGS TURNED OUT FOR NICK

Nick contacted a victims' support group, which helped him realise his problems were not unique. He discussed details of the event with a therapist, who encouraged him to confront his memories and look at the emotional turmoil the attack had caused. With the backing of the group, Nick opened up to Anna and was relieved to find she was very sympathetic. Nick became less anxious, and is slowly regaining his old confidence.

TAKING THE STRESS OUT OF TRAVELLING

The journey to and from work, whether by car or public transport, can be full of annoyances that increase stress. Travelling for pleasure can have its stressful side, too.

TRAFFIC JAM
Slow-moving traffic is a fact of urban life. Use this time constructively: listen to an audiocassette book, learn a language on cassette, or just catch up with the news.

Some people enjoy commuting to and from work each day because it gives them time to become fully alert in the morning or to unwind from the tensions of the day. Others find that commuting affects their well-being and they arrive at their destination tense or drained. If you are in the latter category, the suggestions below may help make commuting less harrowing.

DRIVING STRESS

When road conditions are congested, many people, even those who are normally placid, become antagonistic and irritable behind the wheel and succumb to 'road rage'. This is a blind fury that causes aggressive and reckless driving behaviour, such as travelling at high speeds, lane-hopping, jumping the gun at traffic lights, and generally being obstructive or discourteous. Aside from the obvious risk of having an accident, if road rage recurs continually, it can result in long-term health problems such as high blood pressure and heart disease.

If you feel road rage coming on, say to yourself such things as: 'I am not the only driver on the road', and 'I don't have special rights', or 'Whatever that driver did I've done myself on occasion'. Then distance yourself from your predicament by rising above it. Try to think of the situation as an enormous internal combustion engine, where patience, courtesy, and consideration are the oil that keeps the system lubricated and moving. This will help free you from the shackles of anger.

You may have to weigh the consequences of being late for an important business meeting or appointment against those of angering another motorist or having an accident – all clearly stressful prospects. (Of course, the predicament is less likely to arise if you allow enough time for delays.) In the end, it's better to slow down and drive carefully. You will arrive at your destination more relaxed, yet alert.

Public transport and stress

On public transport, when delays and overcrowding occur, irritation can be compounded by a sense of inability to control your own fate. Besides having to deal with disgruntled fellow travellers, you must place your fate entirely in the hands of others – drivers, pilots, baggage handlers, or flight controllers. This passive acceptance of such impediments can lead to a buildup of toxins and excessive acidity in the body, and the excess hormones released during stress responses can interfere with the body's

---

DRIVING AND YOUR HEALTH

Stress while driving can be measured directly by tests of skin resistance (tautness), eye movement (which reveals how much information is being conveyed to the brain), heart rate, and blood pressure. Even very experienced drivers demonstrate a 50 per cent increase in these measurements when driving in heavy traffic. And when they have to struggle to read road signs, negotiate roundabouts, or wait at red lights or in traffic jams for long periods, there are corresponding surges in these levels.

RACING DRIVER STRESS
Tests on racing car drivers have shown sustained heart rates that are 50 per cent above normal, peaking in excess of 200 beats per minute. Physical effects may include weight loss, dehydration, and exhaustion.

immune system, leaving it vulnerable to bacteria and viral diseases such as flu.

There are a number of coping strategies you can employ to make this type of commuting easier on the nerves. For instance, carry a good book or magazine to read, so that you can tune out aggravations; or if you do needlework, carry a project with you to make productive use of the time; or use the time to catch up on your work. You might also try persuading the company you work for to adopt flexitime so that you can travel outside of rush hour periods.

Safety and emergency measures

The compulsory wearing of seat belts has proved its worth. Statistics from the Department of Transport show that wearing a lap/shoulder seat belt reduces the risk of fatal injury to a front-seat car passenger by 45 per cent. A further level of safety is provided by airbags, which inflate on impact; these can significantly reduce the risk of serious facial and chest injuries for the driver (and for the front-seat passenger in a vehicle fitted with dual-bags).

Making sure that the vehicle you travel in is safe can help reduce stress. It should be serviced regularly and repaired as necessary, with frequent checks especially on brakes and tyre treads and pressures.

If you do have a breakdown, get the car as far off the road as possible, turn on the emergency flashers, and put up a warning triangle if you have one. Open the bonnet and wait in the car until help arrives. If you cannot get the car off the road, you will probably be safer standing by the roadside. Ask a passing motorist to call for assistance at the nearest call box.

LONG-DISTANCE TRAVEL

Travelling for extended periods in a car can result in stresses that are very different from those of daily commuting. For most people, long-distance driving is physically exhausting; regular stops are essential to relieve cramped and tense muscles and keep the driver mentally alert. It is surprising how much benefit can be gained from even a short pause in driving.

Long car journeys are made easier with activity. Singing, listening to audiocassette books, playing word games, following an extended discussion or musical programme on the radio, or just talking can help ward off boredom and irritation. Try to avoid arguments, however, as the stressful atmosphere generated can distract you and negatively influence your driving, exposing you and your passengers to the risk of accident.

One of the hazards of long-distance travel is that it can lead to drowsiness. Of the 50 000 or so deaths from motor vehicle accidents in the United States each year, 13 per cent are caused by drivers falling asleep.

Relax while travelling

Worrying about problems will only increase your stress, so try to steer your thoughts onto more tranquil topics.

If you are a passenger, an inflatable neck pillow will provide comfort and help you to take a nap. When awake, regularly do muscle relaxation exercises, like those below. If you are travelling by public transport, these can be done discreetly so as not to disturb other passengers.

SLEEP PILLOW
An inflatable pillow may help you sleep more easily on a long journey, as it provides support for your neck.

EXERCISES FOR LONG-DISTANCE PASSENGERS

Sitting in an upright position for a long time with limited body movement restricts blood flow and causes stiffness and aches.

These simple exercises can help reduce discomfort and make you feel more alert on arrival at your destination.

Head should be relaxed

Neck should not be forced

Shoulders should be kept loose

1 *Take a deep breath and slowly lean your head to one side. Rest it gently in this position for three seconds, then exhale.*

2 *Follow the same routine with the other side. Repeat these exercises three times. Do not bounce, rotate, or swivel your neck.*

3 *Bend your head forwards; hold for three seconds. Move head to right then left, holding for three seconds on each side. Repeat three times.*

TIPS FOR AIR TRAVEL

Long hours in confined spaces can make air travel unpleasant. The following are a few tips to help lessen the stress.

▶ *Wear comfortable, loose clothing and shoes.*

▶ *In your hand luggage carry a change of underwear and toiletries in case your luggage is delayed or lost.*

▶ *On long flights, limit or refrain from smoking, because cabin pressure is increased to compensate for higher altitudes and your blood will not carry as much oxygen as at sea level.*

▶ *Avoid alcoholic drinks. The air in the cabin is very dry and causes dehydration. Alcohol will dehydrate you more.*

▶ *Drink plenty of water or fruit juice.*

▶ *Every hour or so, get up and walk the length of the aeroplane, if possible.*

*ROSEMARY
AND GERANIUM
The essential oils of these herbs are refreshing and can help alleviate some of the effects of jet lag.*

If you find yourself beginning to nod off behind the wheel, the safest solution is to stop as soon as you can and get some sleep. If this isn't possible, open the window and let fresh air blow on your face. Or stop the car and jog around it a few times. Other wake-up ideas are: tuning into a radio station and turning up the volume (with the window rolled up), talking back to a radio DJ, singing loudly, stopping for a cup of coffee and a brisk walk. Also, sitting with an erect posture and having the top of the head pulling the neck and spine as straight as possible will enable blood to flow more freely and encourage wakefulness.

FEAR OF FLYING

According to the Civil Aviation Authority, flying is one of the safest forms of travel. The systems for controlling air traffic are sophisticated, mechanical safety checks are carried out regularly, and the training of pilots and other crew is demanding. Statistics show that the fatality rate for air travel is negligible compared with most other forms of transport.

Despite the statistics, many people are afraid of flying. Whether or not you are in this group, you will have more peace of mind if you fly with an airline that has a good safety record. Most large, regularly scheduled airlines meet these standards; charter carriers vary. Also, if possible, fly from airports that have stringent security checks. Before takeoff, pay attention to the safety briefing presented and read the safety instruction card.

Even if you have a phobia about flying, there is still hope. Psychotherapy, hypnosis, and desensitisation courses can do much to reduce these fears by getting you used to all aspects of the flying experience. Joining a support group may also be helpful.

JET LAG

When flying across time zones, it is not uncommon to suffer from an interrupted sleep pattern, irritability, and fatigue, which may last several days. Known as jet lag, this results from disruption of the body's internal clock. The time it takes to recover from it depends on what time the flight left and how many time zones were crossed and in which direction. Crossing one to three time zones takes little adjustment (if the trip is a short one, it might be better to stay on your

own time for its duration). Moving across six or seven zones requires much more.

Going from east to west is easier to adjust to if you take a late afternoon or evening flight, stay awake during the flight, then go to bed shortly after you arrive. Travelling west to east, you will lose a vital number of sleep hours on an overnight flight. If you take a daytime flight, then have dinner and go to sleep relatively late in the new time zone, you will be more rested and your time clock will be better adjusted the next day.

If possible, start to readjust your routine several days before your flight – getting up an hour earlier or later and going to bed earlier or later – to mirror what you will need after your journey. Have as little caffeine as possible in the three days prior to departure. Also, eat lightly the day before and during the flight. Allow yourself a day to rest and recover if you have important business to attend to.

Many people suffer from light deprivation when they return from a winter holiday – going from fun in the sun to the artificial light of an office building. Spending time exposed to the sun shortly after landing can help mitigate the effects of jet lag.

HOLIDAY TRAVEL

Going away on holiday does not necessarily mean that you will be able to leave all your stresses behind. But careful planning can help ensure your trip gets off to a relaxing start and continues that way.

Rather than coping with heavy luggage, take along no more than you absolutely need and pack well in advance. Taking just two basic colours, such as black and white or beige and blue, permits you to mix and match items. Including clothing that can be layered will prepare you to meet varying weather conditions comfortably. Leave out things that you are tempted to take 'just in case'. When you are flying and planning to check your bag in, keep a carry-on bag with toiletries, a change of underwear, all medications, and any items of value.

Plan your route in detail to avoid arguments and anxiety. If you are going by bus, train, or plane, allow plenty of time to get to your departure point and avoid last-minute panics. When flying, choose a schedule that allows enough time to make any connections. If a tight connection is unavoidable, find out what the next available flight will be if you should miss your connection. Also, make a hotel booking for at least the first night away, and learn as much as you can about your destination to orient yourself without difficulty.

If you are travelling abroad, make sure that you arrive with sufficient foreign currency to pay fares and tips to your hotel. Include some change, as many bus and taxi drivers will not accept notes in large denominations. If you do not know the language spoken at your chosen destination, buy a traveller's phrase book and practise a few simple phrases to help you with your first few transactions.

Give a neighbour the phone numbers where you can be reached in an emergency, and the numbers of friends or relatives who can deal with unexpected problems. Provide this same person or another trusted friend or relative with a list of the numbers of all your credit cards, traveller's cheques, and passport if you're going abroad.

In cold weather, make sure that your home is heated well enough to prevent the pipes from freezing. You could also ask a friend or relative to stay there while you are away (or check the newspapers for persons advertising to house sit); this would give you an added sense of security.

In case you are stranded

In many parts of the world, tourists are advised to carry cash, cheques, and passports in a bumbag or a hidden money belt, because travellers tend to stand out from the locals and are often vulnerable targets for theft. Despite precautions, thefts still occur. If you are a victim, report the theft immediately to the police; in the case of traveller's cheques, notify the company that issued them (be sure to carry the numbers and record of cheques cashed separately from the cheques themselves). In most cases, you will receive new cheques within 24 hours.

If you need some cash, automatic cash dispensers are widely available today. An alternative is to have a friend or relative transfer some money to you. Depending on the location, this can usually be carried out through a bank, a traveller's cheques agency, or (in the USA) a telegraph office. You might also arrange to have funds transferred from your own bank to a local one.

HOLIDAY CHECKLIST

Before you leave home, you should:

▶ *Cancel newspaper and milk deliveries.*

▶ *Arrange for someone to check letterbox, tend houseplants and garden.*

▶ *Arrange for a pet minder, if necessary.*

▶ *Do not close all blinds, shades, and curtains as this alerts thieves that you are away.*

▶ *Put a few lights and a radio on timers.*

▶ *Tell your neighbours, and perhaps the police, that you will be away.*

▶ *Empty the refrigerator of all perishable foods.*

Star-of-Bethlehem

Cherry blossom

Clematis

Impatiens

Rock rose

RESCUE REMEDY Extracts from these herbs comprise Rescue Remedy, a popular Bach Flower Remedy.

REMEDIES FOR TRAVEL STRESS

There are a number of practical measures that you can take to make travel less stressful for you and your family. For example, to boost your energy, you should eat snacks of nuts, dried fruit, or wholewheat crackers. To prevent dehydration, drink bottled mineral water (you can also use it to brush your teeth if there is any doubt about the local water supply). To accommodate swollen feet when flying, remove your shoes and wear slippers, or thick socks, or go barefoot. To help you sleep, use earplugs and eyeshades.

Alternative therapists also recommend their own travel stress remedies (see the list below). You can use these on their own or in conjunction with the other measures given.

HOMEOPATHIC	AROMATHERAPY
To minimise the effects of jet lag and aid adjustment when flying through a significant number of time zones, take *Cocculus* 6 for three days before departure. *Arnica* 6 may also ease the transition if taken during the flight and for a couple of days afterwards.	To reduce anxiety before the journey, use rose, juniper, or sandalwood essential oils. To relax you during the journey, use lavender oil. To relieve fatigue after the journey, try rosemary, lemon, geranium, jasmine, or bergamot essential oils. Place two or three drops of oil on a tissue and inhale, or add to your bath, or massage into tired muscles (see page 68).

BACH FLOWER REMEDIES	HERBAL
If you are prone to panic and anxiety – particularly when flying or going on long journeys – place three drops of Rescue Remedy on your tongue every hour before, during, and after the journey (see right).	To help you sleep during the journey, take along a pillow that is filled with lavender, camomile, lime blossom, and hops. You can also drink herbal teas, especially camomile or passion flower tea.

Travel sickness

This condition is caused by changes in speed and direction that upset the delicate balance mechanism in the inner ear, which is responsible for informing the body of its position, movement, and acceleration. The roll and pitch of a ship, the undulations of an aeroplane in rough weather, and the motion of fairground rides can all induce travel sickness in varying degrees.

Fluid in inner ear controls balance

THE INNER EAR
The balance of the fluid-filled, semicircular canals in the inner ear becomes disrupted during travel sickness.

GINGER TEA
Any form of ginger – tea, capsules, preserved, or sticks – will help to settle and warm the stomach. Infuse one slice of peeled, fresh ginger in a cup of boiling water.

Report a stolen or lost passport to the police as well as the nearest British embassy or consulate. You may need the police report to obtain a new passport. If you have the number of your original passport (better yet, a photocopy of it) or any other proof of citizenship, then you should receive a new passport within a day. But you will have to spend time standing in queues and filling in forms, which will eat into your holiday.

For a lost airline ticket, go to the office of the company that issued it. You will probably have to buy a replacement and then wait for a refund. Policies vary.

Preventing travel sickness

Even seasoned travellers can be affected occasionally by travel sickness. Sometimes anxiety and fatigue make a person more susceptible. Whatever your travel mode, try to remain still enough to give the body's balance mechanism a chance to settle down. If possible, lie on your back. This position has been shown to reduce the incidence of travel sickness by about one-fifth.

Avoid travelling on a full stomach. Eating a snack may settle it, but a large meal will make you feel worse. Do not read or play games that require close focusing; straining your eyes to cope with the uneven bumping of the journey will exaggerate the sense of erratic movement that the brain receives.

HOMEOPATHIC TREATMENT

Depending on your symptoms, take one to three pills an hour to relieve them, until they disappear.

▶ *Cocculus 6* For nausea with giddiness and a metallic taste in the mouth.
▶ *Sepia 6* For nausea aggravated by the smell of food, alleviated by eating.
▶ *Nux vomica 6* For nausea with chills; symptoms relieved by vomiting.
▶ *Petroleum* For nausea accompanied by dizziness, faintness, and cold sweat.

When travelling by aeroplane, sit towards the front or over the wing for the smoothest ride. Recline your seat and press your head against the headrest. On a ship, stay in the midsection where it is most stable. If you have a cabin, lie down. If you don't, sit on deck or by a window where you can see the horizon to orient yourself.

There are a number of treatments for travel sickness; you may have to try them all to see which one works best for you. Bands are available that put continuous pressure on the wrist acupressure point that alleviates nausea. Patches behind the ears release anti-nausea medication directly into the bloodstream. Ask your pharmacist for advice. A drop of peppermint oil placed on the tongue might also help.

ACUPRESSURE FOR TRAVEL SICKNESS

If you suffer badly from travel sickness, help may be in your own hands. Acupressure can be used to help prevent or alleviate the nausea that is associated with travel sickness (and also morning sickness). Try the methods illustrated below to help make your journey as comfortable as possible.

Use both thumbs to massage – the point may feel very tender

TO PREVENT TRAVEL SICKNESS
Sitting with feet flat on the floor, find a spot on the outside of your calf 10 to 12 cm below the right knee. Massage it firmly with your thumbs for 20 seconds, breathing deeply. Repeat on the left leg. Do each leg three times.

Maintain firm pressure and use a circular motion

TO RELIEVE TRAVEL SICKNESS
Place the right thumb on the inside of the left wrist, three finger widths from the centre of the wrist crease. Massage between the two tendons for 20 seconds, breathing deeply. Repeat on the other wrist.

Overcoming a Fear of Flying

Whether it's the fear of being in open spaces (agoraphobia) or the fear of flying (aerophobia), phobias can create an overwhelming sense of panic. To avoid the stress of phobia-triggering situations, many people curtail their everyday activities. Thanks to stress-reduction techniques and desensitising treatment, phobias can be overcome and a normal life resumed.

Helen is 38 years old and has just been promoted to regional sales manager for her company. Although she is overjoyed, she is suffering a huge amount of stress because she is required to make frequent flights to sales conferences and business meetings. Since her first flight at the age of 19 she has had a terrible fear of flying. Even before she boards an aeroplane she sweats profusely, develops palpitations, and feels like she can't breathe – all symptoms of extreme anxiety. On long flights, she tries to calm her nerves by drinking several cocktails, but that makes her feel worse. On her last flight her panic was so great, she realised that unless she faced up to her fear she would have to quit her job.

WHAT SHOULD HELEN DO?

Helen needs to seek help for her phobia from a qualified therapist who will start her on a course of desensitisation. In the process, Helen will learn how to use deep breathing and relaxation commands in controlled situations designed to trigger her fear. First Helen will be asked to imagine herself in an aeroplane and then she will use relaxation commands to deal with her fright. The next step might be to have her sit in a parked plane. Finally, Helen will use her fear-controlling techniques to calm herself during a real flight. While Helen is undergoing this treatment, it is important that she talk with her boss and explain her problem and how treatment will help.

HEALTH
Any kind of extreme fear or phobia can wreak havoc with your physical and mental health.

WORK
A fear of flying can jeopardise your job, or even your career, if it is not resolved.

LIFESTYLE
Anxiety is made worse by stimulants, such as caffeine, and nicotine. Using alcohol to cope can risk developing a drink problem.

Action Plan

HEALTH
Learn how to relax and deal with anxiety. Practise deep-breathing techniques. Take a stress management course.

WORK
Inform boss of action being taken for problem. Ask if another manager can go to overseas meetings for the next two months.

LIFESTYLE
Drink calming, caffeine-free herbal teas instead of coffee. Cut down on alcohol consumption, especially on planes. Exercise regularly to relieve stress.

HOW THINGS TURNED OUT FOR HELEN

Helen began desensitising treatment for her phobia. In a few weeks she was able to sit in a flight simulator without suffering any crippling bouts of panic. She also joined a phobia therapy group, which helped her feel less alone with her problem. Helen's first flight went well, but she knows that she will have to practise her relaxation techniques regularly if she wants to hold on to her job and keep her fear of flying in check.

TRAVELLING WITHOUT YOUR CHILD

When you go on a trip and leave a small child behind, you can ease anxiety by:

▶ *Discussing the trip with your child, and letting him or her help you prepare a travel plan, perhaps by cutting out pictures of your destination from magazines or brochures.*

▶ *Arranging to have your child's babysitter take him or her to a few special places while you are away.*

▶ *Putting together a package of surprises, one for each day that you will be gone. Include such things as special notes and jokes and small gifts.*

▶ *Making a tape recording of yourself reading one of your child's favourite stories.*

▶ *Marking a calendar with the days you will be away, and asking your child to check off each day as it passes.*

TRAVELLING WITH CHILDREN

Taking a trip with an infant or young child requires careful planning so that neither of you becomes frazzled along the way. As you make arrangements, try to limit the number of activities and build in some flexibility, allowing extra time to rest, for example, or linger at a favourite spot.

When booking a flight, ask for bulkhead seats. If these are unavailable, request aisle seats to avoid crawling over passengers when your child is restless. If you can travel during off-peak times, your chances are far greater of finding an empty seat for an infant or extra seat space for a toddler to play in.

Before leaving for the airport, always call to find out if the flight is on time. You will save the anguish of coping with a restless youngster if there is a delay.

Whenever possible, plan the travel time to coincide with your child's normal sleeping hours; this will limit the amount of time you have to keep him or her occupied.

For waking hours on the road, tie toys for an infant or toddler to the car seat. Provide young children with toys (if possible, include a couple of new ones; these are likely to hold their interest for a longer period than familiar toys), games, and tapes of favourite stories or music.

Those who can read will be entertained with games based on registration plates, such as counting the number of plates from different countries that they spot.

TALK TO YOUR CHILD
Whether your child is travelling with you or staying at home, discussing the trip beforehand should help to reduce anxiety about change and make things easier for everyone.

They can also mark on a map the progress you are making along the route. Plan to stop at least every two hours during a long car trip, and select a place where children can walk around or run off excess energy.

Children, especially up to the age of six, tend to be more prone to travel sickness than adults. Ask your doctor about preventive medication. Car sickness is mainly brought on by excitement or anxiety, so try to keep the child calm before setting out.

Feeding wisely

Always carry a varied supply of nutritious snacks and soft drinks in order to stave off hunger and thirst (and children's attendant bad temper) in case mealtimes are delayed or boredom sets in. Snack foods come in handy even at a restaurant, if you have to wait long for the meal to arrive.

Ask to have your toddler served first, on an aeroplane or in a restaurant, so you can cut up the food or assist with eating before your own meal arrives. Never permit a child to roam unattended through a restaurant; not only is it extremely annoying to other diners, it could be dangerous if the child accidentally trips a waiter carrying food. It may be necessary for you and your partner to take turns eating while the other takes the young one(s) outside for a stroll.

When travelling by air with an infant, offer a bottle or feeder cup during takeoff and landing. Swallowing helps to keep pain-causing pressure from building up in the ears. Having children suck on a boiled sweet or chew gum serves the same purpose.

Sleeping away from home

For the sake of everyone's comfort, stay at hotels or guesthouses that cater for families by providing cots and possibly babysitting services. As soon as you arrive, put all hazardous or breakable objects out of reach.

Any child may have difficulty sleeping in strange surroundings. It will help if you remember to bring a toy or blanket that the child usually sleeps with, and some favourite bedtime storybooks. If you are in a different time zone, expect problems with sleeping routines for at least a day or two.

As difficult as travelling with children can sometimes be, it gives them a chance to explore and adjust to the wider world and helps them develop coping mechanisms that will be valuable to them in the future.

INDEX

ACKNOWLEDGMENTS

Carroll & Brown Limited
would like to thank
Ellen Dupont
Sue Mims
Irena Hoare

John Wiley & Sons, New York
Mosby, St. Louis

Penguin Books, London (chart,
    pages 64–65)
International Management & Reed
    Business Publishing (chart, page 118)

Additional design assistance
Richard Horsford
Paola Bernardi

Additional editorial assistance
Ian Wood

Advice and assistance
Ainsworths Homoeopathic Pharmacy
Aquatonics
Bundeskriminalamtes
Bureau of Justice Statistics
Central Statistical Office
Department of the Environment
Feng Shui Society
Institute of Environmental Health
    Officers
Institut National de la Statistique et
    des Etudes Economiques
Keep Able
National Center for Health Statistics
National Highway Traffic Safety
    Administration
National Institute for Occupational
    Safety and Health
Statistical Office of the European
    Committee
Statistisches Bundesamt
SW2000 Teleworking Studies
Tim Harper, The College of
    Osteopaths
Wingfield Chiropractic Clinic

Photograph sources
8   Range/Bettmann
10 Popperfoto
11 Gregg deGuire/London Features
13 (Top) Popperfoto; (Bottom)
    Robin Kaplan/London Features
14 Range/Bettmann
17 Tony Stone Images
18 Sally and Richard Greenhill
20 Tony Stone Images
22 Wellcome Institute Library,
    London
32 S.T.A.T.
34 Peter Tizzard
36 (Bottom) Eye Ubiquitous
38 Zefa
40 (Top) Tony Stone Images;
    (Bottom) Courtesy Float Systems
    Int. (London)/Tony Isbitt
41 James Watt/Planet Earth Pictures
42 Robert Harding Picture Library
43 Sarah Errington/Hutchison
    Library
50 Peter Tizzard
52 Scofield Chiropractic Clinic
55 (Left) Peter Tizzard; (Right) 'Art
    as Healing,' Edward Adamson
56 Reed International Books
    Ltd./Hawkley Studios
71 Mary Evans Picture Library
78 Mary Evans Picture Library
90 Petit Format/Nestlé/SPL
99 Zefa
100 John Walmsley
102 (Left) Bubbles/Pauline Cutler;
    (Right) Mary Evans Picture
    Library
106 The Feng Shui Network/Harry
    Archer
108 Thalgo UK Ltd.
114 Zefa
127 Drawing after a building by R. H.
    Partnership Architects with Battle
    McCarthy
134 Range/Bettmann

142 Robert Harding Picture
    Library/Earl J. Young
143 Full Spectrum Lighting Ltd.
144 Robert Harding Picture
    Library/Explorer
150 (Top) Eye Ubiquitous; (Bottom)
    Autosport Photographic

Illustrators
Joanna Cameron
Jane Craddock-Watson
Eugene Fleury
John Geary
Christine Pilsworth
Paul Williams
Angela Wood

Charts
Clive Bruton
Lee Maunder
Nick Roland

Photographic assistance
Nick Allen
Ian Boddy
Alex Hansen
Sid Sideris

Make-up
Bettina Graham
Juliana Mendes Ebden

Picture researcher
Sandra Schneider

Research
Laura Price

Index
Sharon Freed